A Nation under God?

A Nation under God?

Essays on the Future of Religion in American Public Life

Edited by
R. Bruce Douglass
and
Joshua Mitchell

ROWMAN & LITTLEFIELD PUBLISHERS, INC.
Lanham • Boulder • New York • Oxford

ROWMAN & LITTLEFIELD PUBLISHERS, INC.

Published in the United States of America
by Rowman & Littlefield Publishers, Inc.
4720 Boston Way, Lanham, Maryland 20706
http://www.rowmanlittlefield.com

12 Hid's Copse Road
Cumnor Hill, Oxford OX2 9JJ, England

British Library Cataloguing in Publication Information Available

Library of Congress Cataloging-in-Publication Data

A nation under God: essays on the future of religion in American public life / edited by R. Bruce Douglass and Joshua Mitchell.
p. cm.
Includes bibliographical references and index.
ISBN 0-7425-0750-5 (cloth : alk. paper)—ISBN 0-7425-0751-3 (pbk. : alk. paper)
1. United States—Religion. I. Douglass, R. Bruce. II. Mitchell, Joshua.

BL2525 .N38 2000
200'.973—dc21

00-028011

Printed in the United States of America

∞™ The paper used in this publication meets the minimum requirements of American National Standard for Information Sciences—Permanence of Paper for Printed Library Materials, ANSI/NISO Z39.48-1992.

Contents

Preface

This volume is the product of a research project on the fate of religion in American public life today that was undertaken under the auspices of the Program in Social and Political Thought of the College and the School of Foreign Service at Georgetown University in Washington, D.C. Funding was provided by a grant from the Mellon Foundation.

The editors wish to express their appreciation to Karen Lautman, an administrative assistant on the staff of Georgetown College, who was responsible for organizing and staffing the two consultations at which the participants in the project defined the relevant issues and presented their papers.

The editors also wish to express their appreciation to Dr. William Gould, Assistant Professor of Political Science at St. Anselm's College in New Hampshire, and to Brad Holst, a doctoral candidate in the Department of Government at Georgetown University, for their assistance in preparing the manuscript for publication.

Introduction

This is a book of a distinctive sort. It is a collection of scholarly papers on the role of religion in American public life today by a group of people who are themselves believers. All the contributors are practicing adherents of one or another of what are sometimes characterized as this nation's three "historic faiths." We are also people who have shown an active interest in religious matters in our scholarly work, and we are known for doing so on terms that reflect our experience as believers. But none of us is a theologian. We all have been trained and done our teaching and research as political or legal theorists.

The book reflects that blend. It is designed to address the kind of concerns that are characteristic of legal and political theorists, and it has to do primarily, therefore, with the health and well-being of civic institutions. But it does so in a manner that is informed by the experience and convictions of the authors as men and women of faith. It should be of interest, therefore, to both scholars and believers. And it is written in such a way as to meet the needs of both audiences.

The contributors share something else in common as well: We are all dissatisfied with the current state of the debate that this nation has been having in the past several decades about the role of religion in public life—and for essentially the same reasons. For we all espouse faiths that are part of what the distinguished church historian Martin Marty has characterized as the "public" church,[1] and as such, we take for granted not only that religious beliefs have relevance to public affairs but that they should find expression in public debate and policy as well. We have that view, moreover, not just because we think that as a matter of principle democracies need to accommodate the voice of faith but also because we are convinced that as a general rule the quality of their public life is enhanced by doing so. So we are not inclined to go along with the thoroughgoing secularization of public life advocated by those who have been responsible for creating what Stephen Carter of the Yale Law School has aptly characterized as a "culture of disbelief."[2]

At the same time, however, we do not respond any better to the idea that has arisen in reaction against that way of thinking—which is that this nation needs now to go the opposite extreme and "reclothe" the public square with drapery drawn from one particular part of our religious heritage.[3] For not only do we believe that it has ceased to be appropriate for the adherents of any particular faith to aspire to such privileged standing in the public life of this nation, but we also believe that it is unnecessary—and unwise. The desired result—which is an authentic and *effective* expression of religious convictions in the public arena—can be achieved, we are convinced, without seeking any sort of religious establishment, even of an informal sort. We are convinced, in fact, that such a purpose is likely to be better served once it is clear that believers do not have power on their minds when they attempt to make their influence felt in public life.

The people who have contributed to this book are hardly alone in thinking this way, of course. The recognition that a way needs now to be found to allow religious beliefs to be brought to bear on the conduct of public affairs without allowing any one faith to dominate is increasingly common these days. It has become so common in the places where this matter is seriously discussed, in fact, that it is appropriate to conclude that the debate has now entered a new and different phase. The alternative views may not have been altogether discredited, but they have been shown to be vulnerable to criticism from which it will not be easy for them to recover.[4] It is no accident that even the courts are now beginning to show signs of recognizing that the matter needs to be rethought.

It is one thing, however, to have such a conviction and quite another to act on it successfully. And the problem now is that even though it is widely acknowledged that we need a new set of terms on which to define the role of religion in our public life, it is not at all clear what they are. Other than as an insistence that it is in fact possible for religious convictions to have an influence in public life without posing a threat to democratic values, the point of view of those who think this way is largely undeveloped. For all the support this view has attracted, at this juncture it amounts to little more than a set of promises that are yet to be met, and the more important objections to it have barely begun to be addressed. So even though it is, in a sense, an idea whose time has come, its proponents are ill equipped to take advantage of the opportunity they now have.

A Nation under God? Essays on the Fate of Religion in American Public Life is designed as a contribution to the resolution of this problem. For what the book seeks to do is advance the argument for such a "third way" in a manner that will allow it to become a fully articulated position and not just a set of loosely-defined intentions. It builds on the claims that have been advanced to date by the proponents of such a view and attempts to come to terms with some of the more important challenges that will need to be met if those claims are in fact to yield a viable alternative to the ideas they are meant to supplant. It does so in five different ways:

1. *The ethics of religious witness in public life*

One is to underscore—and then explain—the fact that it is inappropriate for believers to maintain that the advocacy of views based on religious convictions in the conduct of public life poses no threat to democratic values unless they are prepared to conduct themselves appropriately. The book recognizes that it is not enough just to assert—much less assume—that the fear of such a threat is misguided; it insists that it needs to be shown that there are in fact alternatives to the practices that are the source of the fear. And much of what it has to offer is devoted to identifying what those alternatives are and explaining why they should be accepted. At least half of the chapters in this volume are concerned with this matter, in one fashion or another, and what they have to say goes a long way, we think, towards defining the ethic believers will need to accept if the claim that a more open expression of religious beliefs in the public arena poses no threat to tolerance is to be taken seriously.

2. *Enrichment of the quality of public discourse*

What the book has to offer in this vein is complemented by another set of arguments designed to show what the body politic itself stands to gain from such a development. The authors also recognize that it is not enough just to insist on the right of believers to speak their minds in the public arena; they understand that the effects of what such people can be expected to say (and do) on the health and well-being of the wider society must also be taken into consideration if the matter is to be treated fairly. So another purpose of the volume is to show how the quality of our public life (and indeed our entire way of life) could be enhanced by making room for a more overt reliance on resources derived from our religious traditions—and how it is diminished when we deny ourselves the possibility of calling on them. The arguments that are advanced in this vein are not naive; the people making them understand full well that there are dangers involved in any such public use of ideas and symbols drawn from religious sources. But they do not believe that those dangers are the whole story. For they are convinced that there are other dangers we run in denying ourselves access to such resources that are in their own way just as worrisome, and for that reason they think the whole matter needs to be rethought.

3. *Back to basics: reason and Revelation*

It will take more, however, than just a demonstration of the utility of ideas with a religious pedigree (like "covenant" and "calling") in public discourse and law for such an argument to be effective. For no matter what promise such ideas (and symbols) may be shown to have as tools for dealing with the practical problems we now face in this nation, attempts to make use of them for public purposes are almost certain to be met with suspicion as long as the principled objections to what they represent are not addressed. So another part of the book is devoted to a consideration of issues of that kind. And the thing in particular those essays are designed to do is challenge conceptually the grounds on which those who insist on excluding such themes from our public life are inclined to make their case. The widely-held conviction that "reason" can be neatly distinguished from "Revelation," for example, is subjected to an extended critique. So, too, is the notion that the kind of public life that is now typically held out in the literature of democratic theory as ideal can in fact be achieved on the basis of "reason" thus understood. It is simply not the case, say the authors of the chapters that examine these matters in the pages that follow, that democrats who are honest about their own presuppositions can really dispense with what "Revelation" has to offer. Nor is it to be taken for granted that we shall be able to make much further progress in realizing the ideals that democrats now espouse without relying on the kind of vision that historically has come from appeals to "Revelation," either. All of that needs to be rethought as well, the book suggests, and much of what it has to offer is designed to show how that might be done fruitfully.

4. *Our historical moment*

Still another matter, finally, that needs to be addressed, if arguments in the vein presented in these pages are in fact to make any real headway, is the character of the historical situation in which such issues are being debated today in American life. For if the impression created by the so-called "culture wars" is valid and we have indeed now come to a place in the history of this nation where the only voices that can be expected to count for anything in public life are the dedicated secularists and the Religious Right, talk of any other alternative is beside the point. But that claim, too, is hardly self-evidently true, and for all the respect it has been given in recent years in the literature of political and legal theory, it cannot be said to reflect a very complete understanding of the relevant empirical data. Even less, moreover, can it be said to reflect a very sophisticated understanding of the subject. It is a view that is based on a very selective reading of the relevant facts, and it deals with them in a manner that does not begin to do justice to the complexity of what is actually happening.

Not only is there room for another account, therefore, but a real *need* for it as well. And the reason in particular why that is so is that neither of the positions that have been featured in the culture wars is in fact favored by the vast majority of Americans. If the relevant opinion and electoral data are to be believed, at least, they are both extreme positions that are espoused by small minorities, and they are regarded as such by most of the rest of the population.

As might be expected in a nation that has had a long history of separating but also combining piety and politics in ingenious ways, most citizens, *including most believers*, want and expect the matter to be handled in another way. They are looking, in other words, for just the kind of alternative being explored in this book. And for all that has happened in recent years to alter the character of the religious life of this nation, it is difficult to imagine that being achieved on terms other than something like the way of thinking represented by the communions that comprise the "public church." Especially so, given the ever expanding variety of different religious beliefs and practices in this country. Far from being passe, therefore, the ecumenical style that these communions have adopted in seeking to bring their influence to bear on public affairs would appear to be just what is now called for.

5. *Looking ahead*

The difficulty, however, is that most, if not all, of the churches—and synagogues—in question are suffering from more than a little uncertainty about their identity and purpose these days. So it can hardly be taken for granted that they will have either the vitality or the confidence necessary to take advantage of such an opportunity. But by the same token, neither can it be assumed that they will not. Particularly not in this nation, which has had such a long history of periodic revivals of religious fervor. If the past is at all reliable as a guide, in fact, the odds are distinctly against a perpetuation of the condition in which they now find themselves. They are due for another "reawakening," and that is all it would take to create a situation conducive to the success of ideas of the sort being explored in this book. But the reasons why that is the case—and what it would mean if events were in fact to take such a turn—need to be spelled out. There has been so little recognition of such a possibility in the writing of legal and political theorists to date, in fact, that it needs *extensive* analysis if it is even to be made intelligible. And that is still another purpose this volume seeks to fulfill. Without actually predicting that such a development will occur, it presents several accounts of why such a possibility deserves to be taken seriously, and what in practice it could mean. On that score, too, therefore, the book ends up challenging in a fundamental way the terms on which such matters are currently being discussed.

NOTES

1. Marty uses this concept as a way of referring to a "communion of (Christian) communions" that all share a common way of relating to one another and the wider society. It includes almost all mainline Protestants, Roman Catholics, and some Protestant evangelicals. And it could well be adapted to include people of other faiths

as well. The hallmark of the "public church" is a commitment to engagement of the wider society combined with a willingness to work together with (and learn from) people espousing other faiths. This kind of tolerant and ecumenical behavior is now taken for granted as the norm in the "center" of American religious life, Marty maintains, and it presents a clear contrast to the "tribalism" that has been at work in the so-called "culture wars." Cf. Martin E. Marty, *The Public Church: Mainline-Evangelical-Catholic* (New York: Crossroad, 1981).

2. Stephen L. Carter, *The Culture of Disbelief* (New York: Basic Books, 1993).

3. Cf. Richard John Neuhaus, *The Naked Public Square: Religion and Democracy in America*, 2nd. ed. (Grand Rapids, Mich.: Erdmans, 1984).

4. It is interesting to note how even John Rawls has come around to acknowledging, albeit implicitly, the inadequacy of the view he has espoused about this matter in his recent work. For in the same book where he elaborates most fully his case for excluding references to "comprehensive doctrines" from public life, he ends up conceding, in an examination of the use of religious imagery in public speech by President Lincoln *et al* during the Civil War, the impropriety of excluding such references altogether. The concession ends up being a very small one, admittedly, but it reveals the extent to which even Rawls has a difficult time defending consistently the logic of the exclusionary rule he wants to affirm. And one can well imagine other conclusions being drawn from this particular example than the one Rawls himself is prepared to draw. Cf. *Political Liberalism* (New York: Columbia University Press, 1993), 249f.

1

The Inseparability of Reason and Revelation

David Walsh

We live in an age when the fixity of historical categories has broken down. Gone are the certainties of Enlightenment self-confidence and the even more brittle denominations of ideologies. Terms of debate cannot so readily be assumed as absolute. The resulting fluidity can of course dissolve all modes of discourse, but it can also provide the necessary flexibility through which to view old problems anew. So long as we realize that not everything can be deconstructed, we retain the possibility of illuminating what had previously remained obscure. It is only when the critical gaze is extrapolated toward everything that the boundaries are eliminated and we are left with a limitlessly expanding vacuum. If we stop short of seeing through everything there is still the possibility of seeing something. Just as we cannot reach an absolute standpoint from which a definitive analysis can be rendered, so we cannot dispense with the givenness of boundaries within which our provisional analysis must take place.

The challenge is always to find the middle ground between fixity and dissolution by which some new light might be shed on questions of long invisible familiarity. It is in this sense expansive to realize that our problem of the relation between religion and public life is tied to a specific historical context. It could not arise before human beings had "religion" which can be dated fairly accurately with the creation of the term by Cicero in *De natura deorum* (45 BC). Before he coined *religio* as a means of solidifying the content of theophany, the question could hardly even arise. Of course the Ciceronian distinction between religion and the state remained largely conceptual. It was not until the advent of Christianity that a substantive distinction came to be made between the things of Caesar and the things of God. The Stoic differentiation between types of theology—poetic, civic and philosophic—was brushed aside as unfitting to transcendent divine Being. St. Augustine revised the tripartite division which had come from Varro, to conflate the poetic and civic into mythology, the philosophic became natural theology, and the new theological truth was identified as Revelation.[1]

Even by Augustine's time the civic theology drawn from mythopoetic sources had largely disappeared. The Empire had officially embraced Christianity ever since the edict of Theodosius (380). Now there was only the theology of the philosophers and the supernatural theology of the Church. The tension occurred, not between these two, but between the official aspiration of the Empire to represent Christian truth and the particularistic demands of a pragmatic imperial symbolism. Despite the unqualified Theodosian establishment of Christianity the relationship between ecclesiastical and imperial representatives remained an uneasy one. An empire which had only lately come to the faith could hardly be expected to subordinate itself so thoroughly to the demands of filial obedience. The celebrated confrontations between Ambrose and the emperor, as well as the progressive cooling of Augustine's enthusiasm for anything approaching a Christian empire, testify to the abundant difficulties. The Roman Empire was not capable of becoming a suitable carrier of the Christian truth. It was only in its successor empires in the east and the west that a solution was developed to move beyond a state of uneasy truce into one of deep rooted cooperation.

It is from the background of the orthodox Christian empires, Byzantine and Latin, that the modern discussion of the relationship between religion and public life arises. Despite their differences in character, the medieval empires shared a common nature. Unlike the Roman Empire which saw itself as an empire first and looked toward Christianity to provide the spiritual supports it needed, the medieval successor empires understood their raison d'etre as the preservation of orthodox Christian faith. Their imperial political existence always remained subordinate to that function. As a result it was relatively easy to accommodate the ecclesiastical authorities, whether through the submissiveness of the West or the identification of the two that occurred in the East. Despite the tensions that naturally erupted between political and ecclesiastical, there was rarely any suggestion of a divergence of imperial authority from Christian orthodoxy. The interest of the political community lay precisely in the defense of the spiritual unity of the Church. Heresy was as revolutionary politically as it was religiously.

Despite the closeness of the twin sources of authority in the medieval Sacrum Imperium, it was from that background that the modern constitutional tradition of separation ultimately emerged. This was possible because the medieval tradition already embodied the principle of separate jurisdictions or offices within one embracing order. The larger order was defined by the revelatory truth of Christianity, but it was precisely the unquestioned character of the supernatural that permitted the autonomous freedom of a natural order to fully emerge. It is no accident that the scientific investigation of nature, the agricultural, commercial, political and civilizational flourishing of the West occurred under the sheltering arm of the Church. The success of the monastic foundations reflected in microcosm the success of medieval society as a whole. It was precisely the ascetic disciplines that generated the means of ensuring worldly material success. What better reflection of the simultaneously material and spiritual achievements than the construction of the great cathedrals?[2]

Of course it is precisely the moment of greatest material fruition that begins to erode the spiritual order on which it was based. The struggle for a renewed attainment of balance begins all over again and we are reminded of the degree to which the medieval world was defined more by the search than the achievement of equilibrium. Like the Sacrum Imperium itself, it existed more powerfully in evocation than in realization. It was in the long drawn out jurisdictional struggles that the great political contribution of the medieval world is elaborated. The modern constitutional tradition, we are coming more and more to appreciate, would be unthinkable without that rich background of legal, philosophical and theological reflection.[3] It made possible the only viable separation between spiritual and political authority, because it was based on a mutual recognition of responsibilities within a common understanding of the whole.

This is a point whose centrality cannot be overemphasized. If we think in terms of limited constitutional government, the very cornerstone of the liberal order of rights we have come to cherish, then the limitation must always occur in reference to something beyond the state. The political order must regard itself as restrained by the authority of a spiritual order beyond itself. It is not strictly speaking a separation of the two, so much as it is a recognition of their mutual self-limitation within an embracing order that includes them both. How else can separation occur than with reference to a wider unity? Even our putatively secular world still carries the marks of that earlier whole within itself. It is not simply that the term "secular" previously referred to property that had been withdrawn from religious use.[4] It is that the substance of a finite, natural order depends on the sense of a whole that transcends such limitation. To a very considerable extent our world is formed by the medieval memory of a state which knew and could define its place within the larger order beyond itself. Modernity can be understood as an indefatigable quest for contact with the lost unity of the whole, whether it took the convulsive form of the secular messianic movements or the saner constitutional evocations of an inviolability beyond the political.

The great difficulty is that the authority of the unifying symbolism, revelation, has progressively ebbed from our world. This is what accounts for the increasing sense of disorientation, the endless search for new absolutes, that characterizes the modern historical movement. We live in a world that has emerged from the wholeness provided by the acknowledgement of its transcendent unity. Yet we have neither been able to reestablish contact with that vivifying source nor eliminate the questions that point toward the void in our lives. It is of course possible to maintain a relationship with the God of revelation. In some respects religion is alive and doing extremely well in the modern world, and certainly surpassing the predictions of its obsolescence. The problem is that revelation no longer grounds a world of meaning. It persists as a fragment within a world of fragmentation. Revelation is not the authoritative apex of public truth. Rather it is a more or less vibrant component within a world of equally disconnected parts and, therefore, just as susceptible to cooptation in schemes of mundane utility as anything else within our reach. The stance of prophecy or even of ecclesiastic authority is hardly any longer viable.

Such a sea change did not occur overnight. It was the result of a long series of readjustments and it is well to remind ourselves of the millennial continuities, before we examine the central philosophical dimensions of the problem. We do not live in a postmodern world because in some sense we do not live fully in the modern world. Our world is stratified historically and some of the sediments reach very far back indeed. There is still an arc of mystery surrounding human existence.[5] No matter how far we travel or how many layers of reality we manage to penetrate, the mysterious horizon seems always to remain the same distance from us. We realize that our lives are structured in the same fundamental way as the earliest human beings who symbolized the mystery of the embracing cosmos in the form of spheres. Birthdays, marriages and deaths are still imbued with a sanctity that no amount of rational homogenization can quite erase. It is not surprising, therefore, to discover that the broader revelatory tradition persists even when it is no longer clothed in any definitive public authority. The medieval articulation of the state in terms of limited government, rule of law, and preservation of the inviolability of rights, could in this way continue even after the fragmentation of Christian universalism. A nonexplicated theological consensus could prove sufficient to sustain a constitutional order of rights that was strong enough to resist all varieties of absolutism and overcome the epidemic of religious conflicts. The secularized Christian polity proved to be an enduring symbolic form with reserves of durability that could carry it into our own era of complete religious disconnection. Continuities are so striking, in fact, that it would be difficult to claim that our current valuation of tolerance, respect for difference, and sanctification of rights is truly a postmodern language at all.

What is postmodern, however, is the sense of incoherence in the whole enterprise. Our present moment is characterized, not so much by the absence of religion, or of revelatory traditions, as the incoherent coexistence of all such fragments along with the most vociferously secular components. The medieval wholeness has finally shattered completely and we seem incapable of bringing the fragments together again. We can neither eliminate the inassimilable parts, such as through the relegation of religion to a wholly private sphere, nor make them cohere without violating the necessary autonomy of each. The only thing that is clear is that the incoherence is itself intolerable. Now we can perceive the extent to which the component parts, reason and revelation, suffer from the same incoherence themselves. Chaos infects not just the whole, but the operation of the parts as well. This is why the cry for a public reassertion of religion is as little comforting as the earlier cry for its elimination in the name of reason. Without a means of relating them to one another, the more forceful assertion of either spirit or intellect can only have the effect of exacerbating the anarchy.[6]

That admission is probably the point at which to begin a more structured reflection on the relation between these twin sources of the Western tradition. It is essential to recognize the incoherence of either reason or revelation on their own. One of the striking features of the primacy of scientific and technological rationality is the contrast between instrumental and final reason. Our sense of technology as an omnivorous force outside of our control arises from the gulf between the limitlessly expanding knowledge of means and the virtual absence of knowledge by which to direct its use. We have become knowledgeable about everything except what we are to use our knowledge for.[7] Equally, spiritual conviction lacking any public status as truth is no more than an exercise of private caprice. Without a means of distinguishing between true and false religion, spirituality can neither save itself or the world. It is confined to a consumerized type of religiosity in which all is a reflection of subjective demands and the shifting vagaries of taste. Revelation can no longer constitute the authoritative voice by which we are judged or saved. Now it is an option we select, so long as it fits our needs. It is as crucial for religion to authenticate itself as the truth of reality as it is for rationality to root itself in an order beyond choice. The nihilism of reason and the instrumentalization of faith go hand in hand. That is the deepest level of the modern philosophical dilemma.

The acknowledgment of the twin collapse of reason and of faith is the starting point for that far-reaching reconsideration of their relationship that has been underway for the past two centuries. It is no accident that the greatest thinkers of the period have been engaged with this project. Hegel, for example, presents the anomaly of a modern philosopher who goes against the prevailing secularizing trend to pose the old question of the continuity between reason and revelation. However we may judge the validity of his reconciliation, and I am not inclined to endorse it, we can hardly fault the seriousness with which he took up the challenge. For us the question is, why did Hegel commit his resources so energetically to the task of finding a modern means of connecting the bifurcated worlds of science and of faith? Surely it was because he understood the centrality of that relationship within the whole unfolding of modern and world history. He had understood that a rationality and freedom exercised without reference to any constraints beyond itself was doomed to unfold into the nihilistic abyss. One has only to read his analysis of the connection between absolute freedom and the terror of the French Revolution to recognize his insight.[8] At the same time he understood the vacuum into which the romantic recourse to religious subjectivity was leading. It was an immersion in an absolute in which, as he remarked, "all cows are black."[9] Absorption into the all in which differences no longer signify anything was the abyss that was later to take a wide range of forms from the mysticism of violence to the aesthetic dissolution of feeling. Either way the result was the same. Just as reason without vision is dead, so vision with reason is empty. Hegel was among the foremost to recognize the interdependence of the two. His stature as a thinker is, as it should be, tied far less to the solution he proposed than to the question he made inescapable.

But clearly if our reflection is to bear fruit we must begin, more modestly than Hegel, with the admission that we have only an indistinct understanding of what the familiar terms denote. The closer we approach "reason" and "revelation" the more we realize the multiplicity of meanings included within them. What is the original and therefore the controlling one? It can hardly be the neat dichotomization of the two modes of knowing divine being which has come down to us from the scholastics. Their disjunction of natural reason from supernatural revelation served the primary purpose of differentiating the transcendent component within our knowledge of God and salvation. To the extent that it is a knowledge of transcendent truth it cannot be known through immanent means. Only a self-revelation of the transcendent, supernatural divinity can make us sharers in the knowledge and life of God. A clear line of demarcation between the two realms, natural and supernatural, also fulfilled the secondary function for St. Thomas of facilitating the integration of the two orders. In particular it was essential to discover a means of relating the impressive corpus of natural philosophy derived from Aristotle, which represented a formidable challenge to the dominance of a largely Christian philosophic tradition. So long as Aristotle could be accounted as the exemplar of the limits of natural reason, his speculations could with minimal compression be integrated into the Christian theological framework. Of course it goes without saying that Thomas's central principle, that "grace does not abolish nature but brings it to perfection,"[10] contains a richness scarcely indicated by the foregoing sketch.

Yet despite that deeper complexity, the essential effect was to confine reason within a finite range in which the existence of God might be deduced but never encountered. The ironic consequence was that this autonomously subordinate reason could now operate more independently and, when the authority of revelation was later shaken, assume the primacy of public authority. It is one of the strange historical ironies that the effort to render reason a more reliable handmaid of revelation should end with a reversal of the roles. The pattern is already established in the generation after Aquinas when William of Ockham, in the name of Franciscan spirituality, severs the connection between the two. Ockham already sounds like a modern in the diminished confidence he exhibits in the capacity of reason. Better not to unsettle the certainty of faith by linking it in any way with uncertainties of rational speculation. Nominalism gets under way, not because it is motivated by the discovery of the limitations of reason, so much as it arises from the desire to overcome the insecurities of faith by affirming its wholly transcendent foundation. We are not far from Kant's later formulation that he found it necessary to place a limit on reason in order to make room for faith.[11]

In that poignant aspiration the dissociation of faith and science seemed complete. The Kantian rigidification could only be broken by the opening of a fresh perspective on each of them. In this task one of the signal advances of the past century has been a deeper historical appreciation, not just of the conditions of revelation, but of the nature of Greek philosophy.[12] The symbol of *nous*, we now know, can scarcely be translated by the modern truncated conception of "reason." Logos as the unfolding of nous has none of the later connotation of logical extrapolation within the limits of a closed system, an elaboration that is indifferent to the premises or purposes on which it is exercised. Rather, *logos* as the instrument of speculation is intimately connected with the apprehension of being that is identified with the experience of *nous*. As a whole they refer to the moment of human participation in the divine Nous, the event in which transcendent being erupts into experience and structures individual and political existence. Nous or reason is in this sense not a self-contained faculty nor an instrumental capacity for coordinating means and ends. It is the apex of a meditative unfolding in which the breakthrough of transcendent being occurs. Reason is at its core a form of revelation.

The strange thing is that, despite the manifest differences between the Greeks and the modern world, this constitutive character of reason still holds. Perhaps more correctly, it still holds us. We may no longer be aware of the structure but the originating destiny, in Heidegger's sense, remains impregnated in the differentiation even in its beclouded form. Once we realize the grounding of reason in an order of reality beyond itself and beyond all being, much of the confusion afflicting our modern notion of rationality begins to dissolve. We are, for example, struck by the contrast between formal and substantive rationality. We know the difference between efficiently relating means to ends and disastrously selecting the ends to pursue. Choice of values can be wildly irrational. Yet we lack any means of voicing such a critique because our notion of reason is restricted to formal rationality. The problem is that our conception of reason is too narrow to accommodate the requirements of reason in the full sense. We know or suspect that reason is not reason unless it is rooted in an order of being that is itself the illuminative center of reality. But how do we reach such a radical reconceptualization?

The only way is the one discovered and elaborated by the Greeks. The luminosity of reason is already present within the question itself. Before the inquiry begins there is already a knowledge of that for which it is in search, otherwise there would be no questioning movement. It is the faint glimpse of that which it seeks that draws the search for the ground into its unfolding. Gradually the outline of its goal becomes more apparent. It assumes a larger presence as reason discerns the source which is itself without a source. But a limit is reached. Everything we know points toward that which itself is not a thing like all the others, yet they do not provide a bridge over toward it. Only if the reality of transcendent being pierces the veil of our consciousness, which is accustomed to the finite realities of existence, can we encounter that which is "beyond being in dignity and power" (*Republic* 509b). Neither through our own efforts nor through extrapolation from the series of finite beings is such an illumination possible. Revelation is the flash of transcendent reality that reaches into the mundane consciousness of human beings. Its impact is such that it structures the whole of existence in relation to itself. The art of measuring all things in the light of being is what the Greeks designated by the term *nous.*[13]

Logos is the unfolding of the consequences for order in the cosmos, in individual, and political existence that follow from this unseen measure. But *logos* by itself lacks both its subject and its direction. Only *nous* with its apex in the revelatory glimpse of transcendent being provides the requisite illumination. What guarantees the reliability of *logos* is thus not merely its fidelity to its own rules of operation, the so called laws of logic, but its foundation within the orientation of *nous* that is at one with the *Nous* which is the ground of reality itself. The possibility of an identity between knowledge and being arises from the underlying continuity between human and divine Nous, which has received its illuminative confirmation in the revelatory encounter. Even the modern truncated understanding of reason trades on this background because it operates on the assumption of the compatibility of the instrument it uses to the analysis of reality. Reason itself rests on faith in the regularity of the order it explores. That faith in turn is nothing more than the assurance, dimly sensed by all but made luminous in the flash of revelation, of the participation of human *nous* within the divine Nous that governs all things.

The revelatory outburst is, however, no more than the beginning, although the very important beginning, from which the discovery of reason unfolds self-consciously within history. At its core, the encounter of human and divine Nous is no more than the illuminative event itself. It leaves shrouded in mystery the teeming questions about the meaning, possibility and consequences of the revelatory drama. We do not know how this irruption has been possible, what it reveals about the order of being as a whole or how it bodes for the eventual resolution of the problems of existence. Having broken out of the confines of myth we seem to be thrust deeper within them again. Revelation is in itself a narrow beam and how it is related to the larger whole from which it has emerged is of crucial significance for its gain or loss. If the change in human consciousness is interpreted as a change in the human condition then chaos results, for nothing of the kind has occurred. The preservation of the illumination that has occurred, reason, is crucially dependent on the discovery of the means of integrating it into the myth of the whole in which it occurs. Philosophy is characterized by its turn toward the order of the polis and the cosmos, rather than the exploration of the transfiguring mystery glimpsed at its apex.

A special moment in this divine cosmic drama occurs when the meditative quest for the divine ground has unfolded into the revelatory encounter in the full sense. The breakthrough of transcendent Being makes clear that none of the cosmic analogies are adequate depictions of the reality of God. Philosophy had reached that recognition but still clung to the possibility that the cosmos itself might be the *eikou thou*, the likeness of God. Revelation proper is rooted in the recognition that God is himself the only adequate revelation of himself. It is at that point that the transcendent God enters history in the mode of what we conventionally refer to as revelation. Essentially it turns on the realization that only the voice of God can communicate his meaning. The cosmic drama becomes also an historical drama in which all who hear the voice of God within must struggle to discern the divine disclosure in history as well. Once transcendent revelation has occurred then the transmission of the historically specific encounters becomes integral to the divinely willed order of existence. We cannot simply resort to the book of nature; we are obliged to consult the Book which has been transmitted to us. It is this historically formed continuity that constitutes the people of Israel and later the Christian Church and later still the tradition of Islam, since a book on its own can hardly convey its meaning.

From the moment when the revelation of the transcendent God takes place the historical instances assume a special importance, since they are the only adequate mode of divine representation. With the advent of Christ this claim takes on a unique intensity. He is no longer one of the intermediaries through whom the divine voice is heard and communicated to others. Now it is the fullness of transcendent Godhead that is present in this unique individual man. No more intermediaries or prophets can occur. In an important sense revelation is definitively over with the appearance of Christ. There can be no more adequate carrier of the divine presence than God himself, now incarnate in human nature within history. The unity of divine and human natures within the one person, Jesus Christ, means more than the definitive mediator. It is tantamount to the divine action which is identical with the divine knowledge and will. Christ is more than an exemplar of divine redemption. He is the savior of the world. Just as he is the culmination of the possibility of revelation, so he is also the definitive realization of myth. Inner and outer redemption are one.

The unique significance of Christ places the diversity of responses to him in sharp contrast. If he is the fullness of transcendent revelation why is he not universally embraced? A persistent plurality of responses and the durability of revelational traditions is itself one of the mysteries of the process. It reminds us that revelation is not tantamount to the gnosis of absolute knowledge. We are given no more than an assurance of the reality of the inner drawing of the Spirit. One of the many mysteries that remain concerns the plurality of revelatory outbursts and continuities. All we can know about them is the structure observed in Matthew 16:13-17. Christ asks his disciples who men say that he is. Some say Elijah, some John the Baptist or one of the prophets. But who do you say that I am? When Peter confesses "You are the Christ, the Son of God," Jesus calls him blessed. "For flesh and blood has not revealed this to you, but my Father who is in heaven." Those who are drawn by the Spirit of the Father are the ones who recognize the same divine presence in the Son. Revelation is an inward movement whose illumination enables the recognition of the carrier of divine truth. The interpenetration of the dimensions of grace and freedom, contingency and necessity, within that process cannot be pierced from any human perspective. We can only admit that the plurality of centers of revelation is so inescapable a reality that it too is included within the divinely willed order of being.

The irreducibility of the revelatory traditions, their persistence and interrelation within history, is one of the features of the human condition. Revelatory outbursts are as independent of our systematizing efforts as they are of our equally ineffectual efforts to ignore or eliminate their significance. But whatever the untidiness of multiple revelatory traditions, it is surely rivalled by the dependence of reason on experiences of revelation. Even for the Greeks this derivation of rationality from ordering experiences of Being was a source of difficulty. It made the establishment of the public authority of the philosopher a notorious political problem within a community composed largely of nonphilosophical souls. How could the truth of the vision of the Agathon be mediated to those who had not shared in it? Yet no matter how intractable the dilemma, at least it remained a largely political problem. The case was far different when the other revelatory tradition of Christianity came to deal with the Greek philosophical legacy. Clearly it was not an earlier form of revelation, as Judaism, and it could not be regarded as a separate revelation without diminishing the uniqueness of the Christian line. Thus began the long millennial effort to transform the Greek discovery of reason into a wholly instrumental faculty, with all of its varying consequences up to the present. Only from our own contemplation of the nihilistic outcome does it become apparent that reason cannot be disconnected from the order of being which is disclosed in certain revelatory experiences.

The sense of having come full circle, of having exhausted most of the blind alleys into which our historical categories have led us, is perhaps the most sanguine sign of the times. Less wedded to the rigid demarcations of reason and revelation we are perhaps more prepared to recognize that the reality in which we live is a good deal more mysterious and deeper than our penchant for intellectual neatness would suggest. Having reached the end of the age of reason we are a little more inclined to acknowledge that reason does not exist as a self-contained faculty. We do not possess an instrument of universal analysis capable of comprehending the whole of reality within its dispassionate gaze. Rather science is a capacity for investigating reality within certain boundaries and therefore itself as much dependent on the presence of that larger horizon within which it functions. Reason's capacity is grounded in its movement toward an illuminative source which it does not possess but knows as the goal of its inquiry. Human reason is reliable because it is one with divine reason. But they are not identical, and the preservation of the life of reason is crucially dependent on recognizing the limitations of the human perspective of well. Myth is as much a guardian of reason as revelation is its source.

The readiness to entertain such a more flexible outlook on conventionally solidified categories arises from three sources. We have already mentioned the openness achieved as a result of our vantage point at the end of the modern age, and we have also alluded to the dramatically deeper appreciation of the historical sources that have coincidentally become available to us. But there is a third dimension whose contribution should not be underestimated. That is the impact of practice. If indeed reason and revelation can never be fully separated then it would not be surprising to discover that, even in a world where they are officially held apart, in practice they are deeply intermingled. It is moreover no accident that this unnoticed commingling also coincides with the most formidable success of the modern world. More impressive than the achievements of science and technology is surely the creation of a public order whose stability makes such enterprises possible. In an age when traditional sources of authority have been drained of their public role, it is surely no small achievement to have constructed a political order whose moral authority remains paramount. I refer to the liberal constitutional tradition.

Its status is exemplified by the degree to which its dependence on the transcendent finality of human existence is almost wholly unacknowledged. The moral primacy of a constitutional order anchored in the recognition of the inviolable dignity and worth of each individual is so unquestioned that it is still taken as self-evident. A liberal order of rights is so authoritative that few raise the awkward question of its intelligibility. In a finite world, where calculation has rendered everything subject to our control, how is it possible to assign an infinite value to anything? Why should human beings be treated as inviolable sources of rights, irrespective of the social benefits that might be gained from occasionally overriding them? We are familiar with the hesitations and uncertainties concerning the justification of human rights. Interpretative problems seem to be a feature of our modern liberal regimes. But this incoherence serves only to underline the certainty that attaches to the principle of liberty itself. Validity is largely unaffected by justification.

The impossibility of providing a functional foundation for our liberal order of rights, which has today become philosophically transparent, is often mistaken as evidence of the insubstantiality of such regimes. But the durability and unsurpassability of liberal democratic forms testifies to a formidable inner resource. What is that depth which is so well concealed even from its own carriers? It is none other than the capacity of liberal constitutional forms to embody the core resonances of the revelatory tradition in respect to human beings. Two factors are at work in its emergence. Liberal orders have succeeded in evoking the spiritual consensus concerning human nature that derives especially from the Christian tradition, but is confirmed in all varieties of revelation. That is that man participates in transcendent being. An inescapable dimension of the infinite defines each person and ensures that he or she is never reducible simply to the sum total of their attributes within time. Participation in transcendent life, however it is elaborated, is the source of that resonance which is contained in the liberal reverence for the inviolable dignity and worth of each individual. Emerging in a period of religious conflict and fragmentation, the liberal political symbolism preserved the thread of connection between the political order and its transcendent source. Despite the appearance of a secular separation, its resonances and vitality are still connected to a reality beyond the human.

This continuity is confirmed in the second feature that has characterized the liberal tradition. Correlative to its focus on the spiritual core of human nature, it has also conveyed the sense of constituting a moral advance. The very concentration on the transcendent dignity of each individual heightens the awareness for the conditions and requirements that attach to such an attitude. A greater sensitivity to the universal character of the conception of rights, the necessity that it extend to all human beings, is integral to the sense of moral progress contained within the liberal tradition. Of course we are all familiar with the failure of liberal regimes to observe the principles they espouse, but this does not affect the degree to which the principles assume an independent status by which such regimes are themselves judged. It is noteworthy that the moral language in which all such battles are contested today is none other than the language of individual rights. No other touchstone of moral rectitude has established such a claim. More than a consensus language, liberal respect for the sanctity of each human being is recognized as the authoritative spiritual truth.[14]

We still live, in other words, in a world which is constituted by the awareness of an authoritative spiritual order. It is emphatically not a secular world. The utilitarian rational calculus is only a dimension which is itself surrounded by an horizon of mystery toward which our aspirations are directed. Revelation may not be explicitly and publicly represented, but it is not far from the resonances on which we continue to live. Reason is for us, as much as for our predecessors, illumined by the light of its transcendent source and guarded by the mystery of the whole in which it occurs. What then is missing in the implicitness of the modern as opposed to the explicitness of the medieval conception? Obviously a great deal, since the modern worldview suffers from the enormous confusion and incoherence occasioned by its inability to explain itself to itself. We might consider the fecund history of modern philosophical projects as an effort to come to grips with this impossible challenge. It is no wonder that we are today the inheritors of a postmodern civilization which, if it means anything, surely suggests we have at last resigned ourselves to the impossibility of rendering any coherence. The only problem with that attitude is of course that we continue to live and are really not as confused as we pretend we are.

A more fruitful approach might be to ask, what is gained by the modern silence about transcendent finalities that continue to animate it? While confusion may be one of the downsides, truthfulness may be one of the unnoticed benefits. The medieval world was after all left behind for some very good reasons. Chief among them was the incongruity between a civilization oriented toward man's eternal fulfillment but dedicated increasingly to embodying that goal in tangible material enterprises. By contrast there is something more appropriate about the modern unwillingness to affirm any transcendent reality as its own, a hesitation that seems more deeply grounded in the appropriate reverence that is owed. The great modern danger is of course forgetfulness of the transcendent, with the consequent distortion by which finite purposes are made to support infinite expectations. But so long as the limited and imperfect character of modern life is kept fully in view, then there is less danger of such disequilibrium. An opening is preserved for the transcendent fulfillment toward which all finite satisfactions point.

Awareness of transcendent reality exists, in other words, on the boundary of secular consciousness. This preserves not only the true meaning of secular, the relationship of withdrawal from the sacred, but more importantly the balance by which the eternal scale remains the measure by which this world is judged. Human action is of significance not only because of what it succeeds or fails to accomplish within history, but because it stands within an order of good and evil that transcends time. This is a realization that may not be on the surface of contemporary moral discourse, yet it imposes itself upon us as we engage in the concrete moral struggle. In the practice of living out the intimations of right and resisting the pull to evil an order of being discloses itself in its full transcendent majesty. Our liberal language of rights is an abbreviated attempt to express the awareness of this dimension of transcendent participation. So long as we are willing to trust in the depth concealed in its summary principles, the reality in depth will reveal itself to us in the concrete struggle to extend and realize their implications. It is as a transcendence in practice that the modern world approaches its deepest truth. Rendering that transcendent openness transparent is the core of the public contribution of the revelatory traditions.

The effect, as many of the following essays attest, is to call into question the breezy liberal self-confidence that the order of rights has nothing to do with religion. On the contrary, we suggest, conceptions of human dignity and respect are rooted in an intimation of the transcendent inexhaustibility of each human being. As Eldon Eisenach argues below, we might better understand contemporary liberal discourse as itself a variety of established religion. In such a context one cannot so easily dismiss one's opponents, for instance pro-life objectors to abortion and euthanasia, as merely "religiously" motivated. The truth is that the arguments on all sides are "religious" in some sense, including the insistence that religious arguments ought not to hold public sway. It is a principle that is enunciated with an authoritative certainty, for on a strictly secular basis we would admit whatever arguments were useful irrespective of source. The mask of neutrality has slipped away from contemporary liberalism. Without a hiding place we are compelled to struggle with the substantive questions of human rights themselves. We cannot avoid deciding publicly how the bearers of such rights are to be defined. How will we determine membership in the human race? It is the light of transcendent revelation that has historically generated the awareness of our common humanity. The application of that insight through the language of rights, we are continually in need of reminding, rejects all barriers of status to the transcendent reverence owed to each human being. Our rational articulation of justice cannot in the end be rendered satisfactorily without acknowledging its revelatory continuity.

NOTES

1. Saint Augustine, *City of God,* VI.5.

2. A fascinating overview of medieval civilization is contained in R. W. Southern, *Scholastic Humanism and the Unification of Europe,* vol.1: *Foundations* (Oxford: Blackwell, 1995).

3. Among the many studies by Skinner, Tuck, Tully and others that could be cited the strongest case has surely been made by Brian Tierney. See his *Religion, Law and the Growth of Constitutional Thought (1150–1650)* (New York: Cambridge University Press, 1982) and most recently, *The Idea of Natural Rights* (Atlanta: Scholars Press, 1997). Also, Annabel Brett, *Liberty, Right and Nature: The Language of Individual Rights in Later Scholastic Thought* (New York: Cambridge University Press, 1997) and the older perspective of Charles McIlwain, *Constitutionalism: Ancient and Modern* (Ithaca: Cornell University Press, 1947).

4. Concept histories may be found in F. Dekelat, *Über den Begriff der Säkularisation* (Heidelberg: 1958), and M. Stallman, *Was it Säkularisierung?* (Tübingen, 1960).

5. The work of sociologist Peter Berger has reminded us of this dimension. See his *A Far Glory: The Quest for Faith in an Age of Credulity* (New York: Doubleday, 1992) and *A Sacred Canopy* (New York: Doubleday, 1969).

6. See for example the aptly titled study of Gilles Kepel, *The Revenge of God: The Resurgence of Islam, Christianity and Judaism in the Modern World* (University Park: Pennsylvania State University Press, 1993).

7.Walker Percy portrays our predicament with wry humor in *Lost in the Cosmos: the Last Self-Help Book* (New York: Washington Square, 1983); for a more somber treatment see Martin Heidegger, *The Question Concerning Technology and Other Essays,* trans. William Lovitt (New York: Harper, 1977).

8. Hegel, *Philosophy of Right,* par. 258.

9. Preface to the *Phenomenology of Spirit,* trans. A.V. Miller (Oxford: Oxford University Press, 1977), 9.

10. *Summa Theologiae,* Ia.8.2.

11. Immanuel Kant, *Critique of Pure Reason,* trans. Norman Kemp Smith (New York: St. Martin's, 1968), 29.

12. The following analysis is indebted to the work of Eric Voegelin, especially his "Reason: The Classic Experience," in Ellis Sandoz ed. *Published Essays 1966–1985* (Baton Rouge: Louisiana State University Press, 1990), 265–91; and *Order and History* vols. III and IV. Voegelin's work in turn rests on a preceding generation of Greek scholarship which included Paul Friedlander, Werner Jaeger, and Dietrich von Hillebrand. It is a perspective which is largely shared by Hans Georg Gadamer and there are even remarkable points of convergence with the approach of Leo Strauss. The latter, however, stopped short of integrating the rational and revelatory components. See the inconclusive exchange and essays in *Faith and Political Philosophy:*

The Correspondence Between Leo Strauss and Eric Voegelin, 1934–1964, trans. and ed. Peter Emberley and Barry Cooper (University Park: Pennsylvania State University Press, 1993). My own assessment, "The Reason-Revelation Tension in Strauss and Voegelin," is included as the final essay in the volume (349–68).

13. Plato describes the movement of the soul in the train of the gods: "But when the souls we call immortals reach the top, they move outward and take their stand on the high ridge of heaven, where its circular motion carries them around as they stand while they gaze upon what is outside heaven. The place beyond heaven—none of our earthly poets has ever sung or ever will sing its praises enough! Still, this is the way it is—risky as it may be, you see, I must attempt to speak the truth, especially since the truth is my subject. What is in this place is without color and without shape and without solidity, a being that really is what it is, the subject of all true knowledge, visible only to intelligence, the soul's steersman. Now a god's mind *(dianoia)* is nourished by intelligence and pure knowledge, as is the mind of any soul that is concerned with what is appropriate to it (*Phaedrus* 247c–d). Similarly there is the description of the same experience in the *Symposium* by which man acquires "the privilege of becoming beloved of God, and becoming, if ever a man can, immortal himself" (212c). This is surely the context in which to interpret the remarks of Aristotle at the conclusion of the *Ethics* when he suggests: "We must not follow those who advise us to have human thoughts, since we are only men, and mortal thoughts, as mortals should; on the contrary, we should try to immortalize (*athanatizein*) as far as that is possible" (1177b33–36).

14. This is a line of reflection I have developed in *The Growth of the Liberal Soul* (Columbia: University of Missouri Press, 1997).

2

The Trajectories of Religious Renewal in America: Tocquevillean Thoughts

Joshua Mitchell

What I propose to do here, in a brief compass, is to offer some provocations drawn largely from Tocqueville, which may serve as a prolegomenon to one of the central questions before us today: what is the proper role of religion in public discourse in America? This question already supposes, of course, a certain instability or outright inadequacy lurking in the well-worn answers that presently obtain. I concur. While I can offer no proof, my intuition is that the question of the proper role of religion will become more prominent as the post–World War II liberal understanding—that preferences, but not beliefs, may be voiced in public discourse—begins to look less and less like a fixed reference point by which we may be oriented in this or any other historical moment, and more and more like an artifact of an historically specific set of circumstances to which we cannot return.

"Liberal Thought" is not an entity; it is hermeneutically reconstituted in light of the ever-new contingencies of history. As such, and in view of the predominance of religion over time, the *generic* formulation of the current problem is not whether religion ought to be let in, but rather why religion has been, for a time anyway, ostensibly left out of the public debate.

In the American context this insight seems especially important to remember. America is a land of periodic religious renewal, and public discourse has followed in step.[1] I do not think that this will change. Neither nations nor persons can wholly escape their lineage. However internally coherent the arguments of contemporary liberals within the academy may be for dismissing religion, these will be ignored if they fail to speak to lingering or emerging verities in society as a whole. Should there be something of a twenty-first century "Great Awakening" in America, then liberals who continue to await the imminent death of religion will be heard only by a remnant of fellow scholars who, like them, maintain a naive and irrational hope that the world will be transformed and remade in their own image. Tocqueville's prescient words, spoken in another context, are pertinent for liberals today and in the future:

> Eighteenth-century philosophers had a very simple explanation for the gradual weakening of beliefs. Religious zeal, they said, was bound to die down as enlightenment and freedom spread. It is tiresome that the facts do not fit this theory at all.[2]

I do not, by anticipating the renewal of religion in American life, mean to suggest that liberal thought will be thereby eclipsed. There are resources within liberal thought to address the coming renewal. And I will address those resources briefly in my concluding remarks. More important for our purposes here, however, are several anterior questions, which I outline immediately below, and consider more fully in sections of their own.

First, while writers throughout history have noted that religion is a perennial aspect of human life,[3] a prominent strand of Enlightenment thought presumes (historically) that modernity involves the movement from enchantment to disenchantment; and (normatively) that in the face of this historical truth, if religion is embraced, it is because individuals lack the strength of character to live in a world without God.[4] These claims so pervade the academic literature today that they form the point of departure *for* study rather than the object *of* study in most political theory. If religion is perennial, however, then some account must be given of why the idea of the disenchantment of the world *could* have been plausible for generations of European thinkers (and their intellectual heirs in American universities in the twentieth century), but not, interestingly enough, for Americans as a whole. To address this question I will draw upon Tocqueville's thinking about American exceptionalism. To put the matter succinctly, the *idea* of disenchantment made sense because of the *real-life* political and social transformations that occurred as Europe moved haltingly and with great turmoil out of the age of aristocracy. The categories of thought recapitulated the historical exigencies of the day—exigencies that did not get adequately mapped onto the American experience.[5]

Second, after considering whether the Enlightenment claim about the disenchantment of history is itself historically rooted in the European experience, I will review the account that Tocqueville offers for why religion remained (and still remains) a powerful force in American life. Where the argument concerning disenchantment directs our attention toward the political and social conditions of Europe during the transition from aristocracy to democracy, here the matter under review will be the different relationships that obtained between religion and politics in the American and in the European contexts, and also whether these relationships did or did not corroborate certain rudimentary religious verities Tocqueville thought to be inscribed, as it were, into the human soul—democratic or otherwise.

Third, in light of the foregoing, and after having presumably offered plausible evidence for the continued vitality of religion in the American future, I will survey what I am here calling the trajectories of religious renewal in America—by which I mean the religious topography, as it were, that is generated in the American context. If ideas are rooted in historical experience, then it is important to ask what are the features of democracy, and of the American experience in particular, that lend themselves to the expression of religion in this way rather than that. Religion may be an opening to the Transcendent, but its immanent articulations must comport with extant categories of thought—which, again, are themselves rooted in historical experience.[6]

THE ENLIGHTENMENT PREJUDICE AND AMERICAN EXCEPTIONALISM

Among contemporary political theorists, though less often political scientists, it is taken for granted that religion in America is an anachronism. Yet among Americans as a whole this is not the case. Indeed, by all empirical measures, America is one of the most religious countries in the world.[7] Such statistics do not, of course, tell the entire story, as Emerson duly noted:

> Our religion vulgarly stands on numbers of believers. Whenever the appeal is made—no matter how indirectly—to numbers, proclamation is then and there made that religion is not. He that finds God a sweet enveloping thought to him never counts his company.[8]

Nevertheless, *something* of note is being captured by the empirical measures. The question to be addressed, therefore, is why the American anomaly is possible at all in view of the Enlightenment claim that the beacon of reason will, given enough time, spread forth its light upon the darkness and chaos of religion—and that this will be good?

On Tocqueville's broader historical view, of course, the question must be turned around: the American "anomaly" is actually paradigmatic, and the Europe of his own day is taken to be the anomaly! Disbelief, he says, is an (historical) accident; faith is the only permanent condition of mankind.[9] The interesting question, then, is this: what are the circumstances that made it possible—indeed, likely—for the Europeans to adhere to the historically provincial notion that religion was an anachronism? His answer, as we might suspect, has to do with the political and social circumstances involved with the transition in Europe from aristocracy to democracy, which he thought generated the Enlightenment prejudice which political theorists in our own day so readily adopt.

Consider, as a way of understanding this larger claim, Tocqueville's thinking about patriotism in Europe. European history, he says, evinces a movement away from the enchanted world of instinctive patriotism and toward disenchantment.

> [When enchantment fades] men see their country only by a weak and doubtful light; their patriotism is not centered on the soil, which in their eyes is just inanimate earth; nor upon the customs of their ancestors, which they regard as a yoke; nor upon their religion, which they doubt.[10]

The European disposition of his day, he says, is to fall into a narrow egoism which cannot easily be prompted toward well-considered patriotism. Instinctive affiliation in which the self is caught up, mystically, into something greater than itself, has given way to near-sighted self-interest. The question, politically, is how to get citizens once again to become "apart-of" now that they recognize themselves to be detached—that is, how to move beyond open-eyed separateness. In America, Tocqueville argues, the political world never was enchanted in the way Europe's had been, and so was not subject to its attendant alternative: disenchantment. Politics was the realm of self-interest, rightly understood. It was an aspect of the practical everyday life of the Americans, nothing more or less.[11] The either/or of mystical corporate unity and radical dissolution arose only in the context of the European experience.

Not having had their eyes opened, so to speak, the situation for the Americans was different. Patriotism here *could* supersede the dangerous opposition from which Europe was unable to disentangle itself precisely because the notion of an enchanted politics had no hold on the memory of the Americans. From the outset they knew self-interest rightly understood, and so possessed a healthy form of patriotism in this, the age of democracy. Self-interest rightly understood was the only real alternative to the destructive antinomies that constituted the parameters of the European experience: enchanted, instinctual, patriotism, on the one hand and, on the other, disenchanted egoism.[12]

Guided, then, by self-interest rightly understood, of the sort that becomes *thinkable* only within the confines of a *local* forum in which occurs the practice of face-to-face politics, the Americans did not play out the European antinomies which proved so destructive. In a word, because of the extensive and long-standing hands-on experience with local politics, the Americans, in taking a share in their government, developed a well-considered patriotism. Because government in Europe was largely a top-down affair, this antidote to the disenchantment that occurred as a consequence of the destruction of the aristocratic order was unavailable there. *Practice* with government alone could overcome the experience of disenchantment; absent the forum of local politics where such practice was possible, there was no way out of the sober morass of disenchantment. In Europe, the politics of disenchantment—and attempted reenchantment—was almost inevitable. Not so in America.

It would not be too bold to say, following Tocqueville, that certain intellectual expressions of this experience of European disenchantment were bound to emerge, but at the same time, that these expressions would never wholly capture the American imagination. One thinks of the tortured efforts of Nietzsche in his early writings to return, by way of historical reconstruction, to the enchantment of the Greek World; and in his later writings to demand a brutal honesty regarding things religious, all things not seen with the cold eye of truthfulness—both of which intellectual projects correspond to the antinomies of enchantment and disenchantment[13] about which Tocqueville earlier wrote. Beyond Nietzsche lies Weber's influential attempt to forestall the emergence of an enchanted politics prior to World War I in Germany,[14] which, in turn, so influenced a generation of émigré scholars whose defining experiences were the events surrounding World War II: Strauss, Arendt, Voegelin, to name only the most prominent. Their problematic was constituted by the horizon given fullest expression by Nietzsche—in short, by the European alternatives of enchantment and disenchantment prophetically grasped almost a century earlier by Tocqueville. One hears the muted voices—Gunnell comes to mind[15]—of Americans today crying in the wilderness in the field of political science that it need not follow the lead of the post-World War II émigrés. Nietzsche and Weber, who, despite their own intellectual and personal peculiarities, so well articulate the European experience of disenchantment, do not speak to the American scene. Tocqueville, in his own way, offers corroboration: "[The American]," he says, "has nothing to forget and has no need to unlearn, as Europeans must, the lessons of his early education."[16]

Yet while the Americans did not have the historical burden of aristocracy and its dissolution to bear, they did face difficulties of their own; different from the Europeans, but with peculiar implications for religion nevertheless. I will explore these difficulties below, after attending to the historical differences in the relationship between politics and religion in Europe and in America.

FURTHER EVIDENCE OF AMERICAN IMMUNITY: RELIGION

The matter of patriotism in America, in Tocqueville's view, provides evidence that the disenchantment which occurred in Europe was linked to the absence of institutional forums in which citizens could take an active part in their government. Beyond this, however, there is an additional source of suspicion about religion in Europe: namely, the close alliance of religion and politics.

Tocqueville does not cite Augustine on this matter, but he well could have. The opening paragraphs of the *City of God* contrast the City of Man, which "sways in its temporal instability,"[17] with the City of God, which waits in patience and is known only through faith and hope. No doubt Pascal's important distinction between matters of the *heart* (about which religion speaks) and matters of *interest* (the purview of politics) also lurks in Tocqueville's thoughts.[18] Whatever the pedigree of the idea, it is clear that he thought religion remains powerful only when it resists the temptation to enlist the support of temporal government.

In Europe, Tocqueville argues, the Church had long ago succumbed to that temptation; and so, when the aristocratic order collapsed, so, too, did the Church.[19] The lesson learned by many Europeans who wished to buttress democracy against the old order was that it had to be supported on a wholly secular foundation. This view Tocqueville thought to be a tortured misunderstanding of the ground on which democracy must stand:

> [Today] I find [those] whose eyes are turned more to heaven than to earth; partisans of freedom, not only because they see it in the origin of the most noble virtues, but even more because they think it the source of the greatest benefits, they sincerely wish to assure its sway and allow men to taste its blessings. I think these [men] should hasten to call religion to their aid, for they must surely know that one cannot establish the reign of liberty without that of mores, and mores cannot be firmly founded without beliefs. But they have seen religion in the ranks of their adversaries, and that is enough for them; some of them openly attack it, and others do not dare to defend it.[20]

Religion was one thing, politics another. The Europeans did not heed this distinction; the Americans did.[21] The Europeans, like the sons of the corrupt fathers in Bk. VIII of Plato's *Republic*, saw only part of the truth: religion *aligned with* an anachronistic aristocratic social order was corrupt, but religion itself—that is, the language of hope that speaks eternally to the human heart—was not. The intellectual efforts of those Europeans who were, in the same breath, defenders of democracy and antagonists of religion, misunderstood the larger, necessary, affinity between democracy and Christianity.

It is worth pondering just how much of the philosophy of the European Enlightenment Tocqueville would have thought could be understood in light of the massive social transformation from aristocracy to democracy. Rousseau,[22] Kant,[23] Hegel,[24] Feuerbach,[25] and a host of other thinkers nobly sought to retain the best of what religion had provided without shouldering the weight of its institutional affiliation with an aristocratic social order that could no longer be maintained. Brilliant achievements of thought though they might have been, however, Tocqueville doubted that they could ultimately support democracy.

> I am informed that on the other side of the ocean freedom and human happiness lack nothing but Spinoza's belief in the eternity of the world and Cabinas' contention that thought is a secretion of the brain. To that I have really no answer to give, except that those who talk like that have never been in America and have never seen either religious peoples or free ones.[26]

The dream of the Enlightenment, of "man's release from his self-incurred tutelage,"[27] occupied a certain people with a unique historical burden. In America, the subtext of that historical burden was absent—the intellectual achievements of the Europeans could have no experiential referent here. The Puritans, being a part of the covenantal tradition, in fact, *chose* tutelage of a certain salutary sort![28] Religion did not stand opposed to democracy; it could, therefore, survive the transition from the aristocratic to the democratic age intact. European Enlightenment thinkers fought for disenchantment in order to further the cause of freedom; the Americans, on the other hand, "[see] religion as the companion of [freedom's] struggles and triumphs, the cradle of its infancy, and the divine source of its rights."[29] The European attempt to reject religion, to disenchant the world, was an historical accident, linked as it was to an unholy and temporary alliance between the City of Man and the City of God. In Tocqueville's words,

> It is by a sort of intellectual aberration, and in a way, by doing moral violence to their own nature, that men detach themselves from religious beliefs; an invincible inclination draws them back.[30]

In time, he thought the Europeans, like all the prodigal sons of all the errant sects of Protestantism, would return to the Church of Rome.[31]

The two examples I have given of the way in which the European experience leads to the rejection of religion while the American experience does not—namely, the top-down structural arrangement of politics, and the relationship between politics and religion—open up to the possibility that the question of religious renewal, in America, at least, may be earnestly posed rather than summarily dismissed. On Tocqueville's view, the question in America is not *whether* there can be religious renewal, but rather what are the circumstances which conspire to generate it and what forms is it likely to take. To these questions I now turn.

WHEN DOES RELIGION APPEAR?

I mentioned a few moments ago that the Americans, though immune from the difficulties that the Europeans faced, had to contend with difficulties of their own, which had peculiar implications for the development of religion. First and foremost of these is material prosperity. To be sure, the temptations of the world can and do distract the soul from its return to its spiritual home.

The injunction, "Sell all that thou hast, and distribute to the poor, and thou shalt have treasure in heaven: and come and follow me,"[32] sets up an antinomy the implications of which are not difficult to discern, *viz.*, material prosperity is an enemy to spiritual health.

Yet the matter is more complicated in human existence than it is as a theoretical construct. A more dialectical approach to the relationship between the material and spiritual domains than is set up by the theoretical opposition is warranted. In America material prosperity is, to be sure, a great temptation which makes citizens forget all else. It is *also* the case, however, that far from material prosperity being anathema to religious renewal, it may actually be responsible for it.[33] *Both trajectories—into the world that the soul may lose itself, and into the world that the soul may find itself—are possible.* Because human beings have both a material and spiritual nature, the more they throw themselves into one aspect of their existence the more the other makes its demands felt. It is not an accident, therefore, that in America—the land where material prosperity is loved more than anywhere else—there should be periodic revivals of religion. In Tocqueville's words,

> I should be surprised if, among a people uniquely preoccupied with prosperity, mysticism did not soon make progress. It is said that the emperor's persecutions and the massacres in the amphitheaters peopled the deserts of the Theaid; I should rather hold Roman luxury and Greek Epicureanism responsible.[34]

"The short space of sixty years can never shut in the whole of a man's imagination,"[35] Tocqueville says. The world may captivate human attention, but only for so long. The "instinctive sense of another life without difficulty"[36] makes itself known—and in proportion (if only periodically) to the effort to hide amidst abundance. Hence the periodic revivals in America, which have faint equivalents in Europe. The American experience, in a word, confirms the proposition that materialism is a threat to spiritual health, *and* that it may be a goad to it.

Pointing out the dialectical tension between the material and spiritual domains alerts us to the possibility of religious renewal amidst material abundance. Another reason why religious renewal is likely under these conditions is that such material abundance is necessarily attended by extraordinary complexities—both technological and social—which reinforce the sentiment that the world is in a state of perpetual flux requiring constant management and attention.

Whatever else may be said about the theoretical inadequacies of Hobbes's assessment of the state of nature, its depiction of the exposure and flux associated with the condition of equality accords too well with the experience of the democratic soul: there is no *Finis ultimis*, no *Summum Bonum*, to which we may readily accede; instead there is only "perpetual and restless desire of power after power, that ceaseth only in death."[37] We may wish to attenuate the language somewhat, but what cannot be denied is that the experience of the contingency of all things fills the democratic imagination. Tocqueville agrees. But whereas Hobbes denied the possibility of *any* resting place beyond the flux of existence, Tocqueville knew this view to be a dangerously partial account of the human situation. Hobbes *did* recognize that the impulse of citizens who were confronted with existential uncertainty would be to look toward the awesome power under which they stood—that is, toward that "mortal-God," the Leviathan.[38] (Hobbes, recall, unlike Tocqueville, was not a dualist,[39] and this is a decisive difference.) Tocqueville also knew that the uncertainties that attend equality do indeed direct citizens toward the "One" under whom all are equal, but he did not suffer the illusion that a temporal power, a mortal-God, might offer the solace that is needed. While the state may, like a God, appear to be "a sole, simple, providential and creative force,"[40] it simply cannot manage all of the complexities of democratic life—notwithstanding its promises to the contrary. Hobbes understood that complexity and uncertainty direct the citizens' gaze toward the "One," but not that any and all mortal renditions of the "One" would be insufficient. (One wonders whether Hobbes's theoretical error, while historically behind us, is one over which we in the democratic age will yet actually stumble.)

Tocqueville knew that precisely because the democratic age is one of unheralded complexity, there would be a longing for the "One," for God, of the sort only dimly foreshadowed in the past. The grinding details of democratic life captivate the soul's attention and diffuse its energies; yet the very absence of God in this condition of powerlessness sets into bold relief, again, the "instinctive sense of another life without difficulty"[41] that is written into every human heart. Complexity directs the soul *both* toward the earth and toward heaven, toward a bounded horizon without breathing room and toward the awesome panorama of God's Providence.[42]

> [In democratic ages, every man,] raising his eyes above his country, begins at last to see mankind at large, [and] God shows himself more clearly to human perception in full and entire majesty. [Under these circumstances] God's intervention in human affairs appears in a new and brighter light.[43]

Inscribed into democracy is the myopia and immediacy of commercial impulses, and of soliloquy masquerading as conversation—but also lurking are the more magisterial religious possibilities (and their derivatives) witnessed by Winthrop, Edwards, Melville, Emerson, and Thoreau. These myopic and magisterial propensities are complementary, not antithetical, phenomena. Complexity generates both possibilities.

In addition to the frustrations of complexity, the character of desire in the democratic age also unwittingly[44] yet inexorably directs attention toward religion. The right to pursue "life, liberty, and happiness" may be guaranteed in print, but while we may be able to grasp the document that assures it, the substance of happiness is a far more elusive matter. The Americans, Tocqueville says, "clutch everything and hold nothing fast, and so lose grip as they hurry after some new delight."[45] There is, furthermore, "a cloud [that] habitually [hangs] on their brow."[46] The pleasures of the democratic soul, like its attention span, are short-lived. What is more, like Warhol's fifteen minutes of fame or Orwell's five minute hate, democratic pleasure is set against the ever-present backdrop of the gray on gray of monotony.[47] Pleasure is comparative—something to be had against the background noise and monotonous clamor of democracy in which all are immersed. For this reason, only the greatest of contrasts offers the promise (but not assurance) of certain pleasure. Said otherwise, the only recognized pleasures in a democracy are ecstatic ones—that is, ones in which we are *ec-stasis*, out of our mundane experience.[48] The increasing elevation of the threshold beyond which pleasures may be found in the democratic age cannot, of course, proceed indefinitely; and it is only a question of time before the soul under democracy looks elsewhere—perhaps to "a still small voice"[49] which whispers that true pleasure is to be found in some other place.[50]

THE FORMS RELIGION IS LIKELY TO TAKE

Permanent though this need for religion may be, however, Tocqueville thought that in America the expression of religious renewal would take a variety of somewhat contradictory forms: among them Fundamentalism, Pantheism, and Roman Catholicism. His thinking was, I think, prescient in this regard. I will briefly explain how each may accord with certain democratic sentiments, and then add Mormonism as a fourth type, for reasons that will become clear in due course. What is remarkable in all this is that while Tocqueville thought that "[e]very religion has some political opinion linked to it by affinity,"[51] it is also that case that *the multiple and cross-cutting aspects of the democratic situation have linked to them a plurality of religious possibilities.*

Fundamentalism

The complexities of life cannot be long borne, as I have said, without simple, intelligible, injunctions.[52] Hence, the periodic return to Scripture in America—followed by worldly accommodation, whereupon the complexities of worldly life become too much to integrate and Scripture again finds its way, following Winthrop, into the wounded hearts of truant souls.[53] The history of the mainline Protestant churches evinces this pattern, and there is no reason to expect that this pattern will not continue into the distant future.[54]

The matter of complexity alone does not account for the efflorescence of Fundamentalism, however. Beyond this, there is Tocqueville's interesting, even if undeveloped, idea that in ages of democracy "God's *intervention* in human affairs appears in a new and brighter light."[55] By this I take him to mean, among other things, that the democratic soul, because it recognizes its powerlessness, knows of its need for the transformative *gift* of grace to unloose it from its corporeal constraints. (While the "secularized" version of this transformative gift may take the form of lotteries involving mortal coin, these offer only a pale imitation of what is really needed.) Theologically, what democracy confirms, at least in its mature stage,[56] is that "Pelagianism"—the doctrine that human beings may will their own salvation—misses the mark. The weakness of the will in comparison to the grand promises of unbounded life in late democracy confront the soul with a paradox akin to that about which St. Paul wrote about sin: "But I see another in my members, warring against the law of my mind, and bringing me into captivity to the law of sin which is in my members."[57] The democratic "mind" sees an open field before it, full of possibilities for goodness; yet against this stands its "members," by which is meant the concrete details of life and habit which hold it fast. Infinite possibility conjoined with embodied constraint: here is a prevalent conjunction of experiences in the democratic age that makes sin, in the Protestant sense, *thinkable*. Both the conditions of democracy and the Protestant view of sin render us *responsible* yet *powerless*. American Fundamentalism, with its emphasis on the sinfulness of man, is not an anachronism that stands *against* democracy; rather, it is an idiomatic expression *of* democracy.

There is a third, democratic, component to Fundamentalism, as well; namely literalism. Scriptural literalism is, in part, a response to the problem of complexity, but it is also a response to the problem of authority in a democracy. In ages of democracy, when formality and nuance appear to citizens as a kind of mystification, literal interpretations will always have an appeal.

> Men living [in democratic] times are impatient with figures of speech; symbols appear to them as childish artifices used to hide or dress up truths which could more easily be shown to them naked and in broad daylight.[58]

It is tempting to agree with Nietzsche, and hold Luther[59] responsible for this democratic prejudice for literalism.[60] Whatever its lineage, however, the fact remains that the democratic soul relies strongly on the authority of its own experience; having limited time to solve the manifold problems that daily come before it, the hermeneutic principle relied upon is unlikely to be scholastic. The Scopes Monkey Trial may have driven Fundamentalism underground until its reemergence in the Reagan presidency, but it would be a mistake to see in the trial a proclamation of the incompatibility of Christianity and modern democracy; rather the literal accounts of Creation upon which Fundamentalists relied should be seen as an aspect *of* democracy—or, more precisely, as one of its internal contradictions.[61] Democracy is the real source of literalism; Fundamentalism, for all its opposition to the secular world, unwittingly adopts this democratic "mode" in its very critique of it.

Pantheism

The broad category of Pantheism, the definition of which shall become clear in a moment, is informed, as well, by a quintessentially democratic impulse: in this case, the obsession with unity and the inability to accept *difference*. In Tocqueville's words,

> Not content with the discovery that there is nothing in the world but one creation and one Creator, [the democratic soul] is embarrassed by this primary division of things and seeks to expand and simplify his conception by including God and the universe in one great whole.[62]

In its specifically philosophical form, Pantheism may refer to those doctrines in which there is no separation between Creator and Creation; as a phenomenon of the democratic age it must be understood more broadly to include the general category of thought which is altogether suspicious of distinctions. Socially and politically, the pantheist impulse appears in numerous guises: equality between the sexes in civil and military life, global free trade agreements and uniform tax codes, post-modern thought, internationalism, earth worship and, more recently, the Internet, can all be seen as aspects of democratic Pantheism, notwithstanding their differing political pedigree. Where Fundamentalism finds its experiential root in the embodied particularisms—theologically, in sin—from which the democratic soul cannot be extricated, Pantheism finds its experiential root in the disembodied universalisms that social distance in democracy makes possible. No longer having need of a neighbor (as federalism gives way to the nation-state), the democratic soul may direct its attention to common humanity—and avoid the inconveniences of the face-to-face. Love at a distance is, after all, ever so much easier. In Tocqueville's words: "In democratic ages . . . the duties of each to all are much clearer but devoted service to any individual much rarer. The bonds of humanity are wider but more relaxed."[63] Or as Rousseau earlier tersely put it: "Distrust those cosmopolitans who go to great lengths in their books to discover duties they do not deign to fulfill around them. A philosopher loves the Tartars so as to be spared having to love his neighbors."[64]

On these readings, the peculiar paradox of the democratic age is that amidst the growing pantheist cry for *universal* human rights, particular associations between neighbors fall into disrepair.[65] Social distance from the particular, and universal proximity to the distant: these are the conditions which give rise to the various species of Pantheist thought. And, like the conditions which give rise to Fundamentalism, there is every reason to believe that they will loom ever larger as democracy ages. As the fascination with unity grows, so, too, will the articulations of Pantheism.

Roman Catholicism

I have already commented on the fact that the complexity of life in the democratic age may be redressed, in some measure, by Fundamentalism. Tocqueville knew of this connection, yet believed that in the long run the Roman Catholic Church, and not the sects of Protestantism, would prevail on the religious landscape.[66] His thinking on the matter warrants attention, if only for a point of departure for more extended ruminations.

"In general [Protestantism] orients men much less toward equality than toward independence," Tocqueville says,[67] and it so tends to decompose into a form of solipsism in which the method and object of love cease to correspond. While he doesn't fully develop this latter thought, in conjunction with his observations about the problem of authority in democracy, a critique of Protestantism emerges that accords with a long-standing body of literature on the subject.[68] Hegel, himself a Lutheran, understood the difficulty—though not, as I will suggest momentarily, as acutely as he might have:

> Many Protestants have recently gone over to the Roman Catholic Church, and they have done so because they found their inner life worthless and grasped at something fixed, at a support, an authority, even if it was not exactly the stability of thought which they caught.[69]

And elsewhere:

> The self-tormenting disposition [of Protestantism] in the present day has induced many persons to enter the Catholic pale, that they might exchange this inward uncertainty for a formal broad certainty based upon the imposing totality of the Church.[70]

Notwithstanding these difficulties, of course, he staunchly defended Protestantism:

> Each individual [came to enjoy] the right of deriving instruction for himself from [the Bible], and of directing his conscience in accordance with it. [Because of the Reformation] we see a vast change in the principle by which man's religious life is guided: the whole system of Tradition, the whole fabric of the Church becomes problematical, and its authority is subverted.[71]

Yet for all of Hegel's brilliance on this and other matters, it was Hobbes before him who grasped the problem as fully as any thinker ever has.[72] "After the Bible was translated into English," Hobbes says, "every man, nay, every boy and wench, that could read English, thought they spoke with God Almighty, and understood what He said."[73] Protestantism goes astray, in a word, because of its misunderstanding of the problem of religious authority. Granting such authority to individuals does not save religion, but rather destroys it. Hobbes comments,

> In a commonwealth, a subject that has no certain and assured revelation to himself concerning the will of God, is to obey as such, the command of the commonwealth, *for if men were at liberty, to take for God's commandments, their own dreams and fancies, or the dreams and fancies of private men; scarce two men would agree upon what is God's commandment.*[74]

In our own day we are able to see this phenomenon in the proliferation of sects within Protestantism and, just as importantly, in the proliferation of translations of the Bible. The age of democracy, which privileges the authority of each individual, will only cause this phenomenon to increase, and with it the dissipation of Protestantism. Ironically, if Hegel is correct about the character of Protestantism, the insight that subjectivity is the inner kernel of Christianity evaporates into shining ether as the authority of that very subjectivity destroys its own foundation.[75]

The *longing* for an escape from this dissipating situation, in which the authority of the subject is at once absolute and socially insignificant, leads the soul invariably toward the Roman Church. While Catholics may have been resigning their faith because of the unholy alliance between Church and worldly powers in the Europe of Tocqueville's day, when Protestants reach the abyss of independence and impotence, they are being drawn back toward the Roman Church—in his day and in our own. For this reason, Tocqueville was able to say, "Our grandchildren will tend more and more to be divided clearly between those who have completely abandoned Christianity and those who have returned to the Church of Rome."[76]

It is not by accident, then, that we are now entering into what has been called "the Catholic Moment." Without detracting from the respects in which Fundamentalism will continue to accord with democracy, because the site of authority in democratic ages rests stubbornly with the individual, for all that it may offer in the way of a profound understanding of sin and grace, the likelihood that it can prevail in this age in which the excesses of individualism reign is low. Should it be able to draw anew upon the covenantal tradition inaugurated by Judaism and carried forward by the Puritans, then perhaps there is hope that Protestantism yet has resources upon which it can draw. Short of that the strength of "the Catholic Moment" will likely continue unabated.

And, if the case for the Roman Catholic Church in the late democratic age were not strong enough already, I add, parenthetically, that as the idea of a universal human nature grows in proportion to the extension of democratic tastes and sympathies,[77] the Catholic insistence that Natural Law be used as a guide will be corroborated not so much by the valiant efforts of philosophers as by the convergence of real-life conditions that generate a commonality heretofore unseen in human history.[78]

Mormonism

The Church of Latter Day Saints has not received the attention it warrants among political theorists, in part because the historical purview of the latter is largely the Europe of the past five centuries. In light of its staggering rate of growth in the United States, however, some consideration of it is due here—on theoretical grounds, at any rate.

The Mormons are, of course, a thorough-going American phenomenon; and it is on that basis that I wish to consider them. It is worth recalling that, foreign as it may be to the American imagination, the idea of a national religion has an ancient pedigree, predating Christianity itself. Rousseau writes eloquently of the subject.[79] Yet it is Hobbes who, again, seems to have understood the root of the issue. I have already noted his insights about the crisis to which Protestantism is prone. His sympathies, however, did not lie with the Roman Catholic Church. To the contrary, while he thought that Protestantism suffered the fate of what might be called "radical particularism," he thought that the Roman Church suffered from what might be called "false universalism." Neither alternative can bring peace: the former because of the crisis of authority that attends it; the latter because prior to the End Time there will be nations and national churches, but no universals, whether church or global society.

This may sound like something of an anachronism, yet I wish to suggest that Hobbes may have been more prescient than we have given him credit for. Tocqueville well knew that democracy generated the twin phenomenon of what I have above called radical particularism and false universalism. His defense of civil society, which has received so much attention of late, is the *mediational* antidote to this twin phenomenon. More recently this phenomenon has been articulated in terms of the idiom of "Jihad and McWorld."[80] It is worth considering, however, whether Tocqueville's mechanism of mediation can any longer be effective—as he himself seemed to worry in his concluding chapters of *Democracy in America.* Should this be the case, other modes of mediating between radical particularism and false universalism will be necessary. Should Tocqueville's mode fail, I suspect that Hobbes's will be upon us.

Until the End Time, on this view, peace can be achieved only through strong nations, each with its own lawful interpreter of the state religion.

I say this not with a view to casting suspicion toward the Church of Latter Day Saints, but only with the view to suggesting that *if* Hobbes's mediational mode comes to be adopted because of the intractable differences that radical particularism generates, or because the pseudo-unification wrought by false universalism begins to decompose into violence (as it always has), then we *shall* have a national church. Mormonism is certainly the likely candidate, because it is the only truly *American* church. I suspect that the scenario I have presented lies in the distant future. Whether it comes to pass depends, in great measure, on whether Tocqueville or Hobbes saw the inner workings of democracy more completely.

LIBERAL THOUGHT IN THE NEXT AGE OF RELIGION

It is not by accident, I think, that Tocqueville thought of himself as a "liberal of a new kind."[81] The democratic world, he knew, would require a novel way of thinking about society, politics, and religion. On the one hand, democratic conditions confront citizens with opportunities and challenges to which they must rise with resources of their own—hence the shift from an ethics of virtue to an ethics of self-interest[82] (one is tempted to say *preference*.) Yet on the other hand, democratic conditions render certain thoughts *natural* to the democratic imagination.[83] There are, in a word, certain *habits of thought* that are likely to appear in the democratic age, which are not, strictly speaking, preferences. By these habits I mean such things as notions of equality, unity, autonomy, and the unmediated equality of all under the one.

Importantly, while Tocqueville thought that these habits of thought are generated in part out of the very conditions of democracy to which we are all exposed, he also thought that religion—specifically Christian religion—has a hand in generating these habits.

> There is hardly any human action, however private it may be, which does not result from some general conception men have of God, of his relations with the human race, of the nature of their soul, and of their duties to their fellows. Nothing can prevent such ideas from being the common spring from which all else originates.[84]

For this reason Tocqueville thought Christian religion to be integral to democracy: it generates the habits of thought within which preferences can operate toward democratic ends. Perhaps this sheds light on his claim that,

> Religion, which never intervenes directly in the government of American society, should therefore be considered as the first of their political institutions, for although it did not give them a taste for liberty, it singularly facilitates their use thereof.[85]

The domain of liberty, in which preferences are expressed, is undergirded by habits of thought that are generated by Christian religion.

Tocqueville thought it very important to separate these two domains of preference and habit, politics and religion, yet also knew that there must be an indirect connection. Religion was important to politics because of the *character* it brought forth—a character capable of using its freedom well. The relationship of religion to politics and political discourse must be indirect rather than direct. Democratic citizenship is more a matter of habit than of perspicuity. For this reason he was able to say:

> I am so deeply convinced of the almost inevitable dangers which face beliefs when their interpreters take part in public affairs, and so firmly persuaded that at all costs Christianity must be maintained among the new democracies that I would rather shut priests within their sanctuaries than allow them to leave them. What means are then left to the authorities to lead men back toward spiritual opinions or to hold them within the religion thereby suggested? What I am going to say will certainly do me harm in the eyes of politicians. I think that the only effective means which governments can use to make [religion] respected is daily to act as if they believed it themselves.[86]

In one respect, of course, this Tocquevillean position regarding the relationship between politics and religion is the cornerstone of the contemporary liberal edifice. Politics ought only to be the domain of preferences; belief has no business there. Yet at century's end the besieged liberal embrace of Wittgenstein's injunction: "whereof one cannot speak, thereof one must be silent,"[87] suffers the same misunderstanding it did at the onset of this turbulent century. Wittgenstein did not intend by his injunction, after all, to suggest that we need not listen, but rather that we must do so with *another* ear when the first one fails—as it must. Far from denying the dimension of the "unspeakable," he meant by his injunction to protect it, to grant it its due.

Contemporary liberal thought does not, however, intend to protect religion, to show its indirect yet necessary effect, by its insistence that belief has no business in democratic politics, in the politics of preference. Because liberal theory is blind to what Tocqueville called habits of thinking it can only conceive of religion in terms of the irrationality of dogmatic propositions about belief.[88] This is not the way that Tocqueville, as a "liberal of a new kind," understood Christianity and its relation to democratic politics.

Beyond the need to recognize the Tocquevillean insight that certain habits of thought generated by religion are integral to democratic politics (and that religion will likely be a powerful force in the next century and in centuries beyond), liberal thought must also deepen its great insight that because human reason is tainted by self-interest, politics must set its sights lower than the Aristotelian tradition might allow. While the rhetoric of liberal political thought has sought to be realistic about the human situation, it has confused a normatively correct insight—namely, that human beings ought to be constantly vigilant about their tendency to make into an absolute what is only partial—with the empirical facts of history which reveal that there is a *perennial* tendency to do just that. Liberal political thought, in other words, endorses a political form which disallows absolute claims, but does not have any way of accounting for the fact that human beings do, by their very nature, make such claims. As Reinhold Niebuhr wryly notes, "it is not within the province of the human spirit to choose qualified goods."[89]

Any political formulation that fails to take cognizance of this fact, which simply dismisses the religious impulse as a species of irrationalism that is wholly irrelevant to politics, as much contemporary liberal political thought does, does not have a firm grasp on the human condition. The "complacent finitude"[90] of liberal thought must be deepened to include an account of why, on theological grounds, human beings are not wholly satisfied with partial goods, and always seek to move beyond the finitude of human existence—even if only episodically. Tocqueville, of course, sought institutional mechanisms to avert this tendency toward, in his language, those general ideas which are disembodied from the partials of daily life:

> The best possible corrective [to the extravagance of general ideas] is to make the citizens pay daily, practical attention to it. That will force them to go into the details, and the details will show them the weak points of the theory. The remedy is often painful but always effective. That is how democratic institutions which make each citizen take a practical part in government moderate the excessive taste for general political theories which is prompted by equality.[91]

Important as this insight surely is, however, we also require a theoretical account to supplement the work local institutions perform—and this only a deepened liberal political theory can provide. To put the matter succinctly, only if liberal thought rediscovers that the theological root of its insight about the limits of human reason lies in the doctrine of human sinfulness, will it not only be able to both justify its suspicion of allowing absolute claims to enter into the fray of democratic politics and, to return to my penultimate point, *simultaneously* grant the importance of religion in forming the *character* so necessary for democratic freedom. This twin-insight, which seems to work at cross-purposes, is in my view, written into the liberal project right from its beginning, and must be recovered if it is going to be able to speak to the public verities of the next century. Liberal thought must then, as it always has, oppose theocracies of every sort; yet it must, as George Washington did long ago, acknowledge that the Enlightenment project of supplanting religion with autonomous "reason" in *all* domains of life will not provide what democracy requires:

> Of all the dispositions and habits which lead to political prosperity, religion and morality are indispensable supports. In vain would that man claim the tribute of

patriotism, who should labor to subvert these great pillars of human happiness, these firmest props of the duties of men and citizens. . . . And let us with caution indulge the supposition, that morality can be maintained without religion. Whatever may be conceded to the influence of refined education on minds of peculiar structure, reason and experience both forbid us to expect that national morality can prevail in exclusion of religious principle.[92]

NOTES

1. See *American Rhetorical Discourse,* 2nd Edition, Ronald F. Reid ed. (Chicago, IL: Waveland Press, 1995). See also *Political Sermons of the Founding Era,* Ellis Sandoz ed. (Indianapolis, IN: Liberty Press, 1991).

2. Alexis de Tocqueville, *Democracy in America,* J.P. Mayer trans. (New York: Harper & Row, 1967), Vol. I, Part II, Ch. 9, p. 295.

3. "[The seeds of religion]," Hobbes says, "can never be abolished out of human nature" (Thomas Hobbes, *Leviathan,* Edwin Curley ed. [Indianapolis, IN: Hackett Publishing Co., 1994], Part I, Ch. 12, ¶23, p. 71). See also Tocqueville, *Democracy in America,* Vol. I, Part II, Ch. 9, p. 297: "faith is the only permanent state of mankind." In more biological terms, following Hans Blumenberg (*Work on Myth,* Robert M. Wallace trans. [Cambridge, MA: MIT Press, 1985]), the achievement of upright posture so extended the horizon from which reality can "can come at one" (p. 5) that it became necessary for the imagination to arrest the "existential anxiety" (p. 6) that ensued when the human being nakedly faced the unoccupied, unnamed, horizon. Myth fills that horizon and arrests anxiety. On this reading myth is a permanent need of human beings, diminished perhaps, but never overcome, by the machinations of logos which would tame "the world." Tocqueville, too, seems to have recognized this need of "the human spirit never [to see] an unlimited field before itself" (*Democracy in America,* Vol. I, Part II, Ch. 2, p. 292).

4. Not withstanding his anti-Enlightenment sentiments, Freud, in the twentieth century, shared with many other Enlightenment thinkers this notion. See Sigmund Freud, *Civilization and Its Discontents,* James Strachey ed. (New York: W.W. Norton & Co., 1989), Ch. 2, p. 22, *passim,* where he reluctantly resigns himself to the fact that most human beings will be unable to face reality and so remain in the perpetual childhood that monotheistic religion countenances.

5. Even when the idea of disenchantment has been explored in the American context it lacks the depth found in European philosophy and literature. Henry Miller's *Tropic of Capricorn* is not Friedrich Nietzsche's *Thus Spoke Zarathustra.* It is worth pondering whether the shift in the locus of public discourse in America from Church journals to Social Science journals in the late nineteenth century, a shift which coincides with the Social Gospel movement in America, might be a distant equivalent of the disenchantment witnessed in Europe. In America, however, it is important to note that there was less of a *loss* of the religious voice in public discourse than a transposition of it from the churches to the universities. See Eldon Eisenach, *The Lost Promise of Progressivism* (Lawrence, KS: University of Kansas Press, 1994), especially Ch. 3, pp. 98–103.

6. Consider, in this regard, Tocqueville's observations about the importance of the history of the Roman Empire in accounting for the emergence of Christianity and development of the Roman Catholic Church. Tocqueville is not satisfied with a purely theological or philosophical account; for thought to *make sense* it must in some way accord with the real-life conditions that it articulates. "At the time when Christianity appeared on earth, Providence, which no doubt was preparing the world for its reception, had united a great part of mankind, like an immense flock, under the Caesars. The men composing this multitude were of many different sorts, but they all had this in common, that they obeyed the same laws, and each of them was so small and weak compared to the greatness of the emperor that they all seemed equal in comparison to him. One must recognize that this new and singular condition of humanity *disposed* men to receive the general truths preached by Christianity, and this serves to explain the quick and easy way in which it then penetrated the human spirit" (Tocqueville, *Democracy in America,* Vol. II, Part I, Ch. 5, p. 446 [emphasis added])." See also Alexis de Tocqueville, *The Old Régime and the French Revolution,* Stuart Gilbert trans. (Garden City, NY: Doubleday and Co., 1955), Part I, Ch. 3, p. 13, where the *idea* of equality could not take hold of Europe prior to the eighteenth century because the *real-life* conditions did not yet accord with it. The real-life condition of the Romans (where, as in Roman Catholicism, all are equal under the Pope/Emperor) "disposed" the people toward a religious idea that recapitulates what their lived experience avowed. They could easily come to *think* Christianity because the life they *lived* already evinced the Christian pattern. Being precedes consciousness; real-life conditions of equality dispose thought to accept certain religious notions. For Tocqueville, to put it boldly, thought moves not so much toward disembodied truth, as toward the familiar.

There is more: the breakdown of the Roman Empire into its numerous fragments had precisely the opposite effect on thought than did the unification of Rome under the Caesars. "There soon developed within these nations an infinite hierarchy of ranks. Racial differences became marked, and castes divided each nation into several peoples. In the midst of this communal effort, which seemed bent on subdividing humanity into as many fragments as it is possible to conceive, Christianity did not lose sight of the principal general ideas which it had brought to light. . . . Unable [then] to subdivide the Deity, they could at least multiply and aggrandize his agents beyond measure" (Tocqueville, *Democracy in America,* Vol. II, Part I, Ch. 5, p. 446). There is an account of why Roman Catholics worshipped the saints. The real-life fragmentation of the Roman Empire disposed persons to accept the *idea* of particular mediaries who were God's agents.

Also see Paul Tillich, *Systematic Theology* (Chicago: University of Chicago Press, 1951), Vol. I, Introduction, p. 61: "the divine-human relation, and therefore God as well as man within this relation, changes with the stages of history of revelation and with the stages of every personal development." Tillich's "method of correlation," like Tocqueville's sociology of knowledge, insists that the *whatness* of God *for humankind* can never be other than historically bound, and can only be comprehended in terms of lived experience at any given moment of history.

7. See "World Values Survey, 1991-93."

8. Ralph Waldo Emerson, "The Over-Soul," in *Emerson's Essays* (New York: Harper & Row, 1951), p. 209.

9. Tocqueville, *Democracy in America*, Vol. I, Part II, Ch. 9, p. 297.

10. Tocqueville, *Democracy in America*, Vol. I, Part II, Ch. 6, p. 236.

11. In this light, it is interesting to note that certain political theorists seem rather put off by this unremarkable view of politics. Hannah Arendt, for example, while occasionally praising Tocqueville, never seems to understand that American politics is not the domain where ancient Greek notions of politics can make sense. See Hannah Arendt, *The Human Condition* (Chicago: University of Chicago Press, 1958), Ch. II, §7, pp. 54–55: "if the world is to contain a public space [which gathers men together and relates them to each other], it cannot be erected for one generation and planned for the living only; it must transcend the life-span of mortal men. Without this transcendence into the potentially earthly immortality, no politics, strictly speaking, no common world and no public realm, is possible." The eternity which Christians sought is no substitute for the immortality of heroic deeds and words in the public space that politics offers. For the Americans, on Tocqueville's view, politics has little to do with "heroic deeds."

12. See Carl Schmitt, *The Crisis of Parliamentary Democracy* (Cambridge, Mass.: MIT Press, 1985). Commenting on Marxism's response to bourgeois rationalism Schmitt notes, "as Trotsky justly reminded the democrat Kautsky, the awareness of relative truths never gives one the courage to use force and to spill blood" (p. 64). (See also Jean-Jacques Rousseau, *Emile*, Allan Bloom trans. [New York: Basic Books, 1979], Bk. III, p. 183: "in vain does tranquil reason make us approve or criticize; it is only passion which makes us act." Rousseau's comment, however, pertains to the stage in the development of the soul where reason begins to be awakened by the right exercise of the body, after which we become adults.) Schmitt's opposition to liberalism stems from his assumption that self-interest is weak and unable to make sacrifices. Community must be based on enchantment, not reason and self-interest. Tocqueville would, I think, see in Schmitt further evidence of European categories of thought that do not map onto the American experience.

13. Nietzsche's *The Birth of Tragedy* reflects the fervent attempt to re-enchant the world, while *Ecce Homo* reflects his effort to confront the hard truths of a disenchanted world.

14. See Max Weber, "Politics as a Vocation," in *From Max Weber*, H.H. Gerth and C. Wright Mills ed. (New York: Oxford University Press, 1946), pp. 77–128. While arguing against an enchanted view of the world, Weber was only a reluctant defender of a disenchanted world. It was, for him, the existentially honest posture to adopt at that historical moment.

15. See John G. Gunnell, *The Descent of Political Theory: The Genealogy of an American Profession* (Chicago: University of Chicago Press, 1993).

16. Tocqueville, *Democracy in America*, Vol. I, Part II, Ch. 9, p. 286.

17. Augustine, *City of God*, Henry Bettenson trans. (New York: Penguin Books, 1972), Bk. I, Preface, p. 5.

18. See Peter Augustine Lawler, *Alexis de Tocqueville on the Origin and Perpetuation of Human Liberty* (Savage, MD: Rowman & Littlefield, 1993).

19. See Reinhold Niebuhr, "The Tower of Babel," in *Beyond Tragedy: Essays on the Christian Interpretation of History* (New York: Charles Scribner's Sons, 1951), p. 32: "[the Middle Ages was a] 'Christian' civilization in its own estimation. But it was also a Tower of Babel. It failed to realize that it was also primarily a landlord's civi-

lization which had carefully woven the peculiar economic interests of feudal aristocrats into the fabric of Christian idealism. Its theory of the 'just price' sought to set a religio-moral check upon economic greed. But the theory of the just price was the expression of a consumer's economy at the expense of producers, the aristocrats being the consumers and the city artisans the producers. In the same way its rigorous prohibition of usury was ostensibly the application of a scriptural ideal to the problem of borrowing and lending. It was enforced only as long as the landed gentry were primarily borrowers and not lenders of money." Niebuhr's distinction between "biblical religion" and "culture religions" (Ibid., p. 44) is helpful in clarifying the problem about which Tocqueville worries. On Niebuhr's view, biblical religion warns against the construction of systems of thought which purport to grasp the whole. (The story of the Tower of Babel conveys precisely this message.) Culture religions, on the other hand, succumb too readily to this temptation. Tocqueville thought that the American genius was to have rejected cultural religion in favor of biblical religion.

20. Tocqueville, *Democracy in America*, Author's Introduction, p. 17.

21. Consider, in this light, the warnings of Luther and Locke—both suspicious of a Roman Catholic theology that failed adequately to distinguish between the two realms, political and religious. Luther observed that when the two worlds, spiritual and carnal, are confused "the door is opened for every kind of rascality, for the world as a whole cannot receive or comprehend it" (Martin Luther, "Temporal Authority: The Extent to Which It Must Be Obeyed," in *Luther's Works*, Helmut T. Lehmann ed. [Philadelphia: Fortress Press, 1967], Vol. 45, p. 92). In his own time he thought that the distinction between the two realms had become so confused that bishops ruled over cities while lords ruled over the human souls (Ibid., p. 109).

In Locke's words, "The care of souls cannot belong to the civil magistrate because his power consists only in outward force; but true and saving religion consists in the inward persuasion of the mind, without which nothing can be acceptable to God" (John Locke, "A Letter Concerning Toleration" [Indianapolis, IN: Bobbs-Merrill Publishing Co., 1955], p. 18). Locke echoes this view in the *First Tract*. (See *The First Tract on Government*, in *Two Tracts of Government*, Philip Abrams ed. [Cambridge: Cambridge University Press, 1967]). It is "out of a fond conceit of themselves" (p. 160) that human beings wish to intercede in the spiritual affairs of others. Doing so dishonors God because it supposes that His ways are easily discernible by beings whose judgment is corrupted by the flesh. It is these who believe that "they ought to vindicate the cause of God with swords in their hands" (Ibid., p. 160). Here, the state is given the right to intercede in matters of indifferency. This offers a check upon the human tendency to confuse what is essential and what is accidental in matters of faith.

22. See Rousseau, *Emile*, Bk. IV, "Profession of Faith of the Savoyard Vicar," pp. 266–95.

23. Immanuel Kant's "starry heavens above and the moral law within" (*Critique of Practical Reason*, Lewis Beck trans. [Indianapolis: Bobbs-Merrill, 1956], Part II, p. 166): what are these if not analogs of the two realms—carnal and spiritual—of which Luther speaks? Kant's two-fold division of reality in which the soul finds a respite from the storm of the sensuous world without is as severe in its lines of demarcation between the two realms as is Luther's. Richard Kroner, in his Introduction to Hegel's *Early Theological Writings* (Philadelphia: University of Pennsylvania Press, 1971), notes that "[the] philosophic decision [to deny knowledge of things as they are in themselves]

and the method of reflective subjectivity which it entailed are, according to Hegel, fruits on the tree of Protestantism. The reformers made an end to the confident rationalism of the Scholastics. They cut the bond between knowledge and faith, between human intellect and divine revelation, between the temporal and the eternal. By denying philosophy the power of penetrating into the essence of things, Kant and his disciples gave their blessing to this separation" (p. 37). See Otto Wolff, *Die Haupttypen der neueren Lutherdeutung* (Stuttgart: W. Kohlhammer, 1938) for the argument that Luther discovered the categorical imperative several centuries before Kant.

24. See G.W.F. Hegel, *The Philosophy of History* (New York: Dover Publications, 1956), Part IV, Sec. III, Ch. I, p. 415: "Luther's simple doctrine is that the specific embodiment of the Deity—infinite subjectivity, that is true spirituality, Christ—is in no way present and actual in an outward form, but as essentially spiritual is obtained only in being reconciled to God—*in faith and spiritual enjoyment*" (emphasis in original). The inner truth of Christianity, for Hegel, was subjectivity.

25. See Ludwig Feuerbach, *The Essence of Christianity*, George Eliot trans. (Buffalo, NY: Prometheus Books, 1989), Ch. 1, p. 2: "Religion being identical with the distinctive characteristic of man, is then identical with self-consciousness—with the consciousness which man has of his nature." The relationship between religion and self-consciousness, it should be pointed out, is a peculiarly German phenomenon, traceable to aspects of Luther's thinking.

26. See Tocqueville, *Democracy in America*, Vol. I, Part II, Ch. 9, p. 294. Worth pondering, in this light, is Acts 17:15-18:17. In Athens, where philosophy ruled, St. Paul's proclamation of the Good News was received with derision; in Corinth, where commerce prevailed, Christianity was received more favorably.

27. Immanuel Kant, "What is Enlightenment?" in Kant's Political Writings, Hans Reiss ed. (Cambridge: Cambridge University Press, 1970), p. 54.

28. See Tocqueville, *Democracy in America*, Vol. I, Part I, Ch. 2, pp. 36–39.

29. Tocqueville, *Democracy in America*, Vol. I, Part I, Ch. 2, p. 47.

30. Tocqueville, *Democracy in America*, Vol. I, Part II, Ch. 9, p. 297.

31. Tocqueville, *Democracy in America*, Vol. II, Part I, Ch. 6, pp. 450–51.

32. Luke 18:22.

33. In contrast, think here of Marcuse, who construed the problem of modernity as one in which the future is arrested because the dialectic is unable to proceed. His deepest worry was that in advanced capitalist society, "the space for the transcending historical practice . . . is being barred by a society . . . that has its raison d'être in the accomplishments of its overpowering productivity" (Herbert Marcuse, *One-Dimensional Man* [Boston: Beacon Press, 1964], p. 23, emphasis added). Consider also Nietzsche: "[O]ur modern, noisy, time-consuming industriousness, proud of itself, stupidly proud, educates and prepares people, more than anything else does, precisely for 'unbelief'" (Friedrich Nietzsche, *Beyond Good and Evil*, Walter Kaufmann trans. [New York: Vintage Books, 1966], Part III, §58, p. 69). Both of these ideas are already portended in Rousseau: society has become a closed system. This latter thought is something about which Tocqueville also worries. See Tocqueville, *Democracy in America*, Vol. I, Part II, Ch. 7, pp. 254-56; Vol. II, Part III, Ch. 21, p. 645.

34. Tocqueville, *Democracy in America*, Vol. II, Part II, Ch. 12, p. 535. Cf. G.W.F. Hegel, *The Philosophy of History*, J. Sibree trans. (New York: Dover Publications, 1956), Part III, Sec. III, Ch. 2, pp. 318–19.

35. Tocqueville, *Democracy in America*, Vol. I, Part II, Ch. 9, p. 296.

36. Tocqueville, *Democracy in America*, Vol. I, Part II, Ch. 9, p. 300.

37. Hobbes, *Leviathan*, Part I, Ch. XI, pp. 57–58, ¶¶ 1-2.

38. Hobbes, *Leviathan*, Part II, Ch. 17, p. 109, ¶13.

39. See Hobbes, *Leviathan*, Part III, Ch. 39, ¶5, p. 316: "Temporal and spiritual government, are but two words brought into the world, to make men see double, and mistake their lawful sovereign."

40. Tocqueville, *Democracy in America*, Vol. II, Part IV, Ch. 2, p. 670.

41. Tocqueville, *Democracy in America*, Vol. I, Part II, Ch. 9, p. 300.

42. Laura Ingalls Wilder's *Little House on the Prairie* series conveys the American situation well: on the one hand the enclosed attention to the details of daily life within and immediately surrounding the cabin; and on the other, the awesome, quiet, mysterious yet benevolent landscape upon which is played out the highly personal drama of American life.

43. Tocqueville, *Democracy in America*, Vol. II, Part I, Ch. 17, p. 486.

44. In this regard, consider Plato's intimation, in the *Phaedrus*, that the dark steed, the appetitive steed, drags the soul toward what it mistakenly takes to be true gratification; and that the discovery of true gratification can occur only in virtue of this initial *misunderstanding*—a thought confirmed by the journey to and beyond Rome that Augustine recounts in his *Confessions*.

45. Tocqueville, *Democracy in America*, Vol. II, Part II, Ch. 13, p. 536.

46. Tocqueville, *Democracy in America*, Vol. II, Part II, Ch. 13, p. 536.

47. See Tocqueville, *Democracy in America*, Vol. II, Part III, Ch. 17, p. 614: "[In an aristocracy] nothing changes and everything differs"—to which might be added: in a democracy everything changes and nothing differs!

48. Hence, in the 1940s the expression "Divine," and in the 1960s the phrase "far out!"

49. I Kings 19:12. I shall not here address the question of the place and significance of the Quakers, though the Quaker emphasis on silence offers a welcome antidote to the din of democracy.

50. See Plato, *Republic*, G.M.A. Grube trans. (Indianapolis, IN: Hackett Publishing Co., 1992), Bk. IX, 583b–586c. All mortal pleasures, he says, are relative. As a consequence the possession of them can never fill the void in the soul, and if fact reveals this void in proportion to the alacrity with which mortal pleasures are indulged. The more human beings immerse themselves in mortal pleasures, the more these pleasures reveal their emptiness. This dialectical view is one which modern critics of materialism have, for the most part, ignored. Karl Marx, interestingly, is one of the few thinkers who has understood this connection, as his assessment of late capitalism reveals.

51. Tocqueville, *Democracy in America*, Vol. I, Part II, Ch. 9, p. 287.

52. Here is the basis of Tocqueville's profound difference with J.S. Mill, for whom all matters must be, in principle, open to critical inquiry. For counterpoint to Mill's "On Liberty," see Tocqueville, *Democracy in America*, Vol. II, Part I, Ch. 5, p. 443.

53. See Tocqueville, *Democracy in America*, Vol. I, Part I, Ch. 2, p. 46.

54. See Roger Finke and Rodney Stark, *The Churching of America, 1776–1990: Winner and Losers in Our Religious Economy* (New Brunswick, NJ: Rutgers University Press, 1992).

55. Tocqueville, *Democracy in America,* Vol. II, Part I, Ch. 17, p. 486 (emphasis added).

56. Tocqueville distinguishes between what could be called the age of transition, and the democratic age, proper. The former is characterized by an optimism that is generated by the combination of the destruction of old boundaries, along with the memory of nobility and achievement; the latter is characterized by the competition of all and against all—which institutes new constraints—and a loss of a sense of the possibilities for human greatness. See Tocqueville, *Democracy in America,* Vol. II, Part III, Ch. 21, p. 645.

57. Rom. 7:23 (emphasis added).

58. Tocqueville, *Democracy in America,* Vol. II, Part I, Ch. 5, p. 447.

59. See Friedrich Nietzsche, *On the Genealogy of Morals,* Walter Kaufmann trans. (New York: Random House, 1967), First Essay, §16, p. 54.

60. See Martin Luther, "Lectures on Isaiah," in *Luther's Works,* Vol. 16, p. 327: "faith must be built on the basis of history, and we ought to stay with it alone and not so easily slip into allegories. . . ."

61. Augustine's fifth century account of Creation, recall, was not literal (see Augustine, *Confessions,* Henry Chadwick trans. [New York: Oxford University Press, 1991], Bk. XII), and this because democratic literalism was unthinkable to him.

62. Tocqueville, *Democracy in America,* Vol. II, Part I, Ch. 7, p. 451.

63. Tocqueville, *Democracy in America,* Vol. II, Part II, Ch. 2, p. 507.

64. Rousseau, *Emile,* Bk. I, p. 39.

65. Furthermore, the only community that is difficult to dismantle in the democratic age is the abstract, universal, community. Local communities more readily give way. See Tocqueville, *Democracy in America,* Vol. I, Part I, Ch. 5, p. 62: "The difficulty of establishing a township's independence rather augments than diminishes with the increase of enlightenment of nations. A very civilized society finds it hard to tolerate attempts at freedom in a local community; it is disgusted by its numerous blunders and is apt to despair of success before the experiment is finished."

66. See Tocqueville, *Democracy in America,* Vol. II, Part I, Ch. 6, pp. 450–51.

67. Tocqueville, *Democracy in America,* Vol. I, Part II, Ch. 9, p. 288.

68. See, for example, Friedrich Schleiermacher, *On Religion: Speeches to Its Cultured Despisers,* Richard Crouter trans. (Cambridge: Cambridge University Press, 1988), Second and Third Speeches, pp. 96–161; G.W.F. Hegel, *Phenomenology of Spirit,* A.V. Miller trans. (New York: Oxford University Press, 1977), §658, pp. 399–400; Karl Barth's Introductory Essay in Feuerbach, *The Essence of Christianity,* p. xix; Ernst Troeltsch, *Protestantism and Progress* (Philadelphia: Fortress Press, 1986), pp. 95–99; Max Weber, *The Protestant Ethic and the Spirit of Capitalism,* Talcott Parsons trans. (New York: Charles Scribner's Sons, 1958), Ch. V, pp. 180–83; Robert Bellah, *Habits of the Heart* (New York: Harper & Row, 1985), pp. 243–48, *passim.* In contemporary social science, the "rational choice" paradigm is the latest incarnation. Here, theologically, there is no intermediary between the soul ("actor") and God (the "good" desired); each person *chooses* on the basis of their own conscience ("values"); and the locus of authority is the self. The self-reflective method no longer leads to God, but rather to strictly human "values."

69. G.W.F. Hegel, *Philosophy of Right,* T.M. Knox trans. (Oxford: Oxford University Press, 1967), Addition to §141, pp. 258-59.

70. Hegel, *Philosophy of History*, Part IV, Sec. III, Ch. 1, p. 425.

71. Hegel, *The Philosophy of History*, Part IV, Sec. III, Ch. 1, p. 418.

72. Hobbes complains in *Behemoth*, for example, that the effect of the controversy between the Pope and the Reformed church was, in effect, to bring the word of God within the reach of the Israelites—which Moses, in receiving the word of God *on the Mount*, had not done. The Pope, in keeping Scripture out of the hands of the people, had acted (rightly!) as Moses had. While the Reformed Church may have been correct in denying authority to the Pope, the effect of the controversy between them undermined the authority of both, for now the word of God was in the hands of the people.

73. Hobbes, *Behemoth*, Stephen Holmes ed. (Chicago: University of Chicago Press, 1990), Dialogue I, p. 21. Cf. Hegel, *Philosophy of History*, Part III, Sec. III, Ch. 1, p. 418: "Luther's translation of the Bible has been of incalculable value to the German people. It has supplied them with a People's Book, such as no nation in the Christian world can boast."

74. Hobbes, *Leviathan*, Part II, Ch. 26, pp. 213–14 (emphasis added).

75. Perhaps this is what Nietzsche had in mind in his compact formulation at the end of the *Genealogy of Morals* (Third Essay, §27, p 160): "two thousand years of training in truthfulness . . . finally forbids itself the *lie involved in the belief in God*" (emphasis in original). I add that his understanding of the essence of Christian religion is indebted to Protestant and not Catholic categories.

76. Tocqueville, *Democracy in America*, Vol. II, Part I, Ch. 6, p. 451.

77. See Tocqueville, *Democracy in America*, Vol. II, Part III, Ch. 18, p. 627.

78. On this view, the Democratic age is inaugurated just as the idea of Natural Law is being discredited by the claim that all social relations are conventional. Yet this view of the centrality of convention—a result of the mixing up of peoples of different stations in the transitional period after the fall of aristocracy—is itself superseded by a renewed acceptance of the idea of Natural Law that occurs as uniformity comes to prevail. The content of Natural Law may be different in the Aristocratic and Democratic ages, but the idea that human life accords with a Natural Law does not.

79. See Jean-Jacques Rousseau, *The Social Contract*, Maurice Cranston trans. (London: Penguin Books, 1968), Bk. IV, pp. 176–87.

80. See Benjamin Barber, *Jihad vs McWorld: How Globalism and Tribalism are Reshaping Our World* (New York: Ballentine Books, 1995).

81. Tocqueville refers to himself as a "liberal of a new kind" in a letter to Eugène Stoffels, July 24, 1836, in *Memoirs, Letters, and Remains of Alexis de Tocqueville*, translated from the French by the translator of *Napoleon's Correspondence with King Joseph* (Boston: Ticknor and Fields, 1862), Vol. 1, p. 381.

82. See Tocqueville, *Democracy in America*, Vol. II, Part II, Ch. 8, pp. 525–28. His theory of the destruction of the law of primogeniture also involves the supplanting of virtue by self-interest. See Ibid., Vol. I, Part I, Ch. 3, pp. 52-53.

83. See Tocqueville, *Democracy in America*, Vol. II, Part IV, Ch. 2, pp. 668–670.

84. Tocqueville, *Democracy in America*, Vol. II, Part I, Ch. 5, pp. 442–43.

85. Tocqueville, *Democracy in America*, Vol. I, Part II, Ch. 9, p. 292.

86. Tocqueville, *Democracy in America*, Vol. II, Part II, Ch. 15, p. 546.

87. Ludwig Wittgenstein, *Tractatus Logico-Philosophicus* (London: Routledge and Kegan Paul, Ltd., 1981), p. 189.

88. Like the Protestant thought out of which it evolved, contemporary liberal thought focuses almost exclusively on the perspicuity of choice.

89. Reinhold Niebuhr, *An Interpretation of Christian Ethics* (New York: Harper & Row, 1935), Ch. III, p. 69.

90. Niebuhr, *Interpretation of Christian Ethics*, Ch. III, p. 67.

91. Tocqueville, *Democracy in America*, Vol. II, Part I, Ch. 4, p. 442.

92. George Washington, "Farewell Address," in *George Washington, A Collection*, W.B. Allen ed. (Indianapolis, IN: Liberty Press, 1988), p. 521.

3

Transcendence and the Democratic Prospect

R. Bruce Douglass

> In our age, the I-It relation, gigantically swollen, has usurped, practically uncontested, the mastery and the rule. The I of this relation, an I that possesses all, makes all, succeeds with all, this I that is unable to say Thou, unable to meet a being essentially, is the lord of the hour. This selfhood that has become omnipotent, with all the It around it, can naturally acknowledge neither God nor any genuine absolute which manifests itself to men as of non-human origin. It steps in between and shuts off from us the light of heaven.
>
> Such is the nature of this hour. But what of the next? It is a modern superstition that the character of an age acts as fate for the next. One lets it prescribe what is possible to do and hence what is permitted. One cannot surely swim against the stream, one says. But perhaps one can swim with a new stream whose source is still hidden? . . . The most important events in the history of that embodied possibility called man are the occasionally occurring beginnings of new epochs, determined by forces previously invisible or unregarded.
>
> Something is taking place in the depths that as yet needs no name. To-morrow even it may happen that it will be beckoned to from the heights, across the heads of the earthly archons. The eclipse of the light of God is no extinction; even to-morrow that which has stepped in between may give way.
>
> Martin Buber[1]

It is common these days for democratic theorists to assume that the time when religion mattered to the success of democratic politics is now over. One encounters statements reflecting that view so often in the writing of the more influential figures that it is appropriate to think of it as a kind of conventional wisdom in those circles. Admittedly, those who hold such a view often are prepared to acknowledge the contribution certain religious beliefs have made in preparing the way for the appeal democratic ideas now enjoy. Some of them even go so far as to characterize that contribution as invaluable. But they then insist that it is a thing of the past.

This is why they can proceed as though the subject were one that could now be ignored. For if religion has done its work and is no longer needed to convince people of the value of the aims to which democrats are committed or to motivate them to act in conformity with democratic ideals, then of course it makes sense to think that we can stop talking about it. Especially so, given the complications created by the diversity of people's beliefs on such matters these days.

But what if that is not the case? What if it is a mistake to think that we have arrived as democrats and our willingness and ability to act in conformity with democratic ideals is something that can be taken for granted? To think that way is, after all, to adopt a very sanguine view of the situation in which we now find ourselves. And it is hardly self-evident that it is true. Especially not that it is the *full* truth. Nor is it a claim for which much argument has really been given, either. More often than not it has just been stipulated as though the matter were self-evident.

To anyone who is at all familiar with the history of serious reflection on democratic politics, moreover, what can scarcely help but be apparent is how oblivious are most of the people who think this way to the kind of troubling considerations that have been of concern to the more thoughtful students of the subject in times past. One looks in vain in the works they have written for any reference to, let alone analysis of, the problems posed by such phenomena as the "soft despotism" that concerned Alexis de Tocqueville or the "tyranny of the majority" of which J.S. Mill warned or Max Weber's "iron cage." It is as though they have not given a moment's thought to such matters.

But surely it is not possible to proceed in that way and do justice to the realities of the world we inhabit. There is just too much about our situation that is reminiscent of the problems with democratic regimes discussed in such works as *Democracy in America,*[2] *Considerations on Representative Government,*[3] and *The Protestant Ethic and the Spirit of Capitalism*[4] for us to be able to dispense with that sort of analysis. In fact, now more than ever would the sociological realism it entails seem to be needed, and when that is recognized and acted on, our situation is bound to look different from the impression created by those who would have us think that the battle for democracy has essentially been won in this part of the world.

Indeed, it is the argument of this chapter that things end up looking *altogether* different. For once one begins thinking in such terms, the fate of democratic ideals in our time becomes a much more complex—and uncertain—matter than it would otherwise be. It ceases to be possible, for example, to ignore just how much our lives are subject to the influence of powerful forces beyond our control—and how driven they tend to be. Or to act as though the social pathologies with which we must contend did not exist. Or to turn a blind eye to the fatalism so many people seem now to have in this part of the world. All that (and more) comes back into view, and if it is given anything like the attention it deserves, the mood is bound to change.

So, too, does the theorist's agenda. Instead of celebrating our achievements and acting as though the principal intellectual challenge we now face were to make sense of what we have already accomplished, the task becomes one of trying to understand why events are *not* turning out quite as planned. And if that is done at all well, it can scarcely help but result in a significant recasting of the problematic of democratic politics. For the more carefully one reflects on why it is that we are finding it so difficult to lead lives that do not significantly compromise the ideals we espouse as democrats, the harder it becomes to avoid facing up once again to the tensions and even contradictions that have been emphasized in most of the classic works on the subject. And once that happens, the practical task awaiting the theorist becomes one of figuring out what to do about the resulting predicament.

Much of what is said in this paper is designed, in turn, to show what that means. In particular it is intended to show what is to be gained from recovering a realistic sense of democracy as a distinct *way of life*, which is an idea that all too often has been either ignored or idealized in recent democratic theory. But this is done not just to provide an alternative view of the state of our public life, but to make a case for a different view of what is at stake in the debate we are now having in this nation about the place of religion in the conduct of public affairs as well. For if in fact we are not doing as well in realizing the ideals we espouse as democrats as the more fashionable theories would have us believe, it is not obvious, to say the least, that religious conviction—and even more, piety itself—are resources we can do without. Especially not if there is reason to think that this is the case because of our spiritual condition in some measure. The entire matter will need to be rethought, and that above all is what the argument that is elaborated in these pages is meant to show.

THE DEMOCRATIC ETHOS

The claim that democracy entails a particular way of life presupposes, of course, a certain conception of what it is. For if one conceives of it as nothing more than a set of procedures for allocating power and making decisions, it is not necessary to draw that conclusion. If the procedures in question are expected to be neutral with regard to outcome, it is in fact inappropriate to do so. For the whole point of democracy is to get away from practices that are biased in favor of certain ways of thinking and acting at the expense of others.[5]

The difficulty with that way of thinking about the matter, however, is that it fails to take into account why people are attracted to democratic practices in the first place. It gives the impression that they are for everybody, when as an empirical matter that is simply not the case. Such a view is ahistorical and thus oblivious to the fact that the appeal which democratic practices now enjoy is a result of the triumph of certain ways of thinking and acting over others. One would hardly know, listening to what those who hold such a view typically have to say, that intense battles were fought over the practices they advocate, and that it is only because people of a particular kind prevailed in those battles that we are able to talk about democracy as we know it today.

But these are considerations that must be taken into account if one is to have anything like a realistic view of the subject. And the more they are, the more evident it becomes that in actual practice democracy cannot possibly be neutral in the manner the proponents of a procedural conception would have us believe. For as even those who are most committed to a metaphysically and/or ethically neutral politics now acknowledge, it takes people of a certain sort to make it work.[6] And people of that kind can be expected, in turn, to use the opportunities with which democracy presents them in certain predictable ways.

It is not in the least surprising, therefore, that for all the talk we hear about pluralism, the technologically advanced societies we now recognize as democracies all tend to have the same sort of ethos, and it is one which reflects the same sort of values as the ones that were responsible for making them democracies in the first place. As much room—and encouragement—as these societies provide for diversity, the waking hours of most of their inhabitants are still spent primarily on pursuits that reflect the characteristic concerns of the middle and working classes. They are places where people enjoy unprecedented freedoms but typically end up living their lives in similar ways. They spend most of their time and energy pursuing "happiness" of a certain kind, and they take it for granted that is the right way to live.

Now more than ever, moreover, do the societies in question tend to do so with singleness of purpose. In contrast to the days when "the people" and the political forces representing them actually had some significant differences of opinion about the value of trying to achieve an ever higher standard of living, that tends now to be something almost everyone agrees we must do. There is no going back, leaders and publics alike say, and even if we could somehow extract ourselves from the forward march of progress, it would not be wise for us to do so.[7] For prosperity, understood as "growth," is essential to virtually everything else we want—and need. Whether it be jobs or education or up-to-date health care, we cannot expect to continue enjoying the kind of opportunity and services (not to speak of goods) to which we in this part of the world are now accustomed unless we are prepared to keep up. Especially is that the case if we want to make such benefits available on anything like an inclusive basis.

So even though we increasingly have at our disposal the technological capacity to reduce significantly the role labor plays in our lives while providing everyone with a comfortable standard of living, that is not the direction we are headed at all. Just the reverse. Despite the talk of "post materialist" values,[8] the trend in our time is, if anything, for those of us who live in the "developed" democracies of the world to spend more, rather than less, of our time and energy on "materialist" pursuits. Especially now that women have returned to the paid labor force in such numbers, the investment we are making in "making a living" is, in fact, arguably greater than ever.[9] And most of this is done, of course, for reasons that are thought to be compelling. We just "have" to do it, we say. We have no choice if we are to "keep up."

PROVING OURSELVES

Admittedly there is an element of hyperbole in talk of this kind. As even those who speak this way are usually prepared to acknowledge, it is not literally the case that we *must* follow the course of action they favor. We could conceivably choose to do otherwise. No one—or thing—is forcing us to go on living the way in which we are now in the habit of doing. We could decide to do something else.

But most of us do not, of course. We are very much attached to the assumptions that make the talk of necessity plausible, so we find it difficult even to imagine ourselves doing anything else. Regardless of what we *could* do, therefore, most of us end up falling in line.

Nor is this any accident, either. For the point of view in question is one that comes naturally to democratic peoples. It comes so naturally, in fact, that it might even be thought to be inescapably a part of who and what we are. And now that it has been woven so thoroughly into the fabric of our institutions, it has become even more obviously the right way to think. It is so much a part of our environment that it has become almost second nature to us.

Even if we did not have such encouragement, however, most of us would still be inclined to go along. For unlike certain other comparable projects that have been undertaken in recent memory with less success, the campaign to make us ever more affluent has met with little resistance. Those of us who are affected may have to be trained—and repeatedly induced—to do what is expected of us both as producers and as consumers, but it is hardly alien to us. We take to it so readily that it is difficult not to regard it as a natural inclination.

The reason this is so, however, is not just that it serves a "material" interest for us to do so. No doubt it does that, and the desire to preserve and keep on improving our current standard of living surely forms a big part of our motivation for being so attached to the way we now live. But it is not the whole story, and there is reason to doubt that it is even the most important part. For as much evidence as there may be of the famous cupidity of democratic man, it is not the only thing in evidence.

There is no denying, to be sure, that we are always striving for "more." If there is anything that is quintessentially middle class, it is that. But it is not just more "stuff" we are after. There are other desires and aspirations that are also apparent in our behavior, too, and when they are taken into account, it is not at all obvious that it is acquisitiveness per se that really drives us. To see the matter that way is, in fact, to trivialize what is going on. Even more than for the material rewards it brings, we want to succeed in order to demonstrate what we can do with *ourselves*. For as people living in fluid, "open" societies where social standing is more achieved than given, we very much want and need to "prove" ourselves in that way.[10] And it is for that reason even more that we tend to be as devoted to "growth" as we are. For it is above all in gainful employment that such vindication tends to be found in democracies.

THE PULL OF "NECESSITY"

It is true, of course, that the wealth generated by all this labor could be utilized for almost anything. It could just as easily be used to feed the poor as provide us with ever more consumption opportunities. Or to underwrite poets. Or to build cathedrals. And to some extent it is. There would not be anywhere near as many resources available for philanthropic, cultural and religious purposes as there now are in this and other comparable societies if all we were intent on doing was enhancing our standard of living.

Nor would the range of different kinds of activities in which we are involved be anywhere near as large as it tends to be, either. If we were nothing but dedicated utility maximizers, there could not possibly be as many of us who devote our time and energy to raising children, doing volunteer work, and running for public office as there are. And the fact that there is today more possibility than ever of people being able to devote themselves to such pursuits only underscores the truth of the claim that material progress expands our options. There is no denying that in principle we who today are the beneficiaries of such progress are in a position to do more with our lives than people have ever had the chance to do before.

At the same time, however, one truly has to be a Pollyana not to notice how constrained we tend to be in taking advantage of that opportunity. For it is hardly as though we are exactly leaping at the chance to turn our attention in other directions. There is some evidence now, admittedly, of a desire on the part of a growing number of people for more "balance" in their lives. Some among us, in fact, have even taken certain steps to achieve it. But they tend to be halting—and their importance can easily be exaggerated. For as a general rule they count for much less in determining the actual character of our lives than the tendency most of us now have to do just the opposite.

That tendency is so pronounced, in fact, that it is hard to avoid the conclusion that we are being pulled inexorably in the direction of an ever more complete domination of our lives by economic values and concerns. For in all sorts of different ways what we do—and how we do it—is being dictated by the logic of the market.[11] It is no accident that the assumptions about human motivation made by economists have an increasingly wide range of application. Everything from child care to our sex lives is being arranged to accommodate the demands of economic "necessity," and there does not seem to be any end of it in sight. If anything, the pull in that direction seems to be getting stronger all the time. And the more we complain about it, the more we seem to fall in line.

A SQUANDERED OPPORTUNITY

This does not mean, to repeat, that we need to go on living this way indefinitely, or even that we will be required do so as long as the societies we inhabit remain democratic. But it does mean that we are going to have to exert ourselves if we are to do anything else. The opportunity to do so will not be handed to us. It is something for which we will need to fight. And it will take real effort—and dedication—to succeed.

The idea that it might be good for us to do so comes from more, moreover, than just a recognition of the desirability of relieving us of some of the pressures we are now under. It goes without saying that much of the stress that comes from living as most of us in this part of the world do these days is unhealthy, and we surely would be better off if we could rid ourselves of some of it. It is more appropriate now than ever to regard what "progress" has brought us as a kind of treadmill, and the toll it takes on our health, marriages, families, etc. is all too clear. Whatever else may be said for our being productive on the job, it scarcely can be good for us to achieve it at the expense of the rest of what makes life worthwhile. And the more we are required to do so, the more evident it becomes just how much the resulting way of life leaves to be desired.

This is just the beginning of what is problematic about it, too. For what is also becoming more evident all the time is that there are other, even more troubling phenomena to which this way of life gives rise that cannot be explained away as mere growing pains. There have always been costs imposed by the modern quest for prosperity, of course, but in times past they could plausibly be construed as nothing more than temporary phenomena that had to be endured in order to realize the better future that lay ahead. But less and less do the problems we now face lend themselves to that sort of explanation. When highly sophisticated technology is used to create a popular culture that is *deliberately* designed to be "dumb" (and coarse), it cannot be blamed on our backwardness. Nor can the increasing superficiality of our public life. Or the incivility and crime. Or the reluctance of so many of our young people actually to make use of the educational opportunities they are afforded. All this is evidence that something has gone wrong, and the more of it there is, the more evident it becomes that we are going to have to change directions if we are not to end up betraying systematically the hopes that have been invested in the quest for "progress."

The case for doing so is even stronger, furthermore, if one has other ideas about life's meaning and purpose. If one thinks that human beings have better things to do with themselves than just to keep on making–and enjoying–indefinitely an ever more elaborate "living," the situation in which we now find ourselves cannot help but appear a squandered opportunity. And the more elevated one's conception of the alternative, the greater the sense of loss. To those who think, for example, that the quality of people's lives should be measured primarily in aesthetic or spiritual terms, it has to be a bad joke to hear our current way of life characterized as a (let alone "the") Good Life. The fact, moreover, that we persist in holding on to it as doggedly as we do in the face of mounting evidence of dangers that *most of us acknowledge* can only seem like obsessive behavior. Indeed, even in the clinical sense.

NOT BY BREAD ALONE

The suggestion that religion might have some role to play in solving this problem is not meant to be accepted uncritically, of course. Especially not in this country. Democracies have shown themselves to be every bit as capable as other regimes of using piety for their own purposes, and nowhere more successfully than here. Religion may have flourished on these shores in a manner that has often not been the case in other places where democratic ideas have prevailed, but the price it has paid for doing so is a high degree of conformity to the outlook and aspirations of the people responsible for giving the nation its identity and characteristic ethos.

Nor can the role religious beliefs have played in *creating* the problem we have been discussing here be ignored, either. For even though there is much that is obviously quite secular that is responsible for the commitment we now have to progress, it still owes a great deal to the influence of ideas that have a religious pedigree, and it is doubtful that it could ever have achieved the hold it now has over us were it not for the frame of mind that was created by those ideas. It is no accident that the conception of the meaning and purpose of labor reflected in so much of our activism is still commonly known as the "Protestant" ethic. Or that our allegiance to it is justified, more often than not, in terms that bear a distinct resemblance to the kind of thinking that gave rise to that ethic.

Virtually every faith which enjoys any significant degree of popular support in this nation has now endorsed the "progressive" view of our situation to a large extent, too. Even in communions that used to pride themselves on their antipathy to the modern project is this true. As one might expect in societies which have undergone extensive modernization over many years, even among the pious the influence of ideas that represent any sort of serious challenge to modern thinking is a fraction of what it once was. So the days are over when religious communities could be counted on to provide principled opposition to the advance of progress, and in its place has emerged a situation in which most believers are exposed to, and in turn espouse, a version of their faith that not only allows but even actually encourages them to behave as well-adjusted producers and consumers.

This does not mean, however, that they are encouraged to do so altogether uncritically. Or that as a general rule the role of religion in democratic societies has been merely to sanctify what the people involved would have been inclined to do anyway. As evident as is the tendency of democratic peoples to use ideas and symbols derived from religious sources in that way, it is not the only thing that has happened. As Robert Bellah *et al.* have shown in their studies of civil religion,[12] once people are in the habit of thinking in such terms, they can also be inspired to think and act in ways that are significantly different from what they would otherwise do. Indeed, sometimes even *very* different. Instead of encouraging social passivity, therefore, piety can actually make people more sensitive to the imperfections of the societies in which they live and less willing to tolerate them. The history of democratic politics is full of examples of demands for change generated in that way. Especially in this country it has been so common, in fact, that it is appropriate to think of the influence exercised by the churches and synagogues as one of the more important sources of the reform impulse in our public life.[13]

For all the accommodations people of faith have made with modern thought and practices over the years, it cannot really be said that they have embraced its conceits unequivocally, either. There are exceptions, to be sure, but on the whole believers have been well aware of what is problematic about modern life, and they have done what they could to correct it. As much enthusiasm as they have shown for the pursuit of an improved standard of living, therefore, they have not succumbed to the illusions it has bred. Not easily, at least. And in particular they have not found it easy to accept the notion that prosperity *per se* is the key to a good life. For all the appreciation they have had for hard work and its fruits, they have recognized that there is more to life than just making and enjoying a living, and they have been more aware than most others of the moral and spiritual perils of worldly success.

All along, it needs to be kept in mind, the investment of worldly activity and goods with higher meaning and significance which has been the characteristic feature of religious thought and practice in modern times has been accompanied by pointed warnings about its dangers. As Weber emphasized in his pioneering study of the subject, the same people who were responsible for creating the Protestant ethic were also ascetics of a sort.[14] Even as they praised productivity and all but made it into evidence of righteousness, they made it clear that the last thing they wanted or expected people to do was place much stock in the enjoyment of worldly goods. They went out of their way, in fact, to indicate that such behavior was *not* what the righteous would do. And for all that has happened subsequently to counteract the legacy of that mentality and create a different climate of opinion, it has not been lost. Over and over again the sentiment that gave rise to the Calvinist presumption against consumption has made itself felt in one form or another as people who were themselves serious about their faith have tried to reconcile it with the opportunities—and problems—presented by an ever higher standard of living. So for all the progress that has been made in making the enjoyment of affluence morally—and even spiritually—respectable, it is still something few believers do with an altogether clear conscience.[15]

OBSESSIVE STRIVING

It is one thing, however, for such a sentiment to survive and quite another for it to have the desired effect. And as Weber would surely point out, the difference such sentiments tend to make in the actual conduct of our lives is not all that great. The process of "disenchantment" he expected to accompany the attainment of a way of life devoted to the enjoyment of affluence may not (yet) have proceeded quite as far as he anticipated, but it has certainly succeeded in marginalizing ideas and sentiments that might take us in other directions. No matter how much those of us who still feel the need to pray and worship may be attuned to higher values, therefore, we have a difficult time giving them anything like the influence they deserve.

But it is not just believers who have this problem. It is not as though organized labor, the women's movement, the arts community or any of the other forces that over the years have made a point of espousing values other than commercial ones have proved to be any more effective in upholding those values in the face of the advance of "progress." Quite the contrary. Nor has the performance of intellectuals been all that different, either. In fact, if anything, we have inclined to be even more compliant than others. Despite our confidence in the power of reason (and flirtation with counter cultural ideas), we have shown remarkably little ability to do anything other than go along with—and even lend our enthusiastic support to—the triumph of economic values.

The important exception is, of course, the environmental movement, which has done much more than just flirt with ideas that are at variance with the ongoing quest for an ever greater prosperity. It is the one serious attempt that has been made to date to operationalize a commitment to values other than the ones that now prevail on any significant scale. What cannot escape the notice of anyone who is at all well informed about that movement, however, is how increasingly its leaders have felt it necessary to appeal to religious beliefs—and even to engage in theological reflection. In growing numbers they have acknowledged that they cannot expect to achieve any real change in people's behavior in the things that matter to them unless we undergo a cultural revolution of the sort that in the past has tended to come from movements of religious revival and reformation. So less and less have they been content to make their case in purely instrumental or utilitarian terms, and even public officials associated with the movement have found themselves appealing to considerations that have an unmistakably religious character.

Whatever the actual motivations for this behavior may be (and they are surely mixed), moreover, it is surely no accident. It is a direct result of the character of the challenge the movement has posed for itself. For as the better environmentalist writing now commonly acknowledges, sooner or later any attempt to bring about behavior that departs significantly from the commitment we now have to keep on improving our standard of living is bound to run up against the fact that the roots of that commitment run deep into our culture—and even into our souls. And it is not going to be challenged successfully until it is addressed at that level.

It will take more to do that, too, than just rethinking the way we perceive the natural environment. Environmentalists are surely right to stress the extent to which a particular view of nature is responsible for much of what we do as economic actors, and they are also right in thinking that the view in question is ripe for theological criticism. But they give a wrong (and self-defeating) impression in so far as they imply that our attachment to it is the root of the problem. For our behavior in that regard is surely even more a function of the way we are used to thinking of *ourselves.* Above all it is the restless, obsessive striving that comes so naturally to middle class people that lies behind our inability to give up—or even significantly change—the way of life to which we are now accustomed. And it will be only as the need met by that striving is addressed that we are likely to do anything else.

THE NEED FOR EMPOWERMENT

This is not to suggest that only the pious—much less the conventionally religious—are capable of meeting that challenge. Far from it. With even Nietzcheans talking about "reverence for existence,"[16] it is so obvious by now that the desired insight and motivation can be achieved in a variety of different ways that the matter is no longer worthy of serious argument. At the same time, however, not just any frame of mind will do. It is so much a part of the democratic ethos today to insist on valuing inclusion and celebrating diversity that it is all but taken for granted that any sort of "privileging" of a particular point of view is problematic. But in dealing with the matter at issue here, it simply will not do to say that the desired result can be achieved from almost any position. For it is just not the case. There are points of view people can and do hold that actually *prevent* them from seeing what needs to be seen, and most of us who are living in this part of the world are under considerable pressure to do just that.

As true as it may be in principle, therefore, that there is more than one way to acquire the habits of mind—and heart—that are called for, it can scarcely be taken for granted that we will be able to do either. Most of us will need to be *empowered* if we have any real chance of doing so. And it is difficult to imagine that happening without our having access to something like what believers are exposed to when they are at all serious about the practice of their faith.

It is even harder to imagine it happening on any significant scale without the benefit of the experience of faith itself. For as effective as the process of "disenchantment" may have been in undermining the public authority of religious belief in our time, the fact remains that for most people religion is still the place where they are most likely to be exposed to the claims of beliefs and values that have to do with something higher than the mundane concerns which absorb most of their time and energy. Indeed, now more than ever religious observance is the *one* place where people still have at least some prospect of distancing themselves from the insistent pressures of everyday life to turn their attention to something higher.

It is not just, however, that in the study of sacred texts, prayer, public worship, and the like those of us who still engage in such practices have occasion to *think* about something else besides our mundane concerns and put them in perspective. Even more important for the purposes of this discussion is the fact that through such experiences we are exposed to *realities* that can draw us out of our self-absorption and allow us to see the world around us on terms other than the instrumental ones to which we are so accustomed. Or, as Mircea Eliade put the matter in his classic work on the subject, an encounter with the sacred has a way of opening people up to *experience* reality a different way.[17] And it is one that naturally inspires the reverence we otherwise find it so difficult to come by.

DISENCHANTMENT AS IMPOVERISHMENT

The problem now, however, is that all this tends to be so attenuated. And compartmentalized. So even though we read—and even study—our Bibles and take part in services of worship, what we actually derive from such experiences is a fraction of what we have been led to expect. The condition of our souls is such that we have to strain just to get a taste of what is promised in the beliefs and practices we have inherited. Precisely because we are (late) modern men and women, we have a difficult time relating to the objects of our faith as anything more than ideas. Even with the best of intentions, therefore, these objects end up functioning in our lives as abstractions that all too easily lend themselves to manipulation to serve *our* needs. Indeed, all too often they are deliberately regarded and used that way! And even when they do seem to exert some independent claim on us, more often than not it is, as Weber predicted, in a manner that is relevant only to the most personal and private affairs.

At the same time, however, there is no mistaking the unease people increasingly have with the condition in which this leaves us—and even more, with the modern penchant for construing it as progress. It was, admittedly, not long ago that even a good many influential theologians were still thinking that way. But it is a practice that is going out of style. And there is more than one reason to believe that it may be fading for good. For not only is the modern project seen to be problematic now in a profound manner that is difficult to imagine being overcome, but the modern assault on religious experience is increasingly suspect as well. The days are gone when it could be confidently maintained that everything worth preserving in the religious part of our cultural inheritance can be captured in a secular, or "demythologized" form, and in their place has emerged a climate of opinion in which, if anything, our need to engage in such practices is itself regarded as evidence of a *deficiency* on our part.[18] The difficulty so many of us now have in appropriating religious beliefs on any terms other than literal ones is increasingly taken—and *experienced*—as a sign of spiritual impoverishment. And the clear implication is that we have lost something we very much need to recover.

It would be claiming too much at this point in time to say that we understand well what that is. There is still too much evidence in people's behavior of inchoate seeking and even of an inclination to exploit the spiritual unrest it reflects for other purposes (e.g., meditation as a strategy for "getting ahead") for any such conclusion to be warranted. But old habits die hard, and there is only so much activity of that kind that can occur before people can be expected to begin recognizing what they are really looking for. Especially is that likely, moreover, if the interest that has been shown here and elsewhere in recent years in learning from the experience of other civilizations were to blossom and bear fruit. For as more than one environmentalist has discovered, there is a sense in which the experience that is reflected in the great religions of the non-Western world—especially Hinduism and Buddhism—is more faithful to the real purpose of religion than the ones that are behind their Western counterparts. And the more exposure we have to what they have to offer, the clearer that can be expected to become.

This does not mean, of course, that we can or should take over uncritically what they have to offer, much less actually *become* Hindus or Buddhists ourselves. It is very ahistorical to think that anything like that could—or should—happen on the scale it would take to make any real difference in the handling of the problem under discussion here. But it is by no means out of the realm of possibility that the quality of our spiritual lives could be significantly enhanced by exposure to people whose religious beliefs and practices come from other civilizations.[19] One can well imagine such an encounter prompting some of us in this part of the world, at least, to cultivate anew parts of our own heritage (mysticism, for example) that have been neglected. Already there is some evidence of that. And who knows where it might lead, if in fact it were to prove fruitful? If it were to have a wider impact, it would hardly be the first time that the interaction between civilizations with very different cultures produced profound change in an established set of beliefs and way of life.

Even if that does not happen, however, the very fact that it is possible today seriously to entertain such a thought is the best reason we have for optimism about the democratic prospect. For what it reveals is not only how far we have come from the days when disenchantment could be regarded as an unqualified blessing, but also that the outlook it has produced may not be the last word. At the very least it means that it can no longer be taken for granted that is the case, and it easily can be taken as evidence of a lot more. It is the best evidence yet that the much-discussed waning of modernity may actually be leading us somewhere, and that it could end up producing more, therefore, than just a loss of faith.

A RECOVERY OF AGENCY

Wherever it is that we are headed, however, it is not back in time. No matter how much we may envy the richness and vitality of the spiritual lives of those who have preceded us and draw inspiration from their example, we will not be able to duplicate their experience. That is just not going to happen, and those who insist that a reenchantment of our lives in that sense is not possible are surely right to do so. They are also correct in thinking that if we are in fact democrats, we should not want to experience such a thing, even if it were in our power to bring it about. For along with the epiphanies people underwent in times past went, of course, much that was inimical to an appreciation, much less realization, of democratic values, and the last thing anyone who has a principled commitment to such values should want is to bring that back.

Where such people are not right, however, is in assuming (as they so often do) that is the end of the matter. For as certain as it is that we are not in a position to turn back the clock, it is not obvious at all that we are precluded from moving *forward* to recover something of what we have lost on a new basis. Indeed, if anything should be clear by now, it is that history does in fact keep advancing and in ways that are hard to foresee. And it is the modern tendency to deny that is the case and insist that events can only proceed in one direction—and have one outcome—that is one of the main reasons why modern thought increasingly seems so dated. For who, after all, can presume these days to know what history has in store for us, much less what we are capable of experiencing? In the heyday of the Enlightenment it may have made a certain amount of sense for informed people to think that way, but not any more.

Even less is it appropriate, moreover, to go on thinking of disenchantment as though it were unambiguously a source of human emancipation. One can appreciate, to be sure, why forward-looking people could see the matter that way in the days when ignorance and superstition were pervasive. One can even understand why it remained possible to do so as late as the middle years of this century, when even in the most technologically advanced societies an educated citizenry and a secular culture were still novelties and there was still some reason to think events were inexorably moving towards the realization of the emancipatory ideals of the Enlightenment. But not any more. Not when there is so much about the situation in which we find ourselves which suggests just the opposite is true.

Nor is it just that we continue to be subject to powerful forces we find difficult to control, either. That goes without saying. But what even more gives the lie to any suggestion that disbelief naturally makes for the kind of autonomy Kant had in mind is that we find ourselves caught up in a way of thinking that makes it difficult for us even to imagine mounting any sort of serious resistance to the pressures we are under. Most of us are so invested in the cluster of projects represented by "the market," "science," "technology," and above all "progress" that even when we recognize the value of doing something else, we are powerless to do much about it. Indeed, even when we acknowledge that it is likely to be *detrimental* to our well-being to continue doing some of the things being asked of us in the name of those forces, we find it difficult to do anything about it.

The trend, furthermore, is for us to behave this way *more* rather than less. This is what is so very ironic about all the emphasis now being placed on our ability to function as choosing agents. For it is not as though we are asserting ourselves more and taking control of our fate more effectively than those who have preceded us. Not in the things that should matter most to political theorists, at least. There may be a good deal of initiative being taken in matters pertaining to personal identity and relationships. But when it comes to the more public ones our tendency is to do just the opposite. Despite the fact that we are all too well aware of the shortcomings—and even dangers—of our current way of life, we show little inclination to do the things it would take to change it significantly, much less abandon it. Indeed, more often than not we actually pride ourselves on our skepticism about the utility of taking any such action! And we then justify the resulting fatalism by congratulating ourselves on our "realism" about the limits of our ability to change things for the better.

Whatever we might like to believe about ourselves and the situation in which we now find ourselves, therefore, the fact of the matter is that we are nowhere near as willing—or able—to make the most of the opportunities we have been given as we could be. For all the freedoms we enjoy and all the resources at our disposal, we seem to be incapable of doing much more with them than we have already achieved. So we are stuck in an historical rut. We just keep on keeping on. And the reason above all for this being the case is that we have lost the capacity to believe in anything that really transcends the way of life to which we are accustomed. We have lost historical agency because the range of things we are able to believe in has steadily shrunken. And we are not likely to get it back unless that trend can be reversed.

Unless, therefore, one is willing to settle fatalistically for our current way of life and assume that it is the best we can possibly do (as so many democratic theorists now do), it is not obvious at all that a spiritual reawakening would necessarily be a development committed democrats should regard as retrograde. In fact, it could well have just the opposite effect. It could be just the thing we need to move forward and realize the promise of the opportunity with which the rights and liberties we currently enjoy presents us. For more than anything else, what we need if we are to do that is *vision*—and not just in the weak sense of another "point of view," either. We need an alternative way of seeing things that *commands our assent*—and does so in a manner that reaches into the very depths of our being. For that above all is what it takes to be empowered. And it is hard to see how we are going to experience it these days in the absence of a more direct exposure to the movements of the Spirit.

NOTES

1. Martin Buber, *The Eclipse of God* (London: Victor Gollancz, 1953), 167.
2. Alexis de Tocqueville (trans. by George Lawrence & ed. by J.P. Mayer), *Democracy in America* (Garden City, New York: Doubleday/Anchor, 1969).

3. John Stuart Mill (ed. by Currin V. Shields), *Considerations on Representative Government* (Indianapolis/New York: Library of Liberal Arts/Bobbs Merrill, 1958).

4. Max Weber (trans. by Talcott Parsons), *The Protestant Ethic and the Spirit of Capitalism* (New York: Charles Scribners' Sons, 1958).

5. It has been the hallmark of much recent liberal political thought to emphasize this idea, of course, and even to make it into one of the principal defining features of democracy as the authors in question conceive of it. Virtually all those who have followed John Rawls's lead in insisting on the priority of the "right" over the "good" have taken this position. But there is nothing in principle new about it. Especially in this country it has long been common in both scholarly and popular circles to define democracy as nothing more than a set of procedures which are available to people with any and all views. But those who have adopted that view usually have ended up conceding at some point (as Rawls now has) that they expect the procedures in question to yield only certain kinds of outcomes, which can, in turn, be expected to appeal only to certain kinds of people. Nor is this a practice which is confined to political philosophers, either. It is just as common among political scientists, whose work is designed to be more descriptive and explanatory. For a good example, cf. Samuel P. Huntington, "The Modest Meaning of Democracy" in Robert A. Pastor, ed., *Democracy in the Americas: Stopping the Pendulum* (New York: Holmes and Meier, 1989), 11–18.

6. After going to great pains to show how important it is for liberals to get away from espousing anything like the sort of "comprehensive" claims about life's meaning and purpose made by such figures as Kant and J.S. Mill, John Rawls, for example, ends up conceding that when all is said and done, even what he is proposing can be expected to appeal only to people who think a certain way *and also* that it cannot be left to chance that citizens do in fact end up thinking that way. So for all he has to say about the value of pluralism, he ends up frankly admitting the need to enforce a certain outlook on children via the schools, *even if it means contradicting the firmly held convictions of their parents.* Cf. *Political Liberalism* (New York: Columbia University Press, 1993), 199.

7. It is one of the several virtues of Michael Sandel's recent book *Democracy's Discontent* (Cambridge, Massachusetts: Harvard University Press, 1996) to remind us how recent this development is. Far from being something everyone has embraced since the rise of popular government as we now know it, the priority we now tend to attach to economic "growth" is, as he shows, a result of events that have taken place *in this century*, and it could not possibly have happened if other currents of thought that had previously played a significant role in the public life of this nation had not been eclipsed. The claim he makes in this regard is even stronger, moreover, if the experience of other comparable nations is taken into account. Sandel's argument has to do almost entirely with the American experience, so he refers only to the resistance to the "political economy of growth" mounted by republicans and populists. But in other countries there were plenty of others (socialists, Catholics, etc.) who did the same thing, and for much the same sort of reasons. And the striking thing about the present moment is how much those dissenting voices have been marginalized, if not silenced.

8. Cf. Ronald Inglehart, *The Silent Revolution* (Princeton: Princeton University Press, 1977) and *Culture Shift in Advanced Industrial Society* (Princeton: Princeton University Press, 1990).

9. Cf. Juliet B. Schor, *The Overworked American* (New York: BasicBooks, 1991). The specific claims Schor makes about the "decline of leisure" in this country in the past few decades have been a source, admittedly, of methodological controversy that has not been satisfactorily resolved. As John P. Robinson and Geoffrey Godbey show in *Time for Life* (University Park, Pennsylvania: The Pennsylvania State University Press, 1997), the matter looks somewhat different when detailed records are kept of the specific uses people *actually make* of the time available to them. But only somewhat. Schor's fundamental point, which is that we could have chosen to use the technological advances of the last several decades to reduce significantly the amount of time (and energy) we invest in gainful employment but chose not to do so, stands. We could have kept reducing the length of the work day and expanded the amount of time available for other pursuits, which had been the trend up to the second half of this century. But we chose to move in just the opposite direction. Up to a point, moreover, it is undeniable that the reason this happened is, as she suggests, that, under the influence of the post-war economic "miracle," the societies in question opted instead for a steadily expanding standard of living.

10. This is an old theme of sociological analysis, of course, and it is no accident that sociologists still tend to have a better feel for the phenomenon than others. The problem it poses has been well explained recently by Peter Berger in these terms: "The idea that the self is some sort of central entity, and that every individual therefore has a 'true' self, is an illusion. Perhaps an individual may, through great effort, acquire such a center; but it does not exist as a given of human nature. Rather, the self is a 'hole' which must somehow be 'filled,' both by oneself and by others. . . . In practice, for most people, the best way to 'fill' this hole is by means of action." *A Far Glory* (New York: The Free Press, 1992) p. 111. What Berger has in mind entails much more, needless to say, than just filling psychic space. It is a matter of creating an identity that is in some appropriate sense *worthy*. And nowhere is this better illustrated than in our behavior as producers of economic goods. For as Robert Wuthnow has shown, the claim that we invest ourselves as heavily as we now tend to do in our careers just for the money will not stand up to careful scrutiny. Having devoted considerable attention to the subject in a whole series of carefully designed empirical studies, he insists that the relevant evidence demonstrates that something deeper is involved. Above all, he says, people work as hard as they are now inclined to do in societies like this one because they feel a need to "give a legitimate account of themselves." *Poor Richard's Principle* (Princeton: Princeton University Press, 1996) 92.

11. For an accessible account of what this means and the economic reasons why it is happening, cf. Robert Kuttner *Everything for Sale* (New York: Alfred A. Knopf, 1997). But the sociological reasons are better explained in Fred Hirsch's older but still relevant *The Social Limits to Growth* (Cambridge, Massachusetts: Harvard University Press, 1976). Robert Wuthnow's *Poor Richard's Principle* does a good job of putting the cultural dynamics at work in this process in its American manifestations in historical perspective.

12. Cf. Robert Bellah, *The Broken Covenant* (New York: The Seabury Press, 1975). The great merit of Bellah's work on this subject is that he has consistently emphasized—and shown convincingly in dealing with the experience of this country—the extent to which civil religion can have a critical, or prophetic, edge.

13. Cf. Peter N. Carroll, ed., *Religion and the Coming of the American Revolution* (Waltham, Massachusetts: Ginn & Co., 1970); Robert A. Handy, *A Christian America* (New York: Oxford University Press, 1971); H. Richard Niebuhr, *The Kingdom of God in America* (New York: Harper & Bros., 1937); Timothy L. Smith, *Revivalism and Social Reform in Mid-Nineteenth Century America* (Nashville, Tennessee: Abingdon Press, 1957).

14. Weber characterized the people in question as *worldly* ascetics, of course, but there is no mistaking the extent to which their lives were dominated by other-worldly concerns.

15. Wuthnow, for example, reports a "deep ambivalence" about the value placed on economic goods in American society by the people of faith who were interviewed in his research project on Religion and Economic Values. They were not opposed, as a general rule, to enjoying the fruits of prosperity, but they were convinced that Americans emphasized money and consumer goods too much for their own good. They also tended to be critical of their churches and synagogues for failing to address the subject more directly. Cf. "Pious Materialism—How Americans View Faith and Money," *The Christian Century*, March 3, 1993, 238–242.

16. Admittedly, this is usually couched in terms that complicate somewhat the meaning of what is being said. William E. Connolly, for example, appeals to what he characterizes as a "non-theistic reverence for *ambiguity* of existence (emphasis added)." But it does not take much exposure to the rest of what he has to say in this vein to see that he is doing roughly the same thing as what others who have invoked the idea of "reverence" have meant to do. Cf. "Identity and Difference in Liberalism" in R. Bruce Douglass, Gerald R. Mara and Henry Richardson, ed., *Liberalism and the Good* (New York & London: Routledge, 1990), 81.

17. "Man becomes aware of the sacred," he says, "because it manifests itself, shows itself, as something wholly different from the profane. . . ." Those who have such experiences have access, therefore, to a whole new order of things, and it is one to which they find themselves drawn instinctively. The more they partake of it, not only do they see almost everything differently, but they end up conducting their lives differently as well. "*Access to spiritual life always entails death to the profane condition, followed by a new birth.*" Cf. Mircea Eliade, *The Sacred and the Profane* (San Diego/New York/London: Harcourt Brace Jovanovich Publishers, 1957) 10 and 201.

18. There are any number of different ways of explaining what the deficiency in question is, but none is more effective than the critiques of our moral and spiritual condition provided by Iris Murdoch and Charles Taylor. The former stresses the shrinkage of moral imagination produced by a reductionist approach to symbols, the latter the self disempowerment entailed by our suspicion of anything that might actually have "transfigurative power." For the former, cf. "Against Dryness: A Polemical Sketch" and "On 'God' and 'Good,'" in Stanley Hauerwas and Alasdair MacIntyre, ed., *Revisions* (Notre Dame and London: University of Notre Dame Press, 1983), 43–50 and 68-91. For the latter cf. *Sources of the Self* (Cambridge, Massachusetts: Harvard University Press, 1989), esp. Part I and the Conclusion.

19. A good example of what this could mean has been provided by the Roman Catholic theologian David Tracy in a discussion of his own experience with dialogue with Buddhists. "Surely," he says, "the most powerful and attractive (perhaps even

fascinans et tremendum) aspect of the Buddhist analysis of the human dilemma which appeals to any contemporary Westerner aware of the plague of possessive individualism is the Buddhist analysis of our inevitable clinging to the ego. The Augustinian understanding of the self as *curvatus in se* has certain affinities to the Buddhist insistence of the ego's compulsive clinging to itself. The Christian understanding of the self as being a self capable of being a true, responsible self only by fidelity to the gospel dialectic of 'to gain the self, one must lose the self' can be radicalized by the Buddhist notion that only by letting go of the utter unreality of the ego and its compulsive clinging can we possessive individualists break the law of the infinite desire of the compulsive ego." *Dialogue with the Other* (Louvain: Peeters Press/Grand Rapids, Michigan: William B. Eerdman's Company, 1990), 77–78.

4

Recovenanting the American Polity

Daniel J. Elazar

THE COVENANTAL ORIGINS OF THE AMERICAN EXPERIMENT

The American experiment was born in federal liberty, birthed by covenant. In the first epoch of its existence, encompassing the roughly 300 years from the first British, Dutch, and Swedish settlements along the eastern seaboard prior to the mid-seventeenth century and until America's emergence as the predominant world power in the mid-twentieth, the American people formed themselves through and around covenants and compacts, their more secular derivative, as they founded their settlements from coast to coast, established their social and political institutions, and developed a comprehensive American civilization based on federal liberty; that is to say, the liberty to live up to the terms embodied in their covenants (as opposed to natural liberty of everyone doing what he or she wished). Elsewhere, this writer and others have described all of this in detail.[1]

It is a central contention of this chapter that the covenantal tradition in both theory and practice presents a compelling framework for articulating the common good. Indeed, as Donald Lutz has shown, it is found at the roots of American constitutionalism. Covenantalism acknowledges equally the legitimacy of individual projects and associative loyalties. It does not rigidly subordinate the personal and the local to either an hierarchical or a collective whole. The covenantal tradition as it has developed respects the private sphere and requires that persons be secure in their liberty to fulfill their chosen projects of life. But it also urges that one of the uses of liberty is for persons to bond together in mutual association. A fully private life is not worth living. Consequently, covenantal liberty is a bonded liberty. It is not the unconditional autonomy of the new morality, but a liberty of self-willed limits. The common good requires that a point of self-sacrifice is always reached. The wise individual, imbued with a covenantal ethos, knows that, in contrast to the ideal-typical ethos of Millsian liberty (an antecedent of the new morality) humans owe each other more than to stay out of one another's way. Covenantalism, which emphasizes relationships over structures, makes thematic our debt and obligation to one another, our expectation from one another. It constitutes the public realm not on an anthropology of discrete individuals and their rights, but on the equilibration of negative and positive liberty. It does not fetishize "freedom from" or valorize "freedom to." It sees both as requisite to human fulfillment and opens up a democratic conversation in which the balance is continuously negotiated. Thus, unlike the new morality's advocacy of diversity as an end in itself, a covenantal perspective both celebrates and orders difference. It celebrates diversity insofar as its ontology postulates a world of diverse beings with irreducibly concrete projects. But it orders this diversity in light of a common good, that is, it urges people to orient their projects toward mutual and public benefit.

This idea of covenant, of a lasting yet limited morally grounded agreement between free people, entered into freely by the parties concerned to achieve common ends or to protect common rights, has its roots in the Hebrew Bible. There the covenant principle stands at the very center of the relationship between man and God and also forms the basis for the establishment of the holy commonwealth. The covenant idea passed into early Christianity only after losing its political dimensions, which were restored during the Protestant Reformation, particularly by Reformed Protestantism (including Calvinism), the same groups that dominated the political revolutionary movements in Britain and America in the seventeenth and eighteenth centuries.

Much of the American reliance upon the covenant principle stems from the attempts of religiously inspired settlers on these shores to reproduce that kind of covenant in the New World and to build their commonwealths upon it, reflecting the intellectual continuity of the concept from ancient times via the great biblically based religions. The Yankees of New England, the Baptists, especially in the North, the Scotch-Irish of the mountains and piedmont from Pennsylvania to Georgia, the Dutch of New York, the Presbyterians, and to a lesser extent, the Quakers and German sectarians of Pennsylvania and the Middle States were all nurtured in churches constructed on the covenant principle and subscribing to the federal theology as the means for properly delineating the relationship between man and God (and by extension between man and man) as revealed by the Bible itself.

While later immigrant groups were on the whole less directly and overtly included in the covenantal tradition, virtually all of them had elements of that tradition embedded in the cultural baggage they brought with them, ranging from Jews, the first biblical covenantal people who had allowed many covenantal ideas to sink into latency in order to enter Western culture as it was manifested in early modern Europe, to Catholics who as Christians were heirs to that covenantal tradition which had been submerged through 1500 years of hierarchical thinking and acting in Europe but which reemerged under the American experience, to many east Asians who found their way to covenantal Christianity when proselytized in the old country based on either old cultural similarities or new social and political aspirations.

One might object that this characterization of the covenantal tradition of biblical religion is altogether too benign, that, after all, biblical religion mandates a certain more or less severe exclusivism. Boldly put, the Israelites had their liberty while the Canaanites met their deaths. Nor were black slaves or many aboriginal peoples subject to liberty under the terms of the initial national covenant. Are not these hypocrisies a cause of the discrediting of the older, biblical ethos by the partisans of the new morality? How can the covenantal perspective with its innate exclusivism serve as a basis for a common good in a multicultural society? There is no quick or easy answer to this question, but the outlines of an answer have at least been limned: covenantalism implies an ongoing endeavor by free people to work out their common life in an appropriate balance of the public and private, the mutual and solitary. In the nature of the case, the past is not ideal. The past is formative, not definitive. Covenantalism does not require that citizens subordinate themselves to the explicit terms of an ancient original contract, but rather that they understand themselves as bound to one another by covenant in a common endeavor.

A central issue in this discussion should be the covenant tradition in democratic republicanism at the present time. One pressing problem is how to allow the maximum amount of freedom while at the same time allowing communities to protect themselves. As a result of these conflicting issues and also in spite of them, there is a new recognition that humans need these ties of community as well as some degree of openness. Civil society needs to find ways and means to balance the two.

The very willingness to covenant and thereby to think in covenantal terms has a moderating influence on extremism, since any joining with other human beings in common purpose involves some willingness to compromise to overcome human differences. Thus, while covenanting may seem in some historical cases to promote exclusivity, as much as it may do so, it also promotes moderation and inclusion for it to happen at all. As such, it is a rejection of fanaticism, not necessarily by denying the truth of fanatics' claims, but by recognizing the necessity for prudence if humans are to live together.

There have been other efforts to balance freedom with the needs of the community. Liberal communitarianism's emphasis on the group has argued that this balance is achieved by emphasizing the needs of the group and those individual freedoms that make the community better. Conservative political ideas have argued that freedoms that are good for the individual will make for a healthier community. Freedoms that do not promote virtue in the individual do no good for the community either.

We have been exploring an old idea that has proven very useful in the past and shows sings of being useful again—the idea of covenant. Covenant is an important foundation of both morality and community for public, civic, and communal purposes, and it is within this paradigm that we can find the balancing tools necessary for a healthy civil society. Covenant is an idea which defines political justice, shapes political behavior, and directs humans toward an appropriately civic synthesis of the two. As such, covenant is an idea whose importance is akin to natural law in defining justice, and to natural right in delineating the origins and proper constitution of political society.

COVENANT AND FEDERAL LIBERTY

The essence of the covenant ideal and the system it established is the idea of federal liberty. John Winthrop, founding Governor of the Massachusetts Bay Colony, defined federal liberty as follows:

> There is a two fold liberty, natural (I mean as our nature is now corrupt) and civil or federal. The first is common to man with beasts and other creatures. By this, man, as he stands in relation to man simply, hath liberty to do what he lists; it is a liberty to evil as well as to good. This liberty is incompatible and inconsistent with authority and cannot endure the least restraint of the most just authority. The exercise and maintaining of this liberty makes men grow more evil and in time to be worse than brute beasts: *omnes sumus licentia deteriores.* This is that great enemy of truth and peace, that wild beast, which all of the ordinances of God are best against, to restrain and subdue it. The other kind of liberty I call civil or federal; it may also be termed moral, in reference to the covenant between God and man, in the moral law, and the politic covenants and constitutions between men themselves. This liberty is the proper end and object of authority and cannot subsist without it; and it is a liberty to that only which is good, just and honest. This liberty you are to stand for, with the hazard (not only of your goods, but) of the lives if need be.[2]

While the idea of covenant is often thought of in religious terms, it is more than a sectarian concept. Rather than merely "religious in the narrow sense," covenant is based on moral commitment. Thinkers from Hobbes onward recognized it as a political moral commitment necessary for people to live in a civil society. Indeed, the American founders recognized covenant as an important ingredient in building a balanced democratic society. Covenant depends on civic capital. Civic capital and community lead to commonwealth.

Commonwealth promotes civil responsibilities and obligation. These values are important in conjunction with civil society. Civil society promotes liberal democracy and freedom while commonwealth promotes responsibility. Covenant can bring back a balance between freedom and responsibility. Covenant creates bonds between individuals and one another, peoples and states, groups with other groups.

Covenantal societies tend to be both simultaneously closed and open. A closed covenant is one that limits interaction and inclusion of those outside of the relationship. An open covenant has an inclusive characteristic that emphasizes bringing outsiders into the relationship. In fact, the openness even limits the use of concepts like outside. In reality, there are degrees of openness and exclusivity and covenants can have both open and exclusive characteristics.

The evidence is overwhelming that the covenant principle translated into the larger political realm to produce modern popular government in the form of federal democracy. The history and meaning of the term itself reveal this. The word *federal* is derived from *foedus*, the Latin word for covenant which, in turn, is the Vulgate's translation of the Hebrew word *brit,* meaning covenant. According to the *Oxford English Dictionary*, it was first used, in English, in 1645 in the midst of the English civil war to describe covenantal relationships of both a political and a theological nature. Apparently, as its theological usage indicates, the term implied a closer or more permanent relationship than its slightly older companion *confederal*, a Middle English derivative of the same Latin root.[3]

Covenant (or federal) theory was widely appreciated and deeply rooted in the American tradition in 1787 because it was not the property of philosophers, theologians, or intellectuals alone. In its various adaptations, it was used for a variety of very public enterprises from the establishment of colonial self-government to the creation of the great trading corporations of the seventeenth century. Americans regularly made covenants or compacts to establish new civil societies. Witness the Mayflower Compact (1620):

> In the name of God, Amen. We whose names are under written . . . Having undertaken for the Glory of God, and Advancement of the Christian Faith, and the Honour of our King and Country, a Voyage to plant the first colony in the northern Parts of Virginia; Do by these Presents, solemnly and mutually in the Presence of God and one another, covenant and combine ourselves together into a civil Body Politick, for our better Ordering and Preservation, and Furtherance of the Ends aforesaid.

The Virginia Bill of Rights (written by George Mason in 1776):

> [A]ll men are by nature equally free and independent, and have certain inherent rights, of which, when they enter into a state of society, they cannot by any com-

> pact deprive or divest their posterity, namely, the enjoyment of life and liberty, with the means of property, and pursuing and obtaining happiness and safety.

The Vermont Declaration of Independence (1777):

> We, the inhabitants [of the New Hampshire grants], are at present without law or government, and may be truly said to be in a state of nature; consequently a right remains to the people of said Grants to form a government best suited to secure their property, well being and happiness.

The Constitution of Massachusetts (written by none other than John Adams in 1779):

> The body politic is formed by a voluntary association of individuals. It is a social compact by which the whole people covenants with each citizen and each citizen with the whole people, that all shall be governed by certain laws for the common good. It is the duty of the people, therefore, in framing a Constitution of Government, to provide for an equitable mode of making laws, as well as for an impartial interpretation and a faithful execution of them, that every man may, at all times, find his security in them.

Covenant making remained a part of the settlement process throughout the days of the land frontier. Men gathered together in every one of the thirty-seven states admitted to the Union after the original thirteen to freely frame their constitutions of government in the manner of the first compacts establishing local self-government in the New World. Cities and towns were created by compact whenever bodies of men and their families joined together to establish communities devoted to common ends.

With the rise of modern organizations and associations, the covenant principle was given new purpose. Scientific and reform societies, labor unions, and professional associations as well as business corporations covenanted or compacted with one another to form larger organizations while preserving their own integrity. As a consequence, the American "instinct" for federalism was extended into most areas of human relations, shaping Americans' ideas of individualism, human rights and obligations, Divine expectations, business organization, civic association, and church structure as well as their notions of politics.

While there were differences in interpretation of the covenant principle among theologians, political leaders directly motivated by religious principles, and those with a secular political outlook, among New Englanders, residents of the Middle States, and Southerners, and from generation to generation, there was also a broad area of general agreement that unified all who subscribed to the principle and set them and their doctrine apart within the larger realm of political theory. All agreed on the importance of popular or republican government grounded on a moral base, the necessity to check and balance power to prevent tyranny, and the importance of individual rights and dignity as the foundation of any genuinely good political system. For them covenanting provided a means for free people to form political communities without sacrificing their essential freedom and without making energetic government impossible.

FEDERAL DEMOCRACY AND ITS RIVALS

The moral and political implications of the federal principle are brought home forcefully when it is contrasted with the other conceptions of popular government developed in the modern era. Other revolutionaries in the "age of revolutions"—most prominent among them the Jacobins—also sought solutions to some of the same problems of despotism that perturbed the Americans. But in their efforts to hurry the millennium, they rejected what they believed to be the highly perceptive assumptions of the American constitution makers that unlimited political power could corrupt even "the people" and considered only the problem of autocratic despotism. They looked upon federalism and its principles of checks and balances as subversive of the "general will," their way of expressing a commitment to the organic unity of society, which, like their premodern predecessors, they saw as superior to the interests of mere individuals. They argued that since their "new society" was to be based on "the general will" as a more democratic principle, any element subversive of its organic unity would be, ipso facto, antidemocratic.

By retaining notions of the organic society, the Jacobins and their revolutionary heirs were forced to rely upon transient majorities to establish consensus or to concentrate power in the hands of an elite that claimed to do the same thing. The first course invariably led to anarchy and the second to the kind of totalitarian democracy that has become the essence of modern dictatorship. Although the "general will" was undoubtedly a more democratic concept than the "will of the monarch," it has proved no less despotic and usually even more subversive of liberty since it is unrestrained by tradition as was the *ancien regime.*

The history of the extension of democratic government since the eighteenth century has been a history of the rivalry between these two conceptions of democracy. Because of the challenge of Jacobinism, the meaning of the American idea of federal democracy takes on increased importance, especially the moral dimension built into federalism. Today these resonances have been made weaker because we have lost the awareness of the covenantal tradition. Yet the tradition itself persists in more ways than we often recognize.

COVENANT, COMPACT, CONTRACT

Covenant is tied in an ambiguous relationship to two related terms: compact and contract. On one hand, both compacts and contracts are in a sense derived from covenant, and sometimes the terms are even used interchangeably. On the other hand, there are very real differences between the three that need clarification.

Both *covenants* and their derivative, *compacts*, differ from *contracts* in that the first two are constitutional or public in character and the last is private. As such, covenantal or compactual obligation is relationship-oriented and broadly reciprocal while the reciprocity of contracts only follows the letter of the law or the agreement because contracts are task-oriented. Those bound by covenant or compact, on the other hand, are obligated to respond to one another beyond the letter of the law rather than to limit their obligations to the narrowest contractual requirements. Hence covenants and compacts are inherently designed to be broad and flexible in certain respects as well as firm in others. As expressions of private law, contracts tend to be interpreted as narrowly as possible so as to limit the obligation of the contracting parties to what is explicitly mandated by the contract itself. It may be said that covenants imply a different moral psychology than contracts.

A covenant differs from a compact in that its morally binding dimension takes precedence over its legal dimension. In its heart of hearts, a covenant is an agreement in which a higher moral force—traditionally God—is a party, usually a direct party to or guarantor of a particular relationship, whereas when the term compact is used the moral force is internal to the pact itself. A compact, based as it is on mutual pledges rather than the guarantees of a higher authority, rests more heavily on a legal though still ethical grounding for its politics. In other words, the compact is a secular phenomenon. This can be verified historically by examining the shift in terminology that took place in the seventeenth and eighteenth centuries. While those who saw the hand of God in political affairs in the United States continued to use the term covenant, those who sought a secular grounding for politics turned to the term compact. Though the distinction is not always used with strict clarity, it does appear consistently. The issue was further complicated by Rousseau and his followers, who talk about the social contract, a highly secularized concept that, even when applied for public purposes, never develops the same level of moral obligation as either covenant or compact.

Covenant is also related to constitutionalism. Normally a covenant precedes a constitution by establishing the people, public, or civil society that then proceeds to adopt a constitution of government for itself. Thus a constitution involves implementing a prior covenant—effectuating or translating a prior covenant into an actual frame or structure of government.

America's first covenants were both religious and civil. This combination was perhaps best reflected in the historically most widely recognized of all seventeenth century America covenants, the Plymouth Combination, which after the American Revolution became known as the Mayflower Compact. This exemplary covenant, drawn up on the decks of the Mayflower off the coast of New England, bound all of the ships' householders together in a civil society based upon their consent, which included both the churched and the unchurched among them, though it was couched in religious terms with God included as an active guarantor, and New England, where covenanting was most widespread and formal, had both church and civil covenants. Indeed, the two kinds were interdependent. Elsewhere, church covenants were widely used, formal civil covenants more sparsely, and the two kinds were usually kept quite separate.

Where actual covenants were made, they have followed a formula that has been passed down from generation to generation and epoch to epoch essentially unchanged (since earliest times in the ancient Near East). This form has been described by students of ancient Near Eastern history as containing the following elements:

1. a preamble naming the parties to the covenant;
2. a prologue, historical or ideological, establishing the setting or grounding of the covenant;
3. the operative section of the covenant including stipulation of what is agreed;
4. provisions for public reading (proclamation) and deposit of the text for safekeeping;
5. the divine witness to the covenant; and
6. the advantages of performance (blessings) and sanctions for nonperformance (curses).[4]

In place of formal covenanting, constitutions of governance were developed based upon covenantal principles; that is to say, based on the consent of those to be bound by them, delineating the republican institutions through which those so bound and their heirs would be organized, a sense that those constitutions of governance also served to constitute the peoples being governed, a definition implicit or explicit of the terms of federal liberty expected from those bound by those constitutions, all under Divine guarantee and/or protection, but for civil purposes alone.

The coming of the American Revolution transformed this original system and network of covenants in three ways.

1. It became statewide and national in character, not merely local and state, and more civil in content with the Declaration of Independence,

although a civil document, coming to serve as the national covenant, as Abraham Lincoln was to wisely observe four score years later.[5]

2. Formal covenanting began to be expressed through secular civil compacts. The Declaration of Independence, although it uses neither word, is a good example of this. The form it follows is almost exactly the same form as covenants had taken since the days of the first vassal treaties in ancient Mesopotamia four millennia earlier, but while Divine guidance and support was invoked at the close of the document, it was clearly more of an obeisance than a stated reliance on active Divine partnership.[6] The key element was the mutual pledge of lives, fortunes, and sacred honor. No doubt, with more than half of the population supporting revolution, those who were associated with Reformed Protestant congregations saw it as a further manifestation of covenantal assertions of human liberty, but the influence of the Enlightenment had been such that the formal grounding of the effort had to be in the more neutral compact mode to reach all segments of the newly emergent American society.
3. At the same time, the idea of federal liberty was also transformed from a liberty to live by Divine law as defined by Divine grant to a liberty shaped by the mutual consent of humans. James Wilson of Pennsylvania, himself born into the Scottish covenantal tradition as reshaped by the Scottish Enlightenment, provided the redefinition, specifically to define the appropriate, compactual relationship between the states and the federal government, just as Winthrop had provided the original covenantal one defining the relationship between man and God.[7]

For Wilson, federal liberty was the means of sharing the attributes of sovereignty, with both the states and the federal government deriving their powers by delegation from the sovereign people through constitutional compacts in such a way that each remained an instrument of the people while at the same time checking the other. His argument was that just as individuals entering a political compact gained greater liberty by surrendering part of their natural rights in exchange for a limitation on the liberty of others to do them harm, so too did the constituent states gain more by surrendering part of their freedom of action to a general government in return for being partners in a larger whole. "Federal liberty then is the liberty to enter into a covenant or compact through which each party surrenders certain of its natural liberties in order to gain more from the new partnership created, to whose rules the parties are then obliged to follow.

The apogee of the impact of the formal use of compact theory in early American history came with the Northwest Ordinance of 1787 which included a specific compact of six articles to be accepted by each new state carved out of the territory as part of its admission to statehood.[8]

Articles of Compact

It is hereby ordained and declared, by the authority aforesaid, that the following articles shall be considered as articles of compact, between the original States and the people and States in the said territory, and forever remain unalterable, unless by common consent, to wit:

Article I: No person demeaning himself in a peaceable and orderly manner shall ever be molested on account of his mode of worship, or religious sentiments in the said territories.

Article II: The inhabitants of the said territory shall always be entitled to the benefits of the writs of habeas corpus, and of the trial by jury; of a proportionate representation of the people in the Legislature; and of judicial proceedings according to the course of the common law. All persons shall be bailable, unless for capital offenses, where the proof shall be evident or the presumption great. All fines shall be moderate, and no cruel or unusual punishments shall be inflicted. No man shall be deprived of his liberty or property, but by the judgment of his peers, or the law of the land, and should the public exigencies make it necessary, for the common preservation, to take any person's property, or to demand his particular services, full compensation shall be made for the same. And, in the just preservation of rights and property, it is understood and declared that no law ought ever to be made or have force in the said territory, that shall, in any manner whatever, interfere with or affect private contracts, or engagements bona fide and without fraud previously formed.

Article III: Religion, morality, and knowledge being necessary to good government and the happiness of mankind, schools and the means of education shall forever be encouraged. The utmost good faith shall always be observed towards the Indians; their lands and property shall never be taken from them without their consent; and in their property, rights and liberty they never shall be invaded or disturbed unless in just and lawful wars authorized by Congress; but laws founded in justice and humanity shall, from time to time, be made, for preventing wrongs being done to them, and for preserving peace and friendship with them.

Article IV: The said territory, and the states which may be formed therein, shall forever remain a part of this confederacy of the United States of America, subject to the Articles of Confederation, and to such alterations therein as shall be constitutionally made; and in all the acts and Ordinances of the United States in Congress assembled, conformable thereto. The inhabitants and settlers in the said territory shall be subject to pay a part of the federal debts, contracted, or to be contract, and a proportional part of the expenses of government, to be apportioned on them by Congress, according to the same common rule and measure by which apportionments thereof shall be made on the other States, and the taxes for paying their proportion shall be laid and levied by the authority and direction of the legislatures of the district, or districts, or new States, as in the original States, within the time agreed upon by the United States in Congress assembled, nor with any regulations Congress may find necessary for securing the title in such soil to the bona fide purchasers. No tax shall be imposed on lands the property of the United States; and in no case shall nonresident proprietors be taxed higher than residents. The navigable water leading into the Mississippi and Saint Lawrence, and the carrying places between the same, shall be common highways, and forever free, as well to the inhabitants of the said territory as to the citizens of the United States, and those of any other States that may be admitted into the Confederacy, without any tax, impost, or duty therefor.

Article V: There shall be formed in the said territory not less than three nor more than five States; and the boundaries of the States, as soon as Virginia shall alter her Act of cession, and consent to the same, shall become fixed and established as follows to wit: The western State, in the said territory, shall be bounded by the Mississippi, the Ohio, and the Wabash and Post Vincents, due north, to the territorial line between the United States and Canada; and by the said territorial line to the Lake of the Woods and Mississippi. The middle States shall be bounded by the said direct line, the Wabash from Post Vincents to the Ohio, by the Ohio, by the direct line drawn due north from the mouth of the Great Miami to the said territorial line, and by the said territorial line. The eastern State shall be bounded by the last mentioned direct line, the Ohio, Pennsylvania, and the said territorial line. Provided, however, and it is further understood and declared, that the boundaries of these three States, shall be subject so far to be altered that, if Congress shall hereafter find it expedient, they shall have authority to form one or two States in that part of the said territory which lies north of an east and west line drawn through the southerly bend or extreme of Lake Michigan. And whenever any of the said States shall have sixty thousand free inhabitants therein, such State shall be admitted, by its delegates, into the Congress of the United States, on an equal footing with the original States, in all respects whatever; and shall be at liberty to form a permanent Constitution and state government. Provided, the Constitution and government, so to be formed, shall be republican, and in conformity to the principles contained in these Articles, and so far as it can be consistent with the general interest of the Confederacy, such admission shall be allowed at an earlier period, and when there may be a less number of free inhabitants in the State than sixty thousand.

Article VI: There shall be neither slavery nor involuntary servitude in the said territory, otherwise than in the punishment of crimes, whereof the party shall have been duly convicted. Provided always, that any person escaping into the same, from whom labor or service is lawfully claimed in any one of the original states, such fugitive may be lawfully reclaimed and conveyed to the person claiming his or her labor or service as aforesaid.

Be it ordained by the authority aforesaid, That the resolutions of the 23rd of April, 1784, relative to the subject of this Ordinance, be, and the same are hereby, repealed and declared null and void.

Done by the United States, in Congress assembled, the 13th day of July, in the year of our Lord 1787, and of their sovereignty and independence the 12th.

COVENANTAL THEORY VS. COVENANTAL PRACTICE

Subsequently, compact theory was transformed in the period between the War of 1812 and the Civil War to support the Southern argument that the Constitution was no more than a compact among the states from which any state or states could secede for cause; that is to say, if its people believed the compact to have been seriously violated. In the years immediately prior to the Civil War and during the war itself, Lincoln articulated a contrary position based on covenantal theory particularly as he saw it presented in the Declaration of Independence, on occasion defining the Union in his homely terms as "a regular marriage," i.e., a covenant that could only be dissolved by mutual consent.[9] Unfortunately, in the public debate the Southern use of compact theory discredited the very idea of compact, while Lincoln's covenantal alternative, while successful in mobilizing the North to defend the Union, was abandoned as a theoretical construct in the face of other, presumably more "sophisticated," constructs derived from Jacobinism and Darwinism imported from Europe at the time.

After the Civil War these new intellectual doctrines replaced covenantal thinking almost completely among the American intellectual establishment. At the same time, covenantal behavior persisted in practice throughout the nineteenth century as part of American westward expansion. In the West community after community and state after state were organized on the basis of the same tradition that had served the colonists prior to the American Revolution. This did not cease until the opportunities for that kind of behavior diminished and then disappeared with the end of the rural-land frontier.

Actual seventeenth century-style civil covenants became increasingly rare during the nineteenth century, since few local communities were founded as communal enterprises. Among the few exceptions were the Amana colonies in Iowa; Excelsior, Minnesota; and Greeley, Colorado. Town compacts were not so rare and indeed were routinized through the enactment by state legislatures of general laws of incorporation that both enabled and required residents of a particular locality to come together to establish municipal governments by writing local constitutions (charters) and adopting them by consent.

Although colonial forms of state organization, which combined religious and civil covenants, were replicated only in the case of the Mormon settlement of Utah and, indeed, had to be abandoned, at least formally, even in Utah in order for that territory to be admitted to the Union, no state could be admitted without going through a rather ritualized process of compacting among the residents of the particular territory and then with the federal government. Moreover, in many cases the initiatives for doing so were local rather than federal, initiated by settlers rather than by Congress.

Following the Revolutionary Era disestablishment of the colonial churches, religion came to occupy the public square less in the form of formal denominational support than in the form of a generalized Protestant religious faith, what might be called an optimistic Calvinism formed out of the American experience, combined with a neo-Baconian approach to define the relationship between religious belief and the material world. This was the religion whose spirit Tocqueville observed all around him when he visited the United States in the 1830s.[10] Like the earlier Protestantism it was short on ritual expressions of religion, and strongly emphasized the moral requirements of "true religion," which were defined as including everything from ethical behavior to abstinence from hard liquor, and which in doctrinal form often led to hair-splitting quarrels over the proper form of baptism or others of the few rituals which Protestants observed.

As this generalized Protestant belief system permeated the majority in American society, it lost its explicit covenantal edge in some quarter. Still it continued to rest on underlying principles of consent which were actively expressed through church affiliation or acceptance of some particular idea or practice stimulated by that generalized religious spirit. Individual congregations were still formed by covenanting and new religious sects such as the Latter Day Saints (Mormons) incorporated covenants and covenantal ideas.[11]

As the Catholic population of the United States began to grow from mid-century onward, a new and competing view of religion was introduced, one with a heavy emphasis on ritual and with foundations that did not rest on individual consent but on the idea of a religious community that originated in ancient times and continues organically from generation to generation. Moreover, this new competition to the Protestant spirit was, in its initial stages, far less civic in its orientation, coming as it did from an environment in which rendering unto Caesar was a fundamental church doctrine. The clash between the two traditions was rarely articulated as a theoretical one. Rather it took the form of conflict over different forms of human behavior, whether with regard to the consumption of alcoholic beverages or the nature of involvement in local politics.

THE DECLINE OF RELIGION IN THE PUBLIC SPHERE

By World War I, the opportunities for civil covenants or compacts had almost entirely disappeared and even where possible, did not touch the lives or consciousness of the vast majority of Americans. New opportunities for establishing church covenants also diminished as organized religion came under assault in the twentieth century. Moreover, separation between the two forms became ever more pronounced, while each form became increasingly ritualized and emptied of meaning even for those engaging in it.

Thus, meaningful covenanting essentially disappeared from the American scene except for isolated cases. Intellectually, Americans were increasingly attracted by new organic theories of social organization and practically what survived of covenanting was highly ritualized and devoid of self meaning. As American mores and morals changed, religion came to be seen by many opinion-leaders as an atavistic and oppressive force in American society and believers as clinging to antiquated beliefs that required limits on personal freedom that were no longer deemed acceptable even in the name of appropriate religious or moral behavior. The impact of all this was limited as long as Americans could live off the cultural capital accumulated in the past. Marquis Childs pointed this out in a telling and prescient book published in the late 1930s.[12]

The heritage established by that cultural capital seemed to be still in place during the first two decades after World War II but collapsed quite suddenly in the mid-1960s, showing how much it had become a shell in those intervening years. The collapse took the form of an aggressive assault on the moral claims of the monotheistic faiths in the name of "New Age" beliefs that in many cases became a form of neo-paganism. The public square was radically transformed as the morality of the monotheistic religions was increasingly excluded from public expression either by constitutional decisions of the U.S. Supreme Court presumably responding to the demands of the Bill of Rights to guarantee individual liberty or through public expressions of the sociological transformations brought about by the demands of the "New Age."

While there are some exceptions, what has characterized paganism from the earliest times, especially as it is understood by monotheists, is that it is amoral religion, more concerned with magically manipulating the powers of nature than with doing justice and mercy, accepting one's obligations to one's neighbors, and generally seeking a more righteous world. One might argue that paganism or at least neopaganism has a different morality, one more attuned to preserving the harmonies of the universe as it is, a theme reflected in neopagan environmentalism (as distinct from monotheistic-based environmentalism) today, but the essence of traditional paganism—recognizing the singular power of natural forces, achieving harmony with the powers that be in the universe, and assuring fertility—lies behind all neopagan adaptations which have been influenced in one way or another by monotheistic religion or the world which monotheistic religion has built. On the other hand, monotheistic religion, which may share some of the same practical goals with neopaganism, grows out of the first associations between religion and morality, those expressed in ancient Mesopotamian civilization, of which biblical religion was the apotheosis and which a thousand years before the birth of the latter, had already placed humanity on the road to the association of religion and righteousness by feeling its way towards the first dimensions of righteousness within its own pagan religion. As biblical scholar Yehezkiel Kaufman has pointed out, the differences between monotheism and paganism are not simply a matter of arithmetic but of worldviews, the first based upon righteousness as the principal divine promise and commandment and the second based upon the achievement of human survival through magical manipulation of the powers that be in the universe.

THE REASSERTION OF MONOTHEISTIC MORALITY

The first immediate response to this was the politicization of many Protestant fundamentalists. Until the 1960s, Protestant fundamentalists had, perhaps more than any other Protestants, separated religion from the public square, having responded to the assault on their beliefs of the earlier twentieth century by withdrawing into their own private realm where they had survived, protected by the larger framework of monotheistic morality that dominated the American scene. With that framework shattered, the fundamentalists regrouped under a new leadership who understood that only by attempting to regain control of the public square could they hope to protect their beliefs from further assault.

Like other movements, their forward progress has been uneven and even has involved retreat at various times, but this fundamentalist movement has had some startling successes. While it cannot muster a majority, perhaps not even in the Republican party, its chosen vehicle of political action for political engagement in the public square, it has come to represent a very large and vocal bloc both within the GOP and in the public square generally. Perhaps even more important, it has made religion, even fundamentalist religion, respectable again among Americans. Members of mainstream churches, who for years had been led by prevailing intellectual trends to conceal their religious convictions and actions, have in the past decade begun to reveal their true selves, thus making religious involvement and belief respectable again even in the highest circles.

Finally, the fundamentalist drive has led to the reemergence of covenanting in the private sphere as members of specific socio-demographic groups come together to promise that they will maintain certain forms of behavior, or refrain from others, relying upon one another for reinforcement. Two examples come to mind: one, the movement among Christian teenagers to commit themselves to sexual abstinence before marriage, and the other, the movement among Christian men, led by the Promise Keepers, to commit themselves to maintaining certain religiously-based standards of moral behavior in their family, business, and professional lives. These are, by conventional definitions at least, all private actions rather than public ones. What is most significant about them, however, is that all are transdenominational. In this sense they are in the great spirit of American evangelism which sees itself as speaking to the whole people without reference to their denominational divisions, if any.

Second, they recognize that there first must be a network of private or sociological transformations if the public square is to be reshaped. In this they follow the teachings of ancient constitutionalism which begin with the individual and the familial before building up to the public and the political. Both the Bible and the ancient Greek laws concentrate more on the former than on the latter to reinforce the enduring importance of right living on the part of individuals and families in order to have right living in the public square through public activity.[13] Throughout much of the modern age, this emphasis in the Bible led to the widespread view that Scripture had little if anything to say about politics, not recognizing that everything in Scripture deals with the political, but that the Bible is less interested in the specific institutions of different political regimes and more on the social environment in which those regimes function to see to it that the regimes do so in such a way as to maintain proper relationships between God and man and among humans.

RECOVENANTING IN A MULTI-CULTURAL WORLD

In this writer's opinion, the experiences of the past thirty years have shown us the following:

1. Despite the regnant modern view that the monotheistic religions had triumphed over paganism, at least in the West, and that the latter was merely an historic memory, we have come to learn that the biblical teaching that paganism and monotheism are constantly in conflict and lack of vigilance on the part of the monotheistic religions will inevitably lead to a resurgence of paganism in some form, is accurate.
2. Nor as Kaufman has said, is this merely a matter of arithmetic—of one God or many, but rather it is a clash of world views dealing with different moralities, understandings of what courses of action humanity

should pursue, and definitions of good and evil.[14] Thus, pagan and neo-pagan assaults on monotheism are primarily assaults upon the monotheistic understanding of the world and the morality that flows from it, and should be resisted.

3. At the same time, the maintenance of monotheism cannot be simply of the traditional kind, common in the Western or larger monotheistic world until the present century. The world is now sufficiently one and the message of equality sufficiently persuasive that cultures as well as individuals now have some claim to equal treatment. Thus pluralism and multiculturalism are realities which, however problematic from a normative point of view, must be dealt with pragmatically. Thus the rebuilding of a moral consensus must be begin and proceed with a recognition of this multicultural and pluralistic reality and be prepared to come to grips with it appropriate ways.
4. At least for the moment it seems that the most appropriate ways are through the uniting of people around specific goals and acts whereby people, usually as individuals who have different formal affiliations and loyalties come together to pledge or promise to behave in certain ways and to support one another in the pursuit of that behavior. That is covenanting. Those promises or covenants made may rest or be seen to rest on mutual promises or on Divine support. For the most part, at first they will be understood as private rather than public commitments. However, there are areas of agreement, for example, with regard to democracy and human rights, that go beyond the private. Here covenant must provide a basis for dialogue. In those areas we can bring publics together to accept certain standards of behavior in such a way that federal liberty is restored.

FEDERAL VS. NATURAL LIBERTY

One of the most prominent dimensions of this struggle between "New Age" neo-paganism and monotheistic morality has been in the definition of what constitutes liberty and all that flows from it. From the very first, New Age thinking has embraced natural liberty as true liberty, the liberty of everyone to do as he or she pleases on the erroneous premise "as long as it doesn't hurt anyone else." This is a liberty of "doin' what comes naturally" stretched into "let it all hang out." It is a liberty limited only by nature. In the past, when most humans had to confront the raw elements of nature unprotected as it were, that kind of liberty may have had some merit since only the fittest could survive. (Obviously there are great problems regarding the humanness of such a situation.) That is the liberty of the North American "mountain men" encountering the great American West during the first half of the nineteenth century.

However, the truth of human history is that humans have not accepted life under conditions of truly natural liberty precisely because for most individuals it was nasty, brutish, and short. Consequently, from earliest times, humans other than barbarians either have accepted tyranny for protection or have pursued federal liberty, whether understood as the liberty flowing from mutual covenants of the Hobbesian kind or liberty based upon covenants between God and humans of the biblical kind.[15] In both cases liberty became the liberty to live up to one's promises, obligations, tasks, and traits which one freely accepted through covenants freely entered into for reasons of both idealism and self-interest and which then were and are binding and have to be maintained.

Natural liberty still works today in some cases, as witness all the deaths from drug overdoses, alcoholism, and other substance abuse. But, since natural liberty is from nature, its consequences are inevitably random and unjust. Consequently it is impossible to build civilization on the basis of natural liberty.

Only federal liberty offers the possibility of building civilization. Today humanity has in certain respects returned to the state of nature and again must begin to build its covenants from the beginning if we are to have a viable federal liberty. Much of what will have to be rebuilt will be very similar to the covenants which have bound us in earlier ages because they encompass enduring truths, but it seems that every so often humanity must rediscover those enduring truths by reverting to a state of nature and learning about them the hard way. This is one of those times. For these purposes, we may use Hobbes's articles of covenant as a modest but powerful starting point.

RECOVENANTING FOR CIVIL COMMUNITY

To summarize, recovenanting is necessary so as to bring the moral teachings of monotheism back into the public square to define and shape the norms of civil society. That recovenanting must proceed from two directions simultaneously: in the public realm for those matters widely understood to be of common interest by public governmental and nongovernmental bodies and, through the private sphere, for those matters involving individual moral behavior that is less easily visible to all on the basis of private undertakings, on an issue by issue basis. Hopefully through rebuilding in both directions humanity will ultimately restore comprehensive federal liberty that will unite public and private without merging them into one, allowing each to retain its own integrity. Then we will not only have civil society but civil community as well.

The challenge for our time is how to achieve community in an age in which freedom and individualism have become essential characteristics and are valued for their own sake. While the idea of community is important to the covenant principle, this community needs also to emphasize personal responsibility and voluntary decisions. Mutual responsibility based upon a commitment to deal with common concerns or possible problems leads to covenantal relationships. If community is to be achieved, it must be achieved within this environment. Freedom is a desirable and highly valued principle. Individualism, also desirable in many respects, is well imbedded into the American political culture.

Where there are no strong organic ties, covenant can achieve community. To the extent that covenant is both a theological and political concept, it is informed by a moral or ethical perspective that treats political relationships in the classical manner, that is, it links power and justice—the two faces of politics—and preserves the classic and ancient linkages between ethics and politics. Again, the emphasis is on relationships rather than structures, per se, as the key to political justice. Structures are always important, but ultimately, no matter how finely tuned the structures, they come alive (or fail to) only through the human relationships that inform them.

While there have been different interpretations of the covenant principle across various regions and from generation to generation, there also has been a broad area of agreement which has unified those who subscribed to the principle and which set them and their doctrine apart within the larger realm of political theory. For Americans, for example, covenant provided a means for a free people to form political communities without sacrificing their essential freedom and without making energetic government impossible. Federal liberty which is based on covenant, enhances pluralism and makes it workable. Federal liberty limits individual freedom. Those who live in a system of federal liberty live by rules that society has created. These rules limit both the individual and the government.

In order to do all of this, partisans of monotheistic morality need to first, capture the conceptual and terminological high ground in the United States and, for that matter, the world. We are helped in this effort by the revival of the idea of civil society as a result of the Central and Eastern European revolts against Communism of the 1980s. In that sense, 1989 was the kind of watershed year that 1689 and 1789 were in their respective centuries.

The revival of the idea of civil society brings us face to face with the ideational matrix from which it developed originally, itself derived from the covenant tradition in Western politics, an idea so well enunciated in the seventeenth century by Hobbes, Locke, and others. That ideal held that human beings ended the state of nature in which they found themselves trapped, to their great disadvantage, by coming together and covenanting with one another to establish civil society so that the stronger few could not dominate the weaker many, while the weaker many could band together to protect themselves without having to destroy the stronger few.

More specifically, the original order of civil society also was covenantal in the way that it recognized that humans came together to form political societies by giving up only as much of their independence as they had to, retaining for themselves all the rest, and in connection with that in which they gave up exclusive control, retaining a share of the decision-making power with regard to it as well. Civil society was an idea that spread throughout Western Europe in the seventeenth century, but it took two forms based on the prior experiences of continental Europe and the British Isles.

On the European continent where statism had already emerged as the most powerful political force by the mid-seventeenth century and the idea of the reified state had become dominant, civil society was viewed as that mediating set of associations between the reified state and the private sphere. Most of those intermediate associations were themselves corporations, not so much reflecting the fluidity inherent in human organization but the establishment of rather rigid corporate structures that were neither part of the state nor belonged to individuals, such as the church, the great trading corporations, and the universities.

On the other hand, in the British Isles where kings reigned but were restricted by traditional constitutions and no state in the reified sense emerged, civil society was the term used to describe the entire political-social order, which consisted of three parts: the governmental, the private, and the public but nongovernmental sectors. The last consisted of voluntary associations voluntarily entered into by private individuals seeking to combine for public purposes without turning to invoke the powers of government.

Covenant needs to be examined in three dimensions: as a form of political conceptualization and mode of political expression, as a source of political ideology, and as a factor shaping political culture and behavior. As a form of political conceptualization, covenant shapes the way in which people look at the world and understand the nature of civil society. As a source of political ideology, covenant shapes the world views or perspectives of whole societies, defining their civil character and political relationships, and serving as a touchstone for testing the legitimacy and even the efficiency of their political institutions and those who operate them.

Perhaps most important is the role of covenant as a factor in shaping political culture and behavior. This factor is the most difficult to measure and yet is operationally the most significant dimension of covenant. All evidence points to the existence of certain covenantal peoples whose political cultures are informed by covenantal and related concepts, which in turn influence their political behavior. Adherence to the covenant maintains the health of these peoples.

Any study of covenant as a phenomenon must focus on these dimensions. Indeed, the intellectual challenge of studying this phenomenon grows out of the possibility of using covenant as a seminal concept which has been given ideological expression and even more importantly, has shaped political culture and through it, political behavior. Studying the linkages between these and the way in which they occurred in various communities and societies is a major intellectual challenge of political science.

The need exists to re-examine some of the characteristics of covenantal groups in order to regain an understanding of how covenant can be reinvigorated. The question needs to be asked, "Is a synthesis of openness and exclusivity possible?" An understanding of theoretical models of opened and closed covenants will lead to an improved basis upon which to both study and encourage covenantal relationships. Much of what we think regarding partnerships are based on the notion that they are closed. Covenantal relationships, by their very nature, are limiting. However, there are cases of openness in covenantal relationships, such as alliances with respect to nations and adoption with respect to families. Both of these examples show some degree of openness in an otherwise closed covenant.

The question of openness and exclusivity in a particular polity is an important one. This aspect of a polity informs policy as well as perceptions from outside. Institutionalized racism and ideological extremism are just two examples of how the degree to which a given polity is closed impacts upon it. Further, a culturally or ethnically homogeneous society may not intend for its policies to create the reaction they do from the outside.

Returning to covenantal roots reemphasizes civil society and the necessary balance between the private and public spheres. A reassessment of the covenantal idea would change the way contemporaries view important questions and contribute to citizenship. No doubt any resolution to the issue of religion in the public square will rest heavily on public nongovernmental action rather than governmental, but action sustained by governmental backing of a certain kind.

To move into a recovenanting mode we need to reemphasize that second theory which is also the American theory, namely, that even government, although it has been granted coercive powers by its constituents, is basically no more than a comprehensive association in a world of associations established by agreement and responsible to those who establish them. This is the theory of federal democracy. Viewing the polity and public nongovernmental associations within it in this manner serves to promote the diffusion of conflicts, the understanding of constitutions as both tools of empowerment and tools of restraint.

Federal democracy is a pluralistic means to deal with the problem of pluralism. Pluralism taken alone essentially rests on sociological foundations which are neither limited nor protected. In other words, the sociology of pluralism can permit an "anything goes" society because it has no way to judge from among the various pluralistic options. At the same time, pluralism will exist only as long as the society maintains it. There are no constitutional restraints on the elimination of pluralism if circumstances otherwise permit it.

Federal democracy, on the other hand, because it involves organization by covenant and the establishment of covenants and constitutions that both empower and restrain, can make collective decisions as to what is legitimate and what is not, and can protect what it determines as legitimate. Federal democracy and federal liberty also enable humans to move from overemphasis on rights and rights language alone to a serious consideration of obligations as well. Covenantal obligations are not the obligations of a subordinate to a superior as in a hierarchical system, but rather the shared obligations of humans to a mutually accepted agreement.

In the monotheistic religions such agreements rest upon a concept antecedent to and larger than both rights and obligations, namely the idea of human dignity, that all humans as God's creatures have a certain inherent dignity which is maintained by endowing them with obligations whose exercise confirms that they are human and turns their dignity into something meaningful. It is through the fulfillment of those obligations that humans gain rights. For example, if the Bible demands that we protect the widows and the orphans, that is our obligation to God. As a result of that obligation, the widows and the orphans gain certain rights to gleaning fields and to otherwise partake in the produce of the community in order to live. But the obligation is prior to the right.

Covenants themselves must be based upon mutual trust. In the last analysis all political society requires some measure of trust, but covenantal societies rest on a minimum of coercion and a maximum of consent which means that they require more trust than others. Perhaps that is why Hobbes referred to the pacts which humans made to remove themselves from the state of nature as covenants, appreciating the amount of trust required to execute and maintain them. The cultivation of covenantal trust is in itself a major social and political good.

RESTORING MODERATION BY ABANDONING THE EXTREMES

Robert Licht has made the extremely important point that the American founding was a success despite the incipient or actual conflicts in American society because both those Americans who derived their democratic republican views from the Enlightenment and those who derived them from one of the monotheistic faiths were able to find common ground.[16] Licht goes on to suggest that they were able to do so because the moderates from both sides retained dominance. They successfully excluded the extremists from each side so that, rather than exaggerate their differences, they could find the necessary common ground that made it possible to achieve the syntheses of the American Revolutionary era culminating in the Constitution of the United States, and to launch nearly a century in which there was an equally healthy synthesis between religion and the public square.

In the late nineteenth and throughout the twentieth century, those syntheses became unraveled as the extremists among both the contemporary products of the Enlightenment and contemporary supporters of biblical religion gained the upper hand in their respective camps. It is the task of all Americans to restore that synthesis by bringing moderation back into the saddle in both camps so that together they can explore useful ways for the religious spirit to express itself in the public square without bringing about the pernicious effects that organized religion sometimes has had on the body politic.

NOTES

1. See, e.g., Daniel J. Elazar, *Covenant and Constitutionalism*; Donald Lutz, *The Origins of American Constitutionalism* (Baton Rouge: Louisiana State University Press, 1988); Alexis de Tocqueville, *Democracy in America* (New York: Colonial Press, 1989) Ellis Sandoz, ed.

2. John Winthrop, *A History of New England, 1630–1649*, ed. James Savage (Boston: Little Brown & Co., 1853) 2:279–82.

3. *Oxford English Dictionary*, "Federal" and "Confederal." At first the two words were so closely related that they were used synonymously until the American Civil War added an additional dimension to the theory of federalism by sharpening the distinction between them. Federal was not used in its present sense until 1777, during the American Revolution. Its modern usage, then, is an American invention. The invention of the term federalism to indicate the existence of a "federal principle or system of political organization" (quoting the *Oxford English Dictionary*) did not come until 1793, after the principle was already embodied in a great work of political theory and the constitution of a potentially great nation.

4. George Mendenhall, *Law and the Ancient Near East* (Pittsburgh: Biblical Colloquium, 1957).

5. Harry V. Jaffa, "Abraham Lincoln" in *American Political Thought*, eds. Morton Frisch and Richard G. Stevens (Itasca, IL: F. E. Peacock, 1983) pp. 195–215.

6. Carl Becker, *The Declaration of Independence* (New York: Vintage, 1958); Gary Wills, *Inventing America: Jefferson's Declaration of Independence* (New York: Vintage Books, 1979); Daniel J. Elazar, *The American Constitutional Tradition* (Lincoln: University of Nebraska Press, 1984).

7. James Wilson at the Pennsylvania ratifying convention, as quoted in John Bach McMaster and Frederick B. Stone, *Pennsylvania and the Federal Constitution, 1787–1788*, (New York: Da Capo Press, 1970).

8. Peter S. Onuf, *Statehood and Union: A History of the Northwest Ordinance* (Bloomington: Indiana University Press, 1987).

9. Harry V. Jaffa, "Abraham Lincoln" in *American Political Thought*, eds. Morton Frisch and Richard G. Stevens (Itasca, IL: F. E. Peacok, 1983) pp. 195–215.

10. Alexis de Tocqueville, *Democracy in America*, ed. J. P. Mayer, translation by George Lawrence (Garden City, NY: Doubleday, 1969).

11. See, e.g., Paul M. Edwards, *The Doctrines and Covenants* (Independence, MO: Herald Pub. House, 1988).

12. Marquis W. Childs, *Ethics In a Business Society* (New York: Harper & Brothers, 1954).

13. Daniel J. Elazar, "Deuteronomy as Israel's Ancient Constitution: Some Preliminary Reflections," in *Jewish Political Studies Review*, Vol. 4, No. 1 (Spring, 1992).

14. Yehezkel Kaufman, *A Religiao de Israel do inicino ao erilio Babilonico* (*The Religion of Israel)* (Sao Paulo: Associacao Universtaria de Cultura Judaico, 1989).

15. Timothy Fuller, "The Idea of Christianity in Hobbes's *Leviathan*," in *Jewish Political Studies Review, Thomas Hobbes Confronts the Bible*, Vol. 4, No. 2 (Nos. 3–4), Fall 5753/1992.

16. Robert Licht, "Communal Democracy, Modernity, and the Jewish Political Tradition," *Jewish Political Studies Review, Communal Democracy and Liberal Democracy in the Jewish Political Tradition*, Vol. 5, Numbers 1 & 2 (Spring, 1993).

5

An Apt and Cheerful Conversation on Marriage

John Witte, Jr.

"The apt and cheerful conversation of man with woman is the chief and noblest purpose of marriage," wrote John Milton. "Where loving [conversation] cannot be, there can be left of wedlock nothing but the empty husk of an outside matrimony"—dry, shriveled, and dispensable. Aptness can strain cheerfulness: candid conversations between spouses can be very painful. Cheerfulness can strain aptness: blissful domestic ignorance can be very tempting. But aptness and cheerfulness properly belong together in a marriage, Milton tells us. Where they fail, the marriage fails.[1]

An apt and cheerful conversation about marriage must be part of our dialogue of "a third way." For marriage is one of the great mediators of individuality and community, revelation and reason, tradition and modernity—dialectics which any discussion of a third way must parse. Marriage is at once a harbor of the self and a harbinger of the community, a symbol of divine love and a structure of reasoned consent, an enduring ancient mystery and a constantly modern invention.

To be "apt," our conversation cannot wax nostalgic about a prior golden age of marriage and the family, nor wax myopic about modern ideals of liberty, privacy, and autonomy. We cannot be blind to the patriarchy, paternalism, and plain prudishness of the past. Nor can we be blind to the massive social, psychological, and spiritual costs of the modern sexual revolution. To be apt, participants in the conversation on marriage must seek to understand both traditional morals and contemporary mores on their own terms and in their own context—without deprecating or privileging either form or norm. Traditionalists must heed the maxim of Jaroslav Pelikan that "[t]radition is the living faith of the dead; traditionalism is the dead faith of the living."[2] Wooden antiquarianism, a dogmatic indifference to the changing needs of marriages and families, is not apt. Modernists must heed the instruction of Harold Berman that "we must walk into the future with an eye on the past."[3] Chronological snobbery, a calculated disregard for the wisdom of the past, also is not apt.

To be "cheerful," our conversation must proceed with the faith that the crisis of modern American marriage and family life can be overcome. Marriage and the family are in trouble today. Statistics tell the grim story. In the 1990s, a quarter of all pregnancies are aborted. A third of all children are born to single mothers. One half of all marriages end in divorce. Three quarters of all black children are without fathers. The number of "no parent" households doubles each year. The number of "lost children"—born in poverty and in broken households, and more likely than not to drop out of school, out of step, and then out of society altogether—has reached more than fifteen million. So much is well known.[4] It brings little cheer.

What is less well known is that the Western tradition has faced family crises on this scale before. And apocalyptic jeremiads about the end of civil society have been uttered many times before—by everyone from Cicero to Calvin, from Maimonides to Moynihan. What brings cheer is that the Western tradition of marriage has always found the resources to heal and reinvent itself, to strike new balances between orthodoxy and innovation, order and liberty with regard to our enduring and evolving sexual, marital, and familial norms and habits. The prospect of healing and reinvention is no less likely today—so long as academics, activists, and advocates, political, religious, and civic leaders ponder these problems in good faith and direct their resources to good works.

This essay makes a small start at such an apt and cheerful conversation on marriage. In the first part of this essay, I show that modern Anglo-American marriage law was formed out of two traditions—one rooted in Christianity, a second in the Enlightenment. Each of these traditions has contributed a variety of familiar legal ideas and institutions—some overlapping, some conflicting. It is in the overlapping and creatively juxtaposed legal contributions of the Christian and Enlightenment traditions that one sees some of the ingredients of a third way respecting marriage. These are outlined in the latter part of the essay.

THE CHRISTIAN AND ENLIGHTENMENT INHERITANCE

The Western tradition has, for nearly two millennia, offered four perspectives on marriage and the family. A spiritual perspective regards marriage as a religious or sacramental association, subject to the creed, code, cult, and canons of the religious community. A social perspective treats the family as a social estate, subject to special state laws of contract, property, and inheritance and to the expectations and exactions of the local community. A contractual perspective describes the family as a voluntary association, subject to the wills and preferences of the couple, their children, their dependents, their household. Hovering in the background, and often adduced in support of these three perspectives is a naturalist perspective that treats the family as a created or natural institution, subject to divine and natural laws.

These four perspectives are in one sense complementary, for they each emphasize one aspect of this institution—its religious sanction, its social legitimation, its voluntary formation, and its natural origin, respectively. These four perspectives have also come to stand in considerable tension, however, for they are linked to competing claims of ultimate authority over the form and function of marriage—claims by the church, by the state, by family members, and by God and nature. Some of the deepest fault lines in the historical formation and the current transformations of Western marriage ultimately break out from this central tension of perspective. Which perspective of marriage dominates a culture, or at least prevails in an instance of dispute—the spiritual, the social, the contractual, or the natural? Which authority wields preeminent, or at least peremptory, power over marriage and family questions—the church, the state, the couple, or God and nature operating through one of these parties?

Historically, Catholics, Protestants, and Enlightenment exponents alike constructed elaborate models to address these cardinal questions. Each group recognized multiple perspectives on marriage but gave priority to one of them to achieve an integrated understanding. Catholics emphasized the spiritual (or sacramental) perspective on marriage. Protestants emphasized the social (or public) perspective. Enlightenment exponents emphasized the contractual (or private) perspective. In broad outline, the Catholic model dominated Western marriage law until the sixteenth century. From the mid-sixteenth to the mid-nineteenth century, Catholic and Protestant models, in distinct and hybrid forms, dominated Western family law. In the past century, the Enlightenment model has emerged, largely eclipsing the theology and law of the Christian traditions.

STEPHEN V. MILL

A good illustration of the Christian and Enlightenment traditions of marriage, and the tensions between them, is captured in a vigorous literary debate in mid-nineteenth century England. The debate featured James Fitzjames Stephen, a prominent Anglican jurist and moralist, and John Stuart Mill, a leading libertarian and utilitarian of ample Enlightenment learning. Both were distinguished men of letters and occasional legislators. Both came to speak for broad constituencies—Stephen for the old order, Mill for a new order.

The setting for much of their debate was the ferment in Parliament for the reform of the traditional English law of marriage—ferment that found equal force in American state legislatures at the same time. The Stephen-Mill debate was focused by several bills in Parliament that sought to liberalize marriage and divorce rules, to liberate children from abusive households, and to enhance the rights of wives to their property and minor children. For Stephen, the heart of the debate was over the essential character of marriage and the family: Is this institution "a divine, indissoluble union governed by the paterfamilias, or is it a contractual unit governed and dissolved by the wills of the parties?"[5]

Stephen, speaking for the old order, defended the first position. "[T]he political and social changes which have taken place in the world since the sixteenth century [Reformation] have . . . been eminently beneficial to mankind," Stephen wrote. "The terms of the marriage relation as settled by the law and religion of Europe" since that time must be maintained.

The "settled" religious view of Stephen's day—among Anglicans, Catholics, and Protestants alike—was that marriage is a "state of existence ordained by the Creator," "a consummation of the Divine command to multiply and replenish the earth," "the highest state of existence," "the only stable substructure of social, civil, and religious institutions." Marriage was viewed as "a public institution of universal concern," even, for some, "a sacrament . . . of primary concern, transcendent in its importance both to individuals and to society." Marriage was almost universally taken to be a permanent monogamous union between a fit man and woman designed for mutual love and affection, mutual procreation and nurture of children, mutual protection from spiritual and civil harms.[6]

The "settled" legal view of Stephen's day was that marriage formation required formal betrothals, publication of banns, parental consent, peer witnesses, state licenses, and church consecration. Marriage would be annulled if couples were related by various blood or family ties identified in the Mosaic law, or where one party proved impotent, frigid, sterile, or had a contagious disease that precluded procreation or endangered the other spouse. Marriages could also be annulled if one of the parties was under age or had been coerced, tricked, or misled into marriage. Couples who sought to divorce had to publicize their intentions, to petition a court, to show adequate cause or fault, to make permanent provision for the dependent spouse and children.

The "settled" natural view, Stephen maintained, was that men are created with superior power, ability, and opportunity in life, which they must discharge with due restraint and accountability to God. Women have a special calling to be wives and mothers, teachers and nurturers of children, which calling they must discharge in the household. Our law and religion reflect these natural sentiments, said Stephen, "by prescribing monogamy, indissoluble marriage on the footing of the obedience of the wife to the husband, and a division of labour among men and women with corresponding differences in the matters of conduct, manners, and dress."

Nature is defied if marriage is treated as a simple contract, Stephen argued. This notion assumes falsely that men and women are equal. To allow marriage to become "a simple bargained-for contract," without oversight by parents and peers and by church and state, "will inevitably expose women to great abuse." They will have no protection in forming the bargain with naturally superior men, nor protection from men who dismiss them when barren, old, unattractive, troubled, or destitute. "The truth is," Stephen thundered, "that the change of marriage . . . from status to contract," from divine sacrament to simple partnership, "is not favorable to equality." "Men [and women] are fundamentally unequal, and this inequality will show itself, arrange society [and its law] as you like." "If marriage is to be permanent," and justice and liberty properly guarded, "the government of the family must be put by law and by morals in the hands of the husband."

Nature is also defied if the family is treated as an open contractual society, subject to multiple claims of right by its members. The family, once formed, is an independent institution that "lies at the foundation of both church and state." The husband and father is the head of the family, just as the monarch is the head of church and state. As paterfamilias, he is "clothed with a variety of powers and characters," and must rule the household as God's vice-regent with all benevolence, grace, and Christian devotion. A wife is the husband's co-helper in the family, his "help meet," who must submit to his reasoned judgment in the event of conflict. A child is the father's ward and agent, who must obey his every reasonable command.

Stephen was well aware of the potential abuses in this traditional law of marriage and family. "No one," he writes, "contends that a man ought to have power to order his wife and children about like slaves and beat them if they disobey him." Such abusive conduct must be punished severely, but on a case-by-case basis. These occasional abuses cannot unmake the general rules of marriage and family life forged by learned theologians and jurists over the centuries.

John Stuart Mill attacked Stephen's sentiments with arguments well known in England's liberal circles, especially those influenced by Mary Wollstonecraft's writings of the 1790s onward.[7] In part, Mill's attack was directed against the abuses of the traditional system of marriage and family law. Though sometimes the family is marked by "sympathy and tenderness," said Mill, "it is still oftener . . . a school of willfulness, overbearingness, unbounded self-indulgence, and a double-dyed and idealized selfishness" of the husband and father, with the "individual happiness" of the wife and children "being immolated in every shape to his smallest preferences." No system of marriage law that allows such abuses can be justified.

Mill's deeper attack on Stephen's defense of traditional English marriage law was theological—"laying bare the real root of much that is bowed down to as the intention of Nature and the ordinance of God," as he put it. The prevailing theology and law of marriage and the family supports a three-fold patriarchy, Mill charged. The church dictates to the state its peculiar understanding of nature. The state dictates to the couple the terms of their marital relation, and abandons them once the terms are accepted. The man lords over his wife and children, divesting them of all liberty and license in their person and property, thought and belief. "The aim of the law," Mill charged, "is to tie up the soul, the mind, the sense," and the body of the wife and children, together with their "material extensions."

Nature does not teach bondage and subjection of women, said Mill, but the natural liberty and equality of all men and women. "[T]he legal subordination of one sex to the other is wrong and ought to be replaced by a principle of perfect equality with no favour or privilege on the one side nor disability on the other." "What is now called the [inferior] nature of women" and the superior nature of man "is an eminently artificial thing," born of social circumstances, not natural conditions. "If marriage were an equal contract . . . and if [a woman] would find all honourable employments as freely open to her as to men," marriages could be true institutions of liberty and affection, shaped by the preferences of wife and husband, not the prescriptions of church and state.

Nature also does not teach parental tyranny and commodification of children but counsels parental nurture and education of children. Children are not items of property, to be sold on the market of marriage, nor simple conduits through which to pass the family name and property. Children are also not slaves or "animals" to be worked and whipped into submission and performance by their parents. If the family were an open unit, where children could seek redress from neglect, abuse and arbitrary rule, a real family could be realized and true happiness for all parties involved could be attained. If the paterfamilias does not "fulfill his obligation to feed, nurture, and educate his child with love and patience," said Mill, the paterpoliticus, the state as the child's protector under the social contract, "ought to see it fulfilled, at the charge, as far as possible, of the parent."

Mill sought to infuse these contractarian principles of marriage and the family into the public opinion of Victorian England, America, and beyond, and into the reform of many traditional laws of marriage. He urged the abolition of the requirements of parental consent, church consecration, and formal witnesses for marriage. He questioned the exalted status of heterosexual monogamy and supported peaceable polygamy (though he personally found the practice odious). He called for the absolute equality of husband and wife to receive, hold, and alienate property, to enter into contracts and commerce, to participate on equal terms in the workplace, in education, in political life, in social circles. He called for severe punishment of husbands who assaulted, abused, or raped their wives, and for strict prohibitions against prostitution and pornography. He urged fathers to turn from their public vocations and avocations to assist in the care and nurture of their children. He called for equal rights of husbands and wives to sue for divorce and remarriage, unilaterally and without stated grounds. He castigated the state for leaving annulment and other marital causes to the church, and urged that the laws of annulment and divorce be both merged and expanded under exclusive state jurisdiction. He urged that paternal abuse of children be severely punished, and that the state intervene where necessary to ensure the proper physical and moral nurture and education of children.

LEGAL REFORMS

Mill's Enlightenment-based critique of traditional Christian marriage lore and law helped to transform Anglo-American marriage law. The reforms came in two waves. The first wave, which broke slowly over England and America from the mid-nineteenth to the mid-twentieth centuries, was designed to bring greater equality and equity to the traditional household, without necessarily denying the traditional Christian ideas of marriage that had helped to form this institution. The second wave of reform, which has been breaking in America since the early 1960s, seems calculated to break the preeminence of the traditional family law, and the basic Christian values which once sustained it.

First Wave

The first wave of legal reforms brought greater protection to religious minorities, children, and women. England set the pace of many of these reforms, and its laws were typical of those that emerged in American states at roughly the same time.[8]

First, Parliament authorized both religious and civil forms of marriage. Parties who reached the age of consent could still marry in accordance with traditional English law—featuring the publication of banns of betrothal, the consent of parents and peers, and a public church wedding. But now Jewish, Quaker, Catholic, and other religious minorities could form their marriages in accordance with the religious laws and customs of their own communities. Parties could also forgo a religious marriage ceremony altogether by swearing a simple marital oath before the Superintendent Registrar.

Second, Parliament relieved children of the costs of their parents' extramarital intercourse. Historically, children conceived out of wedlock bore the brunt of their parents' sexual experimentation. Such children were sometimes aborted in vitro or smothered on birth, with the mother incurring rather modest penalties for the offense. If they survived, they were illegitimate bastards with severely truncated civil, political, and property rights. Several statutes eased this burden. Abortions and infanticide were subject to firm new criminal laws. Exploitation of (especially illegitimate) child labor was increasingly restricted and policed. Educational opportunities for illegitimate children were enhanced through the expansion of state and newly chartered private schools. Illegitimate children could be more easily legitimated through adoption or subsequent marriage of their natural parents. Annulments no longer automatically illegitimated children born of a putative marriage.

Third, in 1857, Parliament authorized private suits for divorce on proof of cause, with a subsequent right to remarry for the innocent party—a right which most American states at the time had already recognized. Parties could still press annulment suits on proof of an impediment, and seek orders for separation from bed and board on proof of adultery, desertion, or cruelty. But now innocent husbands and wives could also sue for absolute divorce and remarriage rights on grounds of the adultery of the other party. When later statutes expanded the grounds for divorce to include desertion, cruelty, frigidity, habitual drunkenness, criminal conduct, and other faults, divorce rates slowly rose in England—from 0.05 divorces per 1000 marriages in 1870 to 0.22 per 1000 in 1920, 4.7 per 1000 in 1970, and a high of 13.4 per 1000 in 1985. At the same time, separation and annulment rates slowly dropped, with divorce increasingly viewed as the most effective and efficient remedy for broken marriages—particularly after the 1969 Divorce Act introduced divorce on the ground of "irretrievable breakdown."

Fourth, Parliament provided that, in cases of annulment or divorce, courts had discretion to place minor children in the custody of that parent who was best suited to care for their maintenance, nurture, and education. This reversed the traditional presumption that child custody automatically belonged to the father. The wife could now claim custody, particularly where the children were of tender years or where the husband was found to be cruel, abusive, or unfit as a caretaker. Courts retained the traditional power to order guilty husbands to pay temporary or permanent alimony to innocent wives. Courts were also newly empowered to make additional "reasonable" allocations of marital property to the innocent wife for the support of minor children.

Fifth, Parliament released married women from the traditional bonds of coverture, which, upon marriage, had subsumed a woman's person and property into that of her husband. Married women could now hold independent title and control and exercise independent contractual and testimonial rights over the property they brought into the marriage, or acquired thereafter. They also gained the capacity to sue or be sued in respect of their property, without authorization or intermeddling by their husbands, and without the usual restrictions on testifying against their husbands or kin in cases of family conflict. After their rights to property were enhanced, (married) women slowly gained broader rights and access to higher education, learned societies, trade and commercial guilds and unions, and a variety of professions, occupations, and societies, and the franchise, all of which had been largely closed to them.

This first wave of reforms sought to improve traditional marriage lore and law more than to abandon it. To be sure, the smug mockery of a Mill and the shattering iconoclasm of some of his contemporaries betrayed ample hostility to the tradition. But most of these reformers, Mill among them, still accepted the Christian ideal of marriage as a permanent union of a fit man and fit woman of the age of consent. Most accepted the classic Augustinian definition of the marital goods of fides, proles, et sacramentum—sacrificial love, benevolent procreation, and symbolic stability.

The primary goal of these early reformers was to purge the traditional household and community of its paternalism and patriarchy and thus to render the ideals of marriage a greater reality for all. The reforms which they introduced rendered marriages easier to contract and easier to dissolve. Courts were more deferential to the wishes of the marital parties. Wives received greater protections from their husbands and greater independence in their relationships outside the household. Children received greater protection from parental abuse and greater access to benefit rights. Young women, in particular, received greater freedom to forgo or postpone marriage, and greater social, political, and economic opportunities, regardless of their marital status.

Second Wave of Reforms

Since the early 1960s, American reformers have taken the lead in pressing the Enlightenment contractarian model of marriage to the more radical conclusions that Mill and others had intimated. The same Enlightenment ideals of individualism, freedom, equality, and privacy, which had earlier driven reforms of traditional marriage laws, have come to be used to reject these laws altogether. The traditional Christian ideal of marriage as a permanent spiritual union designed for the sake of mutual love, procreation, and protection is slowly giving way to a new reality of marriage as a terminal sexual contract designed for the gratification of the individual parties.

The Uniform Marriage and Divorce Act—both a "barometer of enlightened legal opinion"[9] and a mirror of current American laws on marriage—reflects these new sentiments. The Uniform Act defines marriage as "a personal relationship between a man and a woman arising out of a civil contract to which the consent of the parties is essential." Historically, valid marriage contracts required the consent of parents or guardians, publication of banns, the attestation of witnesses, church consecration, and civil licensing and registration. The Act requires only the minimal formalities of state licensing, and parental consent for children under the age of majority. Marriages contracted in violation of even these requirements, however, are presumptively valid and immune from independent legal attack, unless the parties themselves petition for dissolution within ninety days of contracting marriage. Historically, impediments of infancy, incapacity, inebriation, consanguinity, affinity, sterility, frigidity, bigamy, among several others would nullify the marriage or render it voidable and subject to attack from either marital party or a third party. It would also expose parties who married in knowing violation of these impediments to sanctions. The Uniform Act makes no provision for sanctions, and leaves the choice of nullification to the married parties alone. The Act does confirm the traditional impediments protecting consent—granting parties standing to dissolve marriages where they lacked the capacity to contract by reason of infirmity, alcohol, drugs, or other incapacitating substances, or where there was force, duress, fraud, or coercion into entering a marriage contract. But the Act limits the other impediments to prohibitions against bigamy and marriages between "half or whole blood relatives" or adopted siblings. In most states that have adopted the Uniform Act, all impediments, save the prohibition against bigamy, are regularly waived in individual cases.

These provisions of the Uniform Marriage and Divorce Act reflect a basic principle of modern American constitutional law, first articulated clearly by the Supreme Court in the landmark case of *Loving v. Virginia* (1967): "The freedom to marry has long been recognized as one of the vital personal rights essential to the orderly pursuit of happiness by free men. Marriage is one of the 'basic civil rights of man,' fundamental to our very existence and survival."[10] Using that principle, the Court has struck down, as undue burdens on the right to marry, a state prohibition against interracial marriage, a requirement that noncustodial parents obligated to pay child support must receive judicial permission to marry, and a requirement that a prisoner must receive a warden's permission to marry.[11] This same principle of freedom of marital contract, the drafters of the Uniform Act report, has led state courts and legislatures to peel away most of the traditional formalities for marriage formation.

The Supreme Court has expanded this principle of freedom of marital contract into a more general right of sexual privacy within and without the household. In *Griswold v. Connecticut* (1965), for example, the Supreme Court struck down a state law banning the use of contraceptives by a married couple as a violation of their freedom to choose whether to have or to forgo children. "The marital couple is not an independent entity with a mind and heart of its own, but an association of two individuals, each with a separate emotional and intellectual makeup," the Court later proclaimed. "If the right of privacy means anything, it is the right of the individual, married or single, to be free from unwanted governmental intrusion into matters so fundamentally affecting the person as the decision whether to bear or beget a child."[12] In *Roe v. Wade* (1973), the Court extended this privacy principle to cover the right of abortion by a married or unmarried woman during the first trimester of pregnancy—without interference by the state, her husband, parent, or other third party. In *Moore v. East Cleveland* (1978), the Court struck down a municipal zoning ordinance that impaired members of an extended family from living together in the same household. In *Kirschberg v. Feenstra* (1981), the Court struck down a state statute that gave the husband as "head and master" of the family the right unilaterally to dispose of property held in common with his wife.

State legislatures and courts have extended these principles of freedom of contract and sexual privacy to other aspects of marriage. Many states, for example, have abandoned their traditional reticence about enforcing prenuptial and marital contracts. The Uniform Premarital Agreement Act, adopted in about half the states today, allows parties to contract, in advance of their marriage, about all rights pertaining to their individual and common property and "any other matter, including their personal rights and obligations, not in violation of public policy or a statute imposing a criminal penalty."[13] The Act does prohibit courts from enforcing premarital contracts that are involuntary, unconscionable, or based on less than full disclosure by both parties. But, within these broad strictures, marital parties are left free to define in advance their own personal and property rights during marriage or in the event of separation, dissolution, or divorce.

Similarly, many states have left marital parties free to enter separation agreements on their own, or with a mediator, respecting the maintenance and distribution of their property, and the support, custody, and visitation of their children. Such agreements are presumptively binding on a court, and, absent a finding of unconscionability, courts will enforce these agreements on their own terms, reserving the right to alter those contract provisions that bear adversely on the couple's children. If the separation ripens into divorce, courts will also often incorporate these separation agreements into the divorce decree, again with little scrutiny of the contents of the agreement.

The same principles of freedom of contract and sexual privacy dominate contemporary American laws of divorce. Every state has now promulgated a "no-fault divorce" statute, and virtually all states allow for divorce on the motion of only one party. Even if the defendant spouse forgives the fault and objects to the divorce, courts must, after a brief waiting period, grant the divorce if the plaintiff insists. The Uniform Marriage and Divorce Act and fifteen states have eliminated altogether consideration of the fault of either spouse—even if the fault proves to be a crime. The remaining states consider fault only for limited questions of child custody, not for the question of whether to grant the divorce.

Virtually all states have also ordered a one-time division of marital property between the divorced parties. Parties may determine their own property division through prenuptial or separation agreements, which courts will enforce after a loose review of its conscionability. But, absent such agreements, courts will pool the entire assets of the marital household and make an equitable division of the collective property based on numerous factors—"the duration of the marriage, any prior marriage of either party . . . the age, health, station, occupation, amount, and sources of income, vocational skills, employability, estate, liabilities, and needs of each of the parties, custodial provisions . . . and the opportunity for each for future acquisition of capital assets and income."[14] These one-time divisions of property have largely replaced traditional forms of alimony and other forms of ongoing support for the innocent or dependent spouse—regardless of the fault, expectations, or needs of either party.

These two reforms of divorce law were introduced, in part, to protect both the privacy and the contractual freedom of the marital parties. No-fault divorces freed marital parties from exposing their marital discords or infidelities to judicial scrutiny and public record—and from the temptation of making or staging spurious charges of fault to escape the marital bond. One-time marital property divisions give parties a clean break from each other and the consequent freedom to marry another. Both reforms, together, allow parties to terminate their marriages as easily and efficiently as they were able to contract them, without much interference from the state or from the other spouse. These two principles of privacy and freedom of contract reforms are qualified only in divorce cases involving minor children: The "best interests of the child" principle can still lead to awards of custody to innocent spouses, and to mandatory ongoing child support payments for the non-custodial parent.[15]

This second wave of reforms has implemented the more radical suggestions of the Enlightenment reformers. A private contractual perspective on marriage now dominates American law, lore, and life. Antenuptial, marital, and separation contracts that allow parties to define their own rights and duties within the marital estate and thereafter have gained increasing acceptance. Implied marital contracts are imputed to longstanding lovers. Surrogacy contracts are executed for the rental of wombs. Medical contracts are executed for the abortion of fetuses. Requirements of parental consent and witnesses to such contracts have largely disappeared. No-fault divorce statutes have reduced the divorce proceeding to an expensive formality. Lump sum property exchanges now often substitute for alimony.

To be sure, these exponential legal changes in part simply reflect the exponential cultural changes that have occurred in the condition of American families in the past three decades—the stunning advances in reproductive and medical technology, the exposure to vastly different perceptions of sexuality and kinship born of globalization, the explosion of international and domestic norms of human rights, and the implosion of the Ozzie and Harriet family born of new economic and professional demands on wives, husbands, and children. But we have also been witnessing the precocious rise of an Enlightenment contractarian model of marriage that has eclipsed Protestant and Catholic models of marriage and the legal ideas and institutions which those models introduced.

SIGNPOSTS OF A THIRD WAY

A Hegelian might well be happy with this antinomy. Christian models of marriage that prioritized religious norms and ecclesiastical structures squared off against Enlightenment models of marriage that prioritized private choice and contractual strictures. Christianity was exposed for its penchant for paternalism and patriarchy, and lost. The Enlightenment was embraced for its promise of liberty and equality, and won. Thesis gave way to anti-thesis. Stephen gave way to Mill. Such is the way of progress.

The story is not so simple. It is true that John Stuart Mill's ideal of marriage as "a private, bargained-for exchange between husband and wife about all their rights, goods, and interests" has become a legal reality in America. The strong presumption today is that adult parties have free entrance into marital contracts, free exercise of marital relationships, and free exit from marriages once their contractual obligations are discharged. Parties are still bound to continue to support their minor children, within and without marriage. But this merely expresses another contractual principle—that parties respect the reliance and expectation interests of their children, who are third party beneficiaries of their marital or sexual contracts.

It is equally true, however, that James Fitzjames Stephen's warning that undue contractualization of marriage will bring ruin to many women and children has also become a social reality in America. Premarital, marital, separation, and divorce contracts too often are not arms-length transactions, and too often are not driven by rational calculus alone. In the heady romance of budding nuptials, parties are often blind to the full consequences of their bargain. In the emotional anguish of separation and divorce, parties can be driven more by the desire for short-term relief from the other spouse than by the concern for their long-term welfare or that of their children. The economically stronger and more calculating spouse triumphs in these contexts. And in the majority of cases today, that party is still the man—despite the loud egalitarian rhetoric to the contrary.[16]

"Underneath the mantle of equality [and freedom] that has been draped over the ongoing family, the state of nature flourishes," Mary Ann Glendon writes.[17] In this state of nature, freedom and privacy reign supreme. But married life is becoming increasingly "brutish, nasty, and short"—with women and children bearing the primary costs. Recall the statistics: In the 1990s, a quarter of all pregnancies are aborted. A third of all children are born to single mothers. One half of all marriages end in divorce. Two thirds of all black children are without fathers. The number of "no parent" households doubles each year. The number of "lost children" in America has reached more than fifteen million. The greater the repeal of regulation of marriage for the sake of marital freedom and sexual privacy, the greater the threat to real freedom for women and children. The very contractarian gospel that first promised salvation from the abuses of earlier Christian models of marriage now threatens with even graver abuse.

What is the way out of this dilemma? There have been, and must be, many learned responses.[18] Mine is the expected response of an historian: "Back to the sources!"—but now newly enlightened. The achievements of the Enlightenment in reforming the theology and law of marriage cannot be lost on us. It took the contractual radicalism of Mill and his contemporaries to force the Western tradition to reform itself—to grant greater respect to the rights of women, children, and religious minorities, to break the monopoly and monotony of outmoded moral and religious forms and forums respecting sexuality, marriage, and the family. While some religious traditions may have retrieved or conceived their own resources to achieve these reforms, it was the Enlightenment critique that forced these traditions to reform themselves and the state to reform its laws. This was no small achievement.

Just as the Enlightenment tradition still has much to teach us today, so do the earlier Christian traditions of the West. Catholic and Protestant traditions have both seen that families are at once natural, religious, social, and contractual units; that in order to survive and flourish, this institution must be governed both externally by legal authorities and internally by moral authorities. From different perspectives, these traditions have seen that the family is an inherently communal enterprise, in which marital couples, magistrates, and ministers must all inevitably cooperate. After all, marital contracts are of little value without courts to enforce them. Marital properties are of little use without laws to validate them. Marital laws are of little consequence without canons to inspire them. Marital customs are of little cogency without natural norms and narratives to ground them.

The modern lesson in this is that we must resist the temptation to reduce marriage to a single perspective, or to a single forum. A single perspective on marriage—whether sacramental, social, or contractual—does not capture the full nuance of this institution. A single forum—whether the church, state, or the household itself—is not fully competent to govern all marital questions. Marriage demands multiple forums and multiple laws to be governed adequately. American religious communities must think more seriously about restoring and reforming their own bodies of religious law on marriage, divorce, and sexuality, instead of simply acquiescing in state laws. American states must think more seriously about granting greater deference to the marital laws and customs of legitimate religious and cultural groups that cannot accept a marriage law of the common denominator. Other sophisticated legal cultures—Denmark, England, India, and South Africa—grant semi-autonomy to Catholic, Hindu, Jewish, Muslim, and traditional groups to conduct their subjects' domestic affairs in accordance with their own laws and customs, with the state setting only minimum conditions and limits. It might well be time for America likewise to translate its growing cultural pluralism into a more concrete legal pluralism.

The Western tradition has learned, through centuries of hard experience, to balance the norms of marital formation and dissolution. There was something cruel, for example, in a medieval Catholic canon law that countenanced easy contracting of marriage but provided for no escape from a marriage once properly contracted. The Council of Trent responded to this inequity in 1563 by establishing several safeguards to the legitimate contracting of marriage—parental consent, peer witness, church consecration, civil registration—so that an inapt or immature couple would be less likely to marry. There was something equally cruel in the rigid insistence of some early Protestants on reconciliation of all married couples at all costs—save those few who could successfully sue for divorce. Later Protestants responded to this inequity by reinstituting the traditional remedy of separation from bed and board for miserable couples incapable of either reconciliation or divorce.

The modern lesson in this is that rules governing marriage formation and dissolution must be balanced in their stringency—and separation must be maintained as a release valve. Stern rules of marital dissolution require stern rules of marital formation. Loose formation rules demand loose dissolution rules, as we see today. To fix the modern problem of broken marriages requires reforms of rules at both ends of the marital process. Today, more than twenty states have bills under discussion seeking to tighten the rules of divorce, without corresponding attention to the rules of marital formation and separation. Such efforts, standing alone, are misguided. The cause of escalating divorce rates is not only "no fault divorce," as is so often said, but also "no faith marriage."

A promising course is suggested by the Louisiana covenant marriage statute, passed on August 15, 1997, which seeks to reform both ends of the marital process. At the time of their marital formation, couples may choose either a traditional contract marriage with attendant rights to no fault divorce, or a covenant marriage, with more stringent formation and dissolution rules. In forming a covenant marriage, the parties must receive detailed counseling from a licensed therapist or religious official, read the entire covenant marriage statute, and then swear an oath, pledging "full knowledge of the nature, purposes, and responsibilities of marriage" and promising "to love, honor, and care for one another as husband and wife for the rest of our lives." Divorce is allowed such covenanted couples only on proof of adultery, capital felony, malicious desertion or separation for more than a year, and/or physical or sexual abuse of the spouse or one of the children. Formal separation is allowed on any of these grounds, as well as on proof of habitual intemperance, cruel treatment, or outrages of the other spouse.[19]

This is a cleverly drawn statute that seeks to respect both the virtues of contractual calculus and the values of the disestablishment clause of the First Amendment. It goes a long way to incorporating the historical lesson that marriage formation and dissolution rules must be balanced. The statute has been attacked, predictably, as an encroachment on sexual freedom and the rights of women and children, as a "Trojan horse" to smuggle biblical principles into American law, and as a throwback to the days of staged and spurious charges of marital infidelity which "no fault" statutes sought to overcome. But, given the neutral language of the statute and its explicit protections of both voluntary entrance and involuntary exit from the covenant union, such objections are largely inapt. The statute should help to inject both a greater level of realism into the heady romance of prospective couples and a greater level of rigor into the state's law of marriage formation and dissolution.

The stronger objection to the Louisiana statute is not that it jeopardizes liberty but that it trivializes covenant. The statute effectively reduces "covenant" to a super marriage contract between the husband and wife alone. Historically, however, marriage covenants involved parents, peers, ministers, and magistrates as well, who served at least as checks on each other and the prospective couple, if not as representatives of God in the covenant formation. Indeed, according to classic Protestant theology, the couple's parents, as God's bishops for children, gave their consent to the union. Two parties, as God's priests to their peers, served as witnesses to the marriage. The minister, holding God's spiritual power of the Word, blessed the couple and admonished them in their spiritual duties. The magistrate, holding God's temporal power of the sword, registered the parties and their properties and ensured the legality of their union. These four parties represented different dimensions of God's involvement in the marriage covenant, and were thus essential to the legitimacy of the marriage covenant itself.[20] The Louisiana law replaces all four of these four parties with a licensed marital counselor. Moreover, the Louisiana law leaves it to the state to decide the terms of the marital covenant, the credentials of the marriage counselor, and the contents of the marriage oath. Historically, however, churches and synagogues defined these matters for themselves, without much state interference.

The Western tradition has learned to distinguish between annulment and divorce. Annulment is a decision that a putative marriage was void from the start, by reason of some impediment that lay undiscovered or undisclosed at the time of the wedding. Divorce is a decision that a marriage once properly contracted must now be dissolved by reason of the fault of one of the parties after their wedding. The spiritual and psychological calculus and costs are different in these decisions. In annulment cases, a party may discover features of their marriage or spouse which need not, and sometimes cannot, be forgiven—that they were manipulated or coerced into marriage; that the parties are improperly related by blood or family ties; that the spouse will not or cannot perform expected connubial duties; that the spouse misrepresented a fundamental part of his or her faith, character, or history. Annulment in such instances is prudent, sometimes mandatory, even if painful. In divorce cases, by contrast, the moral inclination (and, for some, the moral imperative) is to forgive a spouse's infidelity, desertion, cruelty, or crime. Divorce, in such instances, might be licit, even prudent, but it often feels like, and is treated as, a personal failure even for the innocent spouse. The historical remedy was often calculated patience; early death by one spouse was the most common cure for broken marriages. In the modern age of fitness and longevity, this remedy is usually less apt.

The modern lesson in this is that not all marital dissolutions are equal. Today, most states have simply collapsed annulment and divorce into a single action, with little procedural or substantive distinction between them. This is one (forgotten) source of our exponentially increased divorce rates; historically, annulment rates were counted separately. This is one reason that religious bodies have become largely excluded from the divorce process; historically, annulment decisions were often made by religious bodies and then enforced by state courts. And this is one reason that the "no fault" divorce has become so attractive; parties often have neither the statutory mechanism nor the procedural incentive to plead a legitimate impediment. Parties seeking dissolution are thus herded together in one legal process of divorce—subject to the same generic rules respecting children and property, and prone to the same generic stigmatizing by self and others.

The Western tradition has recognized that marriage and the family has multiple forms, that it can change over time and across cultures. The celebrated nuclear family of husband and wife, daughter and son is only one model that the Western tradition has cherished. It was common in the past to extend the theological and legal concept of the family to other kinds of units—the single household with one parent alongside children, stepchildren, adopted children, or grandchildren; the extended household embracing servants, students, and sojourners or embracing three or four generations of relatives with obligations of mutual care and nurture among them; the communal household of siblings or friends, single or widowed, with or without children; the spiritual household of brothers and sisters joined in the cloister, chantry, or charity, and dedicated to service of God, neighbor, and each other.

The modern lesson in this is that we must not cling too dogmatically to an ideal form of household. It was common in the recent past for the establishment to look askance on the commune but approvingly on the community home, to look churlishly at the divorcee but charitably on the widow, to look suspiciously on the spinster but benevolently on the spurned. Today, we accept, sometimes even admire, communes, divorcees, and spinsters—and make provision for them in our laws of taxation, property, and zoning as well as in our pastoral, diaconal, and pedagogical ministries. We now have other targets of suspicion—homosexuals and polygamists prominently among them.

To bring to light this historical wisdom is neither to wax nostalgic about a golden age of Western marriage, nor to write pedantic about arcane antiquities with no modern utility. We cannot delude ourselves with romantic accounts of the Catholic, Protestant, or Enlightenment past. Nor can we seek uncritically to transpose its mores and morals into our day. To adduce these ancient sources is instead to point to a rich resource for the lore and law of modern marriage that is too little known and too little used today. Too much of contemporary society seems to have lost sight of the rich and diverse Western theological heritage of marriage and of the uncanny ability of the Western legal tradition to strike new balances between order and liberty, orthodoxy and innovation with respect to our enduring and evolving sexual and familial norms and habits. Too much of the contemporary church seems to have lost sight of the ability of its forebears to translate their enduring and evolving theologies of marriage and family life into legal forms—both canonical and civil. There is a great deal more in those dusty old tomes and canons than idle antiquaria or secular memorabilia. These ancient sources ultimately hold the theological genetic code that has defined the contemporary family for what it is—and what it can be.

NOTES

I would like to thank Joel Nichols and Henry Kimmel for their able and ample research assistance, and to thank Harold J. Berman, Don S. Browning, and members of the Mellon Seminar at Georgetown University for their many helpful comments. Some paragraphs of this essay are drawn from my volume, *From Sacrament to Contract: Marriage, Religion, and Law in the Western Tradition* (Louisville: Westminster/John Knox Press, 1997), and a planned sequel, *From Contract to Covenant: Reconstructing the American Law of Marriage and Family Life.*

1. John Milton, *The Doctrine and Discipline of Divorce*, 2d ed. (London, 1644), in *The Complete Prose Works of John Milton* (New Haven: Yale University Press, 1959), 2:235–256 (spelling modernized).

2. Jaroslav Pelikan, *The Vindication of Tradition* (New Haven: Yale University Press, 1984), 65.

3. Harold J. Berman, *Law and Revolution: The Formation of the Western Legal Tradition* (Cambridge: Harvard University Press, 1983), v, vii.

4. See, inter alia, Dennis A. Ahlburg and Carol J. DeVita, "New Realities of the American Family," *Population Bulletin* 47 (2) (1992): 15; Larry L. Bumpass, "What's Happening to the Family? Interactions Between Demographic and Institutional Change," *Demography* 27 (1990): 485; id. and Teresa Castro Martin, "Recent Trends in Marital Disruption," *Demography* 26 (1989): 37; Council on Families in America, *Marriage in America: A Report to the Nation* (New York: Institute for American Values, 1995); id., *Closed Hearts, Closed Minds: The Textbook Story of Marriage* (New York: Institute for American Values, 1997); Maggie Gallagher, *The Abolition of Marriage* (Washington: Regnery Publishing, 1996), 3–12; Barbara Whitehead, *The Divorce Culture* (New York: Alfred A. Knopf, 1997).

5. James Fitzjames Stephen, *Liberty, Equality and Fraternity*, ed. Stuart D. Warner (Indianapolis: Liberty Fund, 1993), 151. Quotes from Stephen hereafter are from ibid., 15, 138–153; id., "Marriage Settlements," *Cornhill Review* (December, 1863): 1–6; id., "English Jurisprudence," *Edinburgh Review* (October, 1861): 456-486. See further Sir C.P. Ilbert, "Sir James Fitzjames as a Legislator," *Law Quarterly Review* 10 (1894): 222; James A. Colaiaco, *Sir James Fitzjames Stephen and the Crisis of Victorian Thought* (New York: St. Martin's Press, 1983). Though he initially condoned Mill's views, Stephen soon found Mill's "hot liberalism" and "cold demeanor" to be deeply unsettling. Sir Leslie Stephen, *Life of Sir James Fitzjames Stephen* (London, 1895), 230–231, 308–340. In 1875, Stephen wrote of Mill's writings: "Probably hardly any work of our day has done so much to shake the foundation of theology . . . and to be fatal to all government whatever." "The Laws of England as to the Expression of Religious Opinions," *Contemporary Review* (Feb. 1875): 446–475, at 473–474.

6. Quotes are from W.C. Rogers, *A Treatise on the Law of Domestic Relations* (Chicago: T.H. Flood and Company, 1899), 2; Joel Bishop, *New Commentaries on Marriage, Divorce, and Separation* (Chicago: T.H. Flood and Company, 1891), 1:3–7, 2: 217; Chester G. Vernier, *American Family Laws: A Comparative Study of the Family Law of the Forty-eight States*, 5 vols. (Stanford: Stanford University Press, 1931–1938), 1:45.

7. For quotes hereafter, see John Stuart Mill, *On Liberty, Essays on Bentham*, ed. Mary Warnock (New York: 1974); *Collected Works of John Stuart Mill*, ed. John M. Robson, repr. ed. (Toronto: University of Toronto Press, 1984), 3:952–943; 16;1470; 17:1624, 1668–1694; 19:401; 21:37, 46 261–263, 287–289, 299–322; 23:677–680; 25:1172–1176; Ann P. Robson and John M. Robson, eds., *Sexual Equality: Writings by John Stuart Mill, Harriet Taylor Mill, and Helen Taylor* (Toronto: University of Toronto Press, 1994), 23, 28–34, 53–102.

8. See sources and discussion in R.H. Graveson and F. R. Crane, eds., *A Century of Family Law: 1857-1957* (London: Sweet & Maxwell, 1957); Max Rheinstein, *Marriage Stability, Divorce, and the Law* (Chicago: University of Chicago Press, 1972); Mary Lynn Salmon, *Women and the Law of Property in Early America* (Chapel Hill: University of North Carolina Press, 1986); Mary Lyndon Shanley, *Feminism, Marriage, and the Law in Victorian England, 1850–1895* (Princeton: Princeton University Press, 1989); Susan Staves, *Married Women's Separate Property in England, 1660-1833* (Cambridge: Harvard University Press, 1990); Lawrence Stone, *Road to Divorce: A History of the Making and Breaking of Marriage in England* (New

York/Oxford: Oxford University Press, 1995); Vernier, *American Family Laws,* vol. 2; Witte, *From Sacrament to Contract,* Chap. 5.

9. Carl E. Schneider, "Moral Discourse and the Transformation of American Family Law," *Michigan Law Review* 83 (1985): 1803, 1811.

10. 388 U.S. 1, 12 (1967).

11. Respectively *Loving v. Virginia*; *Zablocki v. Redhail,* 434 U.S. 374 (1978); *Turner v. Safely,* 482 U.S. 78 (1987).

12. *Eisenstadt v. Baird,* 405 U.S. 438 (1972).

13. Uniform Premarital Agreement Act, Section 3.

14. Ibid., Section 307 (Alternative A).

15. Stephen D. Sugarman and Herma Hill Kay, eds., *Divorce Reform at the Crossroads* (New Haven: Yale University Press, 1990); Eleanor E. Maccoby and Robert H. Mnookin, *Dividing the Child: Social and Legal Dilemmas of Custody* (Cambridge: Harvard University Press, 1992).

16. See generally Lenore J. Weitzmann, *The Divorce Revolution: The Unexpected Social and Economic Consequences for Women and Children* (New York: Free Press, 1985); Whitehead, *The Divorce Culture.*

17. Glendon, *The Transformation of Family Law: State, Law, and Family in the United States and Western Europe* (Chicago: University of Chicago Press, 1989), 146.

18. See the monumental effort in Don S. Browning et al., *From Culture Wars to Common Ground: Religion and the American Family Debate,* (Louisville: Westminster/John Knox Press, 1997).

19. Act 1380 (1997), amending and reenacting Louisiana, Civil Code, Articles 102 and 102 (amended) and R.S. 9:235 and 245 (A) (1) and enacting R.S. 9:224 © and 225 (A) (3), Part VII of chap. 1 of Code Title IV of Code Book I of Title 9 of the La. Rev. Statutes (1950).

20. See Max L. Stackhouse, *Covenant and Commitments: Faith, Family, and Economic Life* (Louisville: Westminster/John Knox Press, 1997); Witte, *From Sacrament to Contract,* chap. 3.

6

Where Are We Now? "The Catholic Moment" in American Politics

Mary C. Segers

During much of American history, Roman Catholicism was thought to be incompatible with American democratic ideals, laws, and practices. Throughout the colonial period, and especially during the great immigration of the nineteenth century, Catholics were viewed as poor, ignorant foreigners who owed primary allegiance to the Roman papacy and were therefore potentially, if not actually, subversive. For their part, Catholics bent over backward to prove their loyalty, patriotism, and good citizenship. In the first half of the twentieth century, Catholics' general support of American involvement in two world wars, the New Deal, McCarthyism, and the Korean War often caused the Catholic community to be blamed for an excess rather than a deficiency of patriotism.

Only within the last forty years has the American Catholic church achieved some balance between the function of legitimator and the role of critic in American culture. The election of President John F. Kennedy in 1960 seemed to signal an end to overt anti-Catholicism in American politics. The emergence of a Catholic left opposition to the Vietnam War in the 1960s and the Catholic bishops' search for a new role in the nation's public life during the 1980s and 1990s confirmed the prophetic potential of Catholic Christianity in the United States.

Indeed, several Protestant thinkers have pronounced the present to be a distinctively "Catholic moment" in the nation's history. William Lee Miller urges, "In the late twentieth century, now is the moment for Catholicism to have its desirable effect upon the America within which at last it is coming to be at home." Peter Berger, a sociologist of religion, told a Catholic audience in 1976 (during the bicentennial of the American Revolution) that its church stood as the foremost defender of a central idea of the Declaration of Independence: that men and women have rights independent of the state. Finally, Richard John Neuhaus in his book, *The Catholic Moment: The Paradox of the Church in the Postmodern World,* defined "the Catholic moment" in more detail:

> This . . . is the moment in which the Roman Catholic Church in the world can and should be the lead church in proclaiming the Gospel. This can and should also be the moment in which the Roman Catholic Church in the United States assumes its rightful role in the culture-forming task of constructing a religiously-informed public philosophy for the American experiment in ordered liberty.[1]

On the face of it, this proposal—particularly as formulated by Neuhaus and other Catholic neoconservatives—sounds mildly preposterous. Granted that the decline of liberal Protestantism in the United States is troubling. Still, what does it mean to proclaim that now is "the Catholic moment," that now is an opportune time for the Roman Catholic Church to "assume its rightful role" in shaping American culture? To some, Catholic dominance in a liberal, democratic, pluralist society sounds positively "un-American"—almost as bad as the idea, put forward by some conservative evangelicals, of restoring America as "a Christian nation."

The vast majority of American Catholics themselves, I suspect, have heard very little about this notion of a "Catholic moment" in American history. Church leaders (both individual bishops and the collective National Conference of Catholic Bishops) are not emphasizing this in sermons, publications, and formal statements. Moreover, many American Catholics can remember only too well what it was like to live in a United States suffused with a kind of Protestant ethos. Protestant hegemony meant Protestant bibles, anti-Catholic textbooks and Protestant prayers in public schools; so Catholics formed their separate parochial schools. Protestant hegemony meant nativism, anti-Catholicism, Prohibition, and quotas for the number of Jews admitted to Ivy League colleges. All things considered, maybe it is a good thing that liberal Protestant hegemony has vanished. But who would want to replace it with Roman Catholic hegemony or the combined dominance of an alliance of Catholics and conservative evangelicals? Indeed, why must any one religious tradition be dominant in the United States?

In this chapter, I shall examine this argument of Neuhaus and other commentators that the present is, and should be, a time of Catholic ascendancy in American public life. The argument is more substantial than it seems on first reading. In addition to Neuhaus's proposal, we need to be aware of

William Lee Miller's softer, more general formulation in his *The First Liberty* (published in 1986). Secondly, I raise questions about Neuhaus's argument for Catholic ascendancy in American affairs. I might agree with Neuhaus's general formulation of the need for Catholic leadership in bringing religious and moral considerations to bear in debates about proper public policy, yet disagree with the political implications he draws from this. Thirdly, I sketch in outline what I think is an appropriate model of public participation for the Catholic church in the United States. I offer a few suggestions as to how Catholics might mount an effective, credible, authentic Christian witness at the intersection of religion, morality and politics. This is in keeping with the aims of our general project—to ensure a legitimate religious presence in the public realm and to show how religion can make a more robust contribution to American public life. I believe that Roman Catholicism is a rich tradition which has much to offer in our deliberations about sound law and policy. At the same time, Catholic conduct on certain public policy issues illustrates the dangers of church involvement in politics and public policy formation. The challenge is to determine the difference between appropriate and inappropriate religious involvement in American politics.

THE ARGUMENT FOR CATHOLIC ASCENDANCY IN AMERICAN PUBLIC LIFE

In 1987, in his preface to *The Catholic Moment*, Richard John Neuhaus, a former Lutheran pastor who was recently received into the Catholic Church and ordained a Catholic priest, described himself as "incorrigibly ecumenical" and explained his Lutheranism in this way: "To be a Lutheran Christian is to be ecumenical, for Lutheranism is not so much the Lutheran church as it is a movement of evangelical catholic reform within and for the one Church."[2] Neuhaus' commitment to ecumenism partly explains his assertion of "the Catholic moment" in American affairs. He contends that the Roman Catholic Church at the Second Vatican Council (1962–65) weathered the challenge of modernity by espousing religious liberty, by insisting that Catholics had a duty to address the problems of the modern world, and by emphasizing ecumenical relations with other Christian churches and other world religions. With this *aggiornamento* and updating of itself, Roman Catholicism became "paradigmatic of the testings and trials of Christianity at the edge of its third millennium."[3] Thus every Christian, Neuhaus argued, has a deep stake in the Roman Catholic Church's engagement with the modern world.

While Neuhaus speaks partly from a theological perspective in insisting that now is "the Catholic moment" in American history and culture, he also boasts a reputation as a forceful clerical commentator on public affairs. Associated with the Institute of Religion and Public Life in New York City, Neuhaus edits a monthly journal, *First Things*, which is designed to "advance a religiously informed public philosophy for the ordering of society."[4] Neuhaus has also published many books over the last twenty years, the most famous of which is the 1984 volume, *The Naked Public Square*. Here he argued that the absence of religion in American public life—"the naked public square"—is a relatively new phenomenon, a departure from age-old traditions of mixing religion and politics. In insisting that constitutional separation of church and state does not mean the exclusion of religion from public life, Neuhaus sought to counter the idea that America is a secular society. According to Neuhaus, "The public square will not and cannot remain naked. If it is not clothed with the 'meanings' borne by religion, new 'meanings' will be imposed by virtue of the ambitions of the modern state."[5]

Neuhaus accepted the fact that the United States is a post-Protestant society and that a major factor in the evolution of secular society was the demographic collapse and cultural marginalization of mainline Protestantism. Indeed, he suggested that in the wake of this final disestablishment of liberal Protestantism, "we are witnessing a contention between religious groups—evangelical, fundamentalist, Catholic—to succeed mainline Protestantism as the culture-shaping force that provides moral legitimacy for democracy in America."[6] However, he rejected fundamentalism's claim to provide a new public ethic for the American polity. Fundamentalism, he maintained, was and is essentially a private morality, based not on public reason but on private interpretation of Scripture. While Neuhaus credited fundamentalists and conservative evangelicals with a correct sociological perception of the essential role of religion in public life, he disagreed with fundamentalists on substantive theological grounds.[7] Moreover, he was impressed with the size, diversity, and dynamism of Roman Catholicism both worldwide and in the United States. The above-mentioned changes within Roman Catholicism at the Second Vatican Council led him to decide upon Catholicism as the culture-shaping force which could best assume the role played by the old Protestant ethos in American public affairs. This was the genesis of "the Catholic moment."

Neoconservatism, Political Theory, and "the Catholic Moment"

Neuhaus, together with George Weigel of the Ethics and Public Policy Center and Michael Novak of the American Enterprise Institute, both in Washington, are three of the most prominent Catholic neoconservatives in contemporary society. Like other neoconservatives in American society, Catholic neocons criticize welfare-state liberalism, favor democratic capitalism, and oppose countercultural excesses. Neoconservative American

Catholicism, however, is not a movement, party, school, faction, or camp. George Weigel describes it as "a community of conversation and friendship, institutional cooperation and literary endeavor, built around a convergence of ecclesiastical and public interests and concerns."[8]

Catholic neoconservatives recognize that, if this is "the Catholic moment" in American society and culture, then intellectual Catholics must be able to speak clearly and persuasively to others. Just as they want to develop a convincing theology for the church, Catholic neocons want to develop an adequate public philosophy for the body politic. In emphasizing reason and the common good, they echo strains of Catholic social teaching. They believe that debate about such issues as abortion, homosexuality, and aid to religious schools can be rational and constructive—provided that people respect the philosophical and religious worldviews which underlie and inform such debate.

Indeed, Neuhaus regards Catholic social teaching with its confidence in reason and its steady commitment to the natural law tradition as a strong foundation for ideas of human dignity, human rights, and freedom in contemporary society. Both Neuhaus and Weigel emphasize their indebtedness to the work of John Courtney Murray, the American Jesuit whose creative theologizing made it possible for American Catholics and the Vatican to accept and embrace religious liberty and church-state separation in a pluralist society. These Catholic neoconservatives lay claim to Murray's legacy and see their own work as an extension of the "Murray Project," the practical working out of "the American experiment in ordered liberty." When they are not indulging in a bit of hagiography about Murray, they wisely interpret Murray as a constitutional liberal who believed in limited government and who sought to reconcile the United States to a centuries-old Catholic tradition of constitutionalism influenced by natural law. They also emphasize Murray's conception of freedom as the right to do what one ought. Above all, they stress Murray's view of America as "a proposition country," a distinctive democratic experiment conceived as the working-out of a set of truth-claims. These are the truths of human dignity and human rights stated in the Declaration of Independence and re-stated by Abraham Lincoln in the Gettysburg Address.[9]

The collapse of mainline Protestantism; the acceptance by the Roman Catholic Church at Vatican II of religious liberty; the ecumenical initiatives of a large, diverse, powerful Roman Catholic Church; the leadership and papal encyclicals of Pope John Paul II; the aggressive opposition of the American Catholic church to legalized abortion; and the legacy of John Courtney Murray—all these developments have led Neuhaus, Weigel, and other Catholic neoconservatives to conclude that Roman Catholicism is well-positioned to evangelize society and to counter secularism. A period of Catholic ascendancy is needed in which Catholic ideas and Catholics themselves should play a major culture-forming role in American society.

The Meaning and Plausibility of a "Catholic Moment" in American Society

To say that "the Catholic moment" is the development of a religiously informed public philosophy for the renewal of American democracy is to speak at a very high level of generality indeed. Neuhaus's argument tends to be very vague about practicalities. What does Catholic ascendancy mean concretely? What precisely does Neuhaus think about voting by Catholics, political lobbying by the Church, the conduct of Catholics in high public office, or the relationship between church teaching and public law? And how does Neuhaus think the Roman Catholic Church should go about the task of constructing a religiously-informed public philosophy?

Because Neuhaus is writing from a theological perspective, it is difficult to know what "the Catholic moment" in American affairs means concretely in particular instances. It surely means opposition to legal abortion and to any attempt to legalize physician-assisted suicide. Judging from other political initiatives Neuhaus has endorsed, Catholic leadership also means support for a Religious Equality constitutional amendment which would permit school prayer,[10] forging a Catholic-Evangelical alliance, criticism of legislation legalizing same-sex marriage, opposition to gay rights ordinances, criticism of the role of the Supreme Court in the American system of government, support for educational choice and school vouchers, support for "family values," and a generous reading of the free exercise clause of the First Amendment. If "the Catholic moment" implies this kind of political agenda, this raises problems because such a partisan, neoconservative agenda is not one that many Catholics would support.

Another Version of the "Catholic Moment" Argument

A softer, more gentle version of Catholic ascendancy is proposed by William Lee Miller in his *The First Liberty: Religion and the American Republic*. Miller notes the irony of the Catholic presence in the United States—that, despite years of anti-Catholic bias and nativist railings against the evils of popery, and despite a wall of separation between church and state that Rome originally found difficult to understand, let alone accept, the American Catholic church has flourished, increasing from 25,000 in 1790 to over sixty million members today. As Miller writes:

> In perhaps the most remarkable of all the remarkable developments of this New World's system of religious liberty, the Roman Catholic Christianity against which its founding movements were rebelling has come, after two centuries, to be its single most important religious presence. It is becoming one of the most significant sources of political understanding as well.[11]

Miller envisions the religious situation in the United States as "a reciprocating deep pluralism in which the several communities affect each other for the better." Within this framework, Catholic Christianity can serve as a healthy corrective to sectarian Protestantism and Enlightenment rationalism. With its notions of the common good and its sense of human solidarity, Roman Catholicism brings a "personalistic communitarianism" to counter the individualistic libertarianism of American culture created in part by our Puritan, sectarian Protestantism.

Catholic Christianity also has intellectual resources that American Protestantism has lacked. The heart and feeling of pietistic Protestantism needs the intellect of Catholicism in deliberating about complex matters of collective life. "Where moral issues are complicated, one needs casuistry, not instant certainty. Where there is disagreement, one needs reason, argument, and conversation." Catholicism brings a tradition of moral reasoning about politics, about just war, about political authority, and about natural law—resources which can be very useful to the American republic on all sorts of public policymaking issues.

At the same time, Catholic Christianity can learn from American Protestantism the necessity of "being open to other pieces of truth's body" in order to avoid "an inclination to creeping infallibility" which Roman Catholicism, with its claims to finality in central matters of faith and morals, has sometimes displayed. In this way, Miller argues, American pluralism would work at its best, through a positive internal dynamic in which each religious tradition affected the other for the better.[12]

Thus Miller urges that "now is the moment for Catholicism to have its desirable effect upon the America within which at last it is coming to be at home." In his view, the American experiment in republican government needs the intellectualism and personalistic communitarianism which Catholicism offers. The Roman Catholic community is "the largest and intellectually and spiritually the most potent institution that is the bearer of such ideas."[13]

It is with some regret, then, that Miller points to the abortion issue as an example of a negative dynamic in American religious pluralism in which groups bring out the worst in each other instead of the best. Miller acknowledges that abortion is a deep and serious and complicated moral issue and that simplistic arguments can be found on both pro-life and pro-choice sides. Nevertheless, he writes,

> It is a disappointment to see a considerable segment of the American Catholic world displaying in the 1970s and 1980s, on the issue of abortion, the absolutistic moral-political method that has marked too much of the social and political role of American Protestantism: the isolated, sharply defined crusade, focused on one issue, with its "moral" dimension made final, without compromise or listening; a crusade, rousing the troops, without much recourse to the tradition of reason. This method is deeply flawed, whether it be employed on an issue large or small, whether the adherent be inclined to the right or to the left . . . It is much to be deplored that the dispute over abortion, with all its human quandary, has been heightened, simplified, and vulgarized

> as it has. One wishes that in the debate, in which religious groups have been so much involved, had been displayed more depth, wisdom, and generosity.[14]

Needless to say, this appraisal of Catholic activity in abortion politics is very different from "the Catholic moment" Richard Neuhaus envisions. I doubt that Neuhaus would share William L. Miller's disappointment with the American Catholic crusade against legal abortion. On balance, I agree with Miller that, although American Catholics should be politically active in shaping the larger culture, the church's conduct in terms of abortion policy leaves much to be desired. This is not an effective or positive way of bringing Catholic ideas, or any religiously grounded moral values, to bear upon public policy. To say this is not to dispute Catholic aims of reducing the incidence of abortion but rather to criticize the method and style of religious-political activism the church has used to achieve these aims. If, as Neuhaus thinks, the most telling example of "the Catholic moment" in American culture is the church's struggle to de-legalize abortion, then perhaps we would do better without such Catholic moments.

A CRITIQUE OF THE ARGUMENT FOR CATHOLIC ASCENDANCY IN AMERICAN PUBLIC LIFE

This leads me to the following critique of the argument for "a Catholic moment" in American public life. First, Neuhaus's argument may make good sense theologically, but bad sense politically, because of ordinary Americans' fears of religious dominance in American culture. Second, the argument for Catholic ascendancy does not take into account the broad diversity of views among American Catholics. Third, the Murray Project for the renewal of American democracy is somewhat incomplete in its understanding of democracy and democratic governance. Fourth, the political crusade against legal abortion led by the American Catholic church is misguided and represents a style of political activism which is inappropriate for religious groups in American politics and woefully inadequate as an example of Christian witness. Let us discuss these criticisms in turn.

The Problem of Hegemony

A first objection to the idea of "a Catholic moment" in American affairs is that Catholic ascendancy and Protestant dominance are not all that different, and that such a majoritarian understanding of Christian hegemony does not really protect the religious freedom of minorities. Richard Neuhaus's "Catholic Moment" does not look all that different from the "Christian America" held out as an ideal by the Religious Right.

It may be that in a multicultural, religiously diverse society, no one religion should be dominant or privileged because of the risk of sectarian strife and social conflict. Such fears of sectarian conflict are, of course, a major factor motivating secularists to exclude religion from the public square. Ironically, a recent moment in American Catholic history illustrates the close relation between experience of religious bigotry and a strong desire not to mix religion and politics. The 1960 election of John F. Kennedy as the first Roman Catholic president is a case in point. During his presidential campaign, Kennedy was questioned repeatedly about his Roman Catholic allegiance. Despite his pledge to exercise his office free of Catholic church influence, the questions about his Catholicism continued all through the spring and summer of the campaign. Finally, in September 1960, JFK spoke to a gathering of Texas ministers in the Greater Houston Ministerial Association and fielded their questions and suspicions.

Kennedy took a strong, clear, almost Jeffersonian stand in favor of strict separation. "I believe in an America where the separation of church and state is absolute—where no Catholic prelate would tell the President (should he be Catholic) how to act and no Protestant minister would tell his parishioners for whom to vote." Kennedy insisted that he did not speak for the Catholic church on public matters, and the church did not speak for him. He claimed that, even on controversial issues such as birth control, divorce, gambling, and aid to church-related schools, his decisions in office would be based on his perception of the national interest and not on religious grounds. In accordance with the Constitution, he rejected the idea that religion should be a litmus test for public office. He argued for equal treatment for all creeds: "Do you mean that 40 million Americans lost the chance to be president when they were baptized?" And he noted how divisive religious intolerance could be. "While this year it may be a Catholic against whom the finger of suspicion is pointed, in other years it has been, and may someday be again, a Jew—or a Quaker—or a Unitarian—or a Baptist."[15]

Kennedy's speech was so strong that, in the context of the 1960 campaign, it was generally regarded as the knockout punch on the "Catholic question." Thirty-five years later it is more generally understood that he had little choice but to take the strict separationist position he took. Kennedy had to say what he said in Houston because of anti-Catholicism. Ironically, the anti-Catholic prejudice of Protestants in 1960 forced him to defend his Catholicism and his political career by calling for absolute church-state separation and the privatization of religion. As one commentator has noted, "In a sense, 1960 was a victory for secularism and a naked public square."[16]

Thus, the very privatization of religion which Neuhaus regrets came about in part because of religious prejudice (anti-Catholicism) in American society. To the extent that later Protestants such as Neuhaus reject a religiously-empty public square, they must reckon with the arguments of a Kennedy, and others in the 1990s, who contend that keeping religion out of the public realm is the only way to avoid the dangers of religious prejudice and sectarian strife. Religion has the potential to subvert public order and social comity. This is a serious objection to Neuhaus-type ideas about Catholic hegemony.

The anti-Catholicism of the 1960 election exemplifies the problem of religious dominance in American life. Why should we have a "Christian America" or a "Catholic moment"? Isn't that a formula for sectarian divisiveness? Ordinary Americans, generally pretty fair-minded, favor equal treatment for all creeds. This leads them to fear religious dominance in American culture. They recognize the need for tolerance and mutual respect in a religiously diverse society. The civic duty to respect those who differ from us is essential in a democratic republic. Thus, religious liberals question Neuhaus's preference for hegemony rather than inclusion. "Inclusion means respecting and listening to America's many voices, religious and secular. It rests, like the republic itself, on the proposition that all human beings are created equal."[17] This last point is about as Murrayesque as one can get.

Diversity and Pluralism Within the Catholic Church

A second objection to Neuhaus's "Catholic moment" is that the argument for Catholic ascendancy does not take into account the broad diversity of views among American Catholics. Catholics may be sixty million strong, but they are not a homogeneous group by any stretch of the imagination. As a group, Catholics are divided in almost every conceivable way: by race, gender, age, education, income, political party identification, theology (traditional or progressive), active or inactive, committed or nominal.

In 1996 there were approximately 60,280,454 Roman Catholics who constituted somewhere between 22 percent and 25 percent of a U.S. citizenry estimated to be 268,784,851 in number. Of these Catholics, 53 percent are female and 47 percent male. In terms of race or ethnicity, 88 percent of American Catholics are Caucasian, 3.8 percent are African-American, 7 percent are Hispanic, and 1.2 percent are Asian or other. It would be difficult to talk about "Catholic Power" or a Catholic voting bloc because, in terms of party identification, Roman Catholics are evenly split across political party lines. Caucasian Catholics are 30 percent Republican, 32 percent Democratic, and 34 percent Independent. Diversity is also evident in theological cleavages between Catholics. "While fully 51 percent of Catholics identify themselves as moderates, 25 percent consider themselves "traditional" and 24 percent "progressive" Catholics. Attitudes on social issues vary accordingly. Progressives are far less likely to follow Catholic teachings on issues such as birth control and abortion. Traditionalists are less likely to follow church teachings on the death penalty, nuclear weapons, and economic justice."[18] Given this kind of diversity, it is difficult to conceive that American

Catholics are a voting bloc or that they might act in concerted fashion to communicate a Catholic ethos to American society.

Moreover, some degree of polarization exists among American Catholics along the lines of these theological cleavages. Traditionalists resist modernity and hanker for a pre-Vatican II Church while progressives keep pushing for the implementation of conciliar reform. Charles Morris, author of *American Catholic: The Saints and Sinners Who Built America's Most Powerful Church*, has said that, while researching his book, he found "disconcerting the degree of distaste, and even contempt, that both liberal and conservative partisans often expressed toward each other."[19] The Catholic Common Ground project, sponsored by a committee convoked by the late Cardinal Joseph Bernardin, is working towards reconciliation within the American church. That Catholics need to work on internal reconciliation suggests that they are perhaps too disunited to provide much of a cultural ethos for the larger society.

Finally, the American Catholic church is undergoing profound demographic changes which affect its own internal identity. While the number of Roman Catholics has increased steadily since 1945—from 23 million in 1945 to 60 million in 1995—a precipitous decline in the number of priests and religious (brothers and sisters) coupled with a decline in Catholic elementary and secondary schools and students directly affects how Catholics are socialized into an identifiable Catholic community. Far more Catholic children are being educated in public schools and not in a Catholic parish school environment than was the case thirty years ago.[20] The church is struggling to develop new forms of religious education that will form young Catholics, sustain adult Catholics, and create for all an identifiable Catholic community. It is difficult to replace the parochial schools which taught catechism and inculcated the Catholic values, stories, vocabulary, humor, and shared history which helped to shape Catholic community in the United States. The point is that, as they devote energy and resources to the formation of Catholic identity and community, Catholics may not be all that available for the culture-shaping task Neuhaus envisions for them.

Catholic Neoconservatives' Understanding of Democracy

A third objection to Neuhaus's "Catholic moment" is that the argument for Catholic ascendancy reveals an inadequate understanding of democratic governance. Neuhaus and his neoconservative colleagues seek to inform "the American experiment" with a Catholic vision. They claim that the development of religiously informed public philosophy is essential for the renewal of American democracy. In emphasizing the importance of religion to democracy in the American context, Neuhaus and Weigel are, I believe, making a positive contribution to public debate about the conditions of democracy in contemporary society.

However, their account of the relation between religion and democracy is incomplete; it does not take into account social scientists' findings about churches and political participation in the contemporary United States. Moreover, their conception of democracy is very abstract; it fails to address the nitty-gritty particulars of modern democratic governance and so seems unreal and almost mythic. These neoconservatives run the risk of supporting a majoritarian democracy which rides roughshod over minority rights. And their sometimes uncritical support of democratic capitalism leaves something to be desired. In short, I think they fail to realize that democracy in the United States is *liberal* democracy.[21] In their haste to criticize liberalism, they fail to appreciate how liberalism prevents or softens democratic excess.

Catholic neoconservatives fear that, without morality, democracy will degenerate into a kind of rootless pragmatism. With the end of the Cold War and the apparent triumph of democratic capitalism, they contend that a religiously derived morality must moderate the rapacious greed of capitalism. This is a typically Catholic concern shared by left-liberals and the bishops as well as the neoconservatives.

However, Catholic neoconservatives have little to say about how the nation's moral-cultural foundations are to be strengthened. They are equally vague about the concrete realities of representative democracy. They say almost nothing about the practical details of, for example, campaign finance reform or redistricting election districts in a way that is fair to minorities. Their preoccupation with culture wars over "life issues" such as abortion and euthanasia lends an air of unreality to their discussions of democratic governance. In my judgment, their concern for democracy would be more credible if they addressed institutional as well as cultural factors.

For example, political scientists who specialize in religion and politics have found that religion enhances American democracy in several ways. Their studies suggest that religion broadens political participation, and that religious lobbies provide a much-needed corrective to the bias towards wealth in the American interest group system. In addition, churches train people in the civic skills necessary for effective political participation, they educate citizens in the moral values supportive of democracy, and they serve as mediating institutions and protective buffers between the individual and the state. In this way churches and synagogues serve as agents of resistance to limit the potential tyranny of majoritarian democracy. As A. J. Reichley states, "From the standpoint of the public good, the most important service churches offer to secular life in a free society is to nurture moral values that help humanize capitalism and give direction to democracy."[22] I believe that the arguments of Catholic neoconservatives might be strengthened if they moved beyond cultural commentary to address these institutional and empirical findings about the relation between religion and democracy.

The one institutional consideration Catholic neoconservatives do address is the role of the Supreme Court in the American system of government.[23] Neoconservatives claim to be committed advocates of judicial restraint. While their preoccupation with what they see as an imperial judiciary is fueled by their concern over abortion and euthanasia, it is rooted in their conception of democracy as majoritarian rule. Catholic neoconservatives seem to forget that democracy in the United States is liberal democracy, and that oftentimes it is an unelected federal judiciary which protects the constitutional rights of individuals and minorities against the will of legislative majorities. In their zeal to combat abstract individualism in American culture, Catholic neocons praise majoritarian democracy with little attention paid to the dangers of majoritarian tyranny.

Neuhaus, for example, thinks courts should be concerned about the legitimacy of law which, in the end, is a function of public opinion. When 70–80 percent of the American people favor prayer in public schools, Neuhaus thinks that a democracy should recognize this. But is the Supreme Court always to follow the will of the majority in a liberal democracy? Or is it the duty of the Court to protect the rights of individual children who may be in the minority on the issue of school prayer? Neuhaus agrees that, in the American system, individual and minority rights are, and should be, protected constitutionally against majoritarian tyranny. But he stresses that, in his view, these individual rights also depend on public opinion and public sentiment. I find this an amazing concession—to utilitarianism or positivism—from a Catholic neoconservative who seeks to, in the spirit of John Courtney Murray, use Catholic natural law and Lockean natural rights traditions to reconstruct a public philosophy for the renewal of American democracy.

One final point. Some might expect Neuhaus and company to translate their concern for democracy in the United States into a concern for democratic governance in the Catholic church. If this is "the Catholic moment" in the United States, and if Roman Catholicism is to be the foundational support of human rights and democracy (as Neuhaus suggests), then perhaps the Catholic church will have to exemplify or model democracy in its own deliberations and governance. After all, how a top-down, hierarchical, clerical institution treats ordinary, lay Catholics will speak volumes about the credibility of Catholic influence in the larger society.

Neoconservatives such as George Weigel resist this suggestion that Roman Catholicism reinvent itself as a democratic institution.[24] Yet, perhaps it is time to reconsider the old adage which insists that "the Catholic church is not a democracy." While the church's magisterial teaching on faith and morals is not democratically defined, the practice of the faithful (the *sensus fidelium*) provides a kind of outer limit on what the hierarchy teaches. Perhaps the church should more fully emphasize those quasi-democratic elements in its own tradition: the *sensus fidelium*, and the role of local church officials and members in episcopal appointments. Practices and procedures which emphasize openness and genuine consultation should be preferred. Perhaps the church can bring more women into central administration—at the diocesan level and at the curial level in Rome. The point is that it is difficult to see how we can have complete honesty and integrity in the church until papal monarchy is somehow constitutionalized and collegiality becomes the preferred organizational model.

Above all, if Catholic neoconservatives accept the American proposition as normative for church and society—if they accept the principles and freedoms associated with the founding of the United States and incorporated into official church doctrine in the Declaration on Religious Liberty—and if they look to "the Catholic moment" to renew American democracy, then perhaps they should rethink non-democratic administrative and governing procedures within the institutional church. Being Catholic and American is a two-way street. If Catholics are to teach and evangelize their fellow Americans, they might also learn from the American experience as well. Some contend that the Catholic church's witness to Christian and American ideals is radically compromised by its own anti-pluralist and antidemocratic structures. The hierarchy fails to fully recognize, they complain, that "democratic, participatory forms of government are more appropriate for the expression of respect for persons and safeguarding against abusive relationships than hierarchical and monarchical systems of government that treat the governed as rightless dependents."[25]

POSITIVE AND NEGATIVE ASPECTS OF PUBLIC CATHOLICISM

This essay has reviewed Catholic neoconservatives' arguments that now is "the Catholic moment" in American affairs, that Catholics should assume their rightful role in shaping a religiously-based public philosophy for the renewal of American democracy. This idea has some considerable merit. I agree with Richard John Neuhaus that lay and clerical Catholics should work to bring religiously-derived moral considerations to bear in deliberations about sound public policy.

Yet I disagree with the political implications Neuhaus draws from this. Any argument for Catholic hegemony must contend with the potential for sectarian strife as well as with ordinary Americans' fears of religious dominance. Secondly, diversity within the American Catholic community impedes the development of a public Catholicism. Thirdly, Catholic neoconservatives' understanding of democracy is deficient in several respects: neglect of minority rights; ignorance of studies showing how religion enhances political participation; an emphasis upon cultural confrontation to the neglect of institutional elements of democratic governance; intense preoccupation with the abortion issue as an example of judicial arrogance; and a failure to appreciate the inconsistency between Catholicism's support for a renewal of American democracy and the church's refusal to take seriously methods of democratic governance in its own organizational life. Nowhere is this more apparent than in the bishops' efforts to de-legalize abortion in the United States. I agree with William Lee Miller that the church's preoccupation with abortion policy in the last quarter of the twentieth century resembles a simplistic, self-righteous political crusade which is sadly inappropriate to the complexity of the issue.

What should the public witness of the Roman Catholic Church in the United States be? Following the suggestions of William Lee Miller, let me review briefly those resources of Catholic thought which can enrich American public life. First, what Miller refers to as Catholicism's "personalistic communitarianism" reflects a traditional Catholic concern for social justice that is almost entirely absent in the neoconservative conception of "the Catholic moment." Catholicism offers a conception of the person as a social self, whose identity is shaped from the start by social interdependence, and whose destiny is to develop a sense of community and solidarity in working for the common good. Catholic social thought thus encourages people to work towards economic justice and the alleviation of poverty, to oppose racism and capital punishment, to translate norms such as "give hospitality to the stranger" into practical concern for the homeless, immigrants, and refugees. I agree with Miller that this "personalistic communitarianism" can help to counter the individualistic libertarianism of American culture.

Second, Miller emphasizes that Roman Catholicism has intellectual resources that American Protestantism has lacked—a tradition of moral reasoning about politics, just war, the state and subsidiarity, economic justice, war, and peace. There is, indeed, a long and rich tradition of Roman Catholic thinking about law and politics which can, I think, be very instructive and useful. In particular, theologians have worked out an ethics of public discourse and a tradition of political realism in thinking about the relation between law and morals.

Catholics have always insisted on the primary role of reason in public discourse. Catholic social teaching with its confidence in reason and its steady commitment to the natural law tradition provides a strong foundation for ideas of human dignity, human rights, justice, equality, mutual respect, and tolerance. The church's insistence upon a morality accessible to all through right reason seems to me to be a real contribution to public deliberation in a liberal, religiously diverse democracy. This approach places the burden on Catholics to make plainly intelligible to non-Catholics the moral insights derived from their religious tradition. This conception of public debate as rational deliberation also obligates others (non-Catholic citizens) to listen carefully to what Catholics, and other religionists, have to say.

Regarding the relation between law and morals, a Catholic tradition of political realism, which can be traced to Augustine and Aquinas, has prudently insisted that not every moral norm should be incorporated into civil law. The church has traditionally recognized that, while law and morality are related, they are not coterminous. There are limits to the law as a method of social control. Lawmakers must consider whether measures they enact will be acceptable and evoke compliance, and whether they will achieve their intended effect or result in a situation far worse than the original problem the law was supposed to remedy. These questions of sound lawmaking assume greater significance in a pluralist, religiously diverse society such as the United States, which is committed to religious freedom and church-state separation. In such a society, the church's conception of the pedagogical function of the law—that the law is a moral teacher—is difficult to sustain on controverted issues where there is little consensus.

This Catholic tradition of political realism should have cautioned American Catholic leaders on the vexing question of abortion politics. Unfortunately, it did not prevent them from engaging in a largely counter-productive effort to ban abortion. The American bishops' political agenda has been dominated for the last quarter century by the single issue of abortion. I agree with Miller that the church's political crusade against abortion is a negative example of public Catholicism. If we draw up a balance sheet on the Catholic political campaign to outlaw abortion, I think the costs outweigh the benefits.[26]

On the plus side, it is clear that the Catholic church has kept the abortion issue alive through its social and political activity. It has given the issue top priority and has thereby refused to allow abortion to become routine, an accepted or standard practice, a matter of conventional wisdom. It has managed through its political lobbying to protect Catholic institutions from being required to perform or condone abortions in violation of their conscience rights. It has also restricted access to abortion more generally through passage of such measures as the Hyde Amendment.

The National Conference of Catholic Bishops has also cut its political teeth on the abortion issue. Over the last twenty years, the institutional church has learned some hard lessons about its mode and style of political participation. As the result of their political activism on the abortion issue, the bishops have learned the importance of not being partisan, the necessity of a multi-issue approach to American politics, and the necessity of presenting a rational and convincing case for their position rather than appealing to scriptural or papal authority for justification. As Bishop James Malone, then NCCB president, noted after the 1984 election, "In the public arena of a pluralistic democracy, religious leaders face the same tests of rational argument as any other individuals or institutions. Our impact on the public will be directly proportionate to the persuasiveness of our positions. We seek no special status and we should not be accorded one."[27]

Nevertheless, while the church has been a major force in the anti-abortion movement and has learned valuable lessons about political participation, it has paid a high price for this knowledge. Many of the church's mistakes here stem from a failure to fully appreciate the importance of political freedom in a liberal democracy. First, the bishops' coercive treatment of pro-choice Catholic officeholders indicates a failure to understand the dilemma of being a lawmaker in a pluralist society with traditions of religious freedom and church-state separation. The abortion issue challenges Catholic politicians to reconcile sometimes conflicting duties to conscience, constitution, constituents, and the common good. Such a challenge invites subtle balancing rather than easy, simplistic, one-dimensional answers.

Secondly, with a few exceptions, the bishops have not consulted Catholic feminists about proper abortion policy in any serious, systematic way. Moreover, the church has been willing to sacrifice its support for women's rights legislation—the Equal Rights Amendment, the 1978 Pregnancy Disability Act, and the 1988 Civil Rights Restoration Act—to the anti-abortion cause. Add to this the critique voiced by many Catholic women that historically the church's moral theology on abortion is not informed by the voices and perspectives of women, and it is not difficult to understand how and why the church's anti-abortion campaign has alienated many Catholic women.

Thirdly, while the church trumpets its pro-life call, the NCCB has emphasized the abortion issue to the comparative neglect of other significant "life" issues. For example, despite important pastoral letters about economic justice as well as war and peace in the mid-1980s, the bishops have not conducted the grassroots mobilization or parish-based educational campaigns on these issues which they have pursued on the abortion issue. This uneven treatment of policy issues undermines the church's commitment to a consistent life ethic.

For these reasons, I would argue, the church's conduct in terms of abortion policy is, on balance, a negative instance of public Catholicism. The bishops' strategy and tactics involved a single-issue focus on abortion as the central issue of the NCCB's political agenda. Church leaders have used Catholic masses as political mobilization centers in which parishioners are supplied with postcards to mail to legislators—to lobby against the Freedom of Choice Act in 1993, or for exclusion of abortion coverage from national health insurance in 1994, or for Congressional override of President Clinton's veto of a bill banning "partial birth" abortions in 1996. Catholic pro-choice lawmakers have been penalized, sanctioned, censured in sermons, barred from ministerial activities, refused sacraments, removed from parish councils, denied invitations to speak at church functions, expelled from the Knights of Columbus, and threatened with excommunication. Individual Catholic citizens were told that it was immoral to vote for pro-choice candidates.

In using such heavy-handed tactics to reinstate restrictive abortion laws, church leaders seem to have forgotten the central distinctions between law and morals emphasized in the Catholic jurisprudential tradition of political realism. There are limits to the law as a method of social control. As Aquinas wrote, it is not the proper function of law to repress all vice or command all virtue.[28] Prudent lawmakers must consider whether anti-abortion statutes will be efficacious, effective, enforced, and enforceable. The duty of citizens and lawmakers is to make sound public policy, not to use the coercive power of the state to impose a moral view not shared by a majority of the citizenry.

Fortunately, over the last twenty years, the American church has also displayed positive examples of public Catholicism: these include the bishops' thoughtful examination of nuclear war and deterrence in their 1983 pastoral letter on war and peace, the equally thoughtful analysis of economic justice in their 1986 pastoral letter on the American economy, and the NCCB's quadrennial *Statements on Political Responsibilities in an Election Year.* In these statements, the bishops encourage citizens to vote, emphasize their own nonpartisanship, and address, in alphabetical order (which means abortion is first), a wide range of issues they judge important in the upcoming presidential election. In this way they seek to bring Catholic moral perspectives to bear on public debate during presidential election campaigns.

These efforts of the Catholic bishops to shape political discourse and public policy are noteworthy in two respects. First, they are characterized by consultation with outside policy experts who advise the bishops (this was especially true in the case of the two pastoral letters). Second, the bishops recognize that in a democracy men and women of good will may draw different policy implications from the moral principles the bishops elucidate. In this way, the bishops remain respectful of the different political and policy positions citizens may legitimately take in a liberal democracy. In style and manner, the bishops recognize subtlety, nuance, the importance of listening, and the need for compromise in public policy on these complex issues—whereas on abortion they tend to display an absolutistic moral-political method that leaves no room for maneuver or compromise.

I trust that these positive examples of public Catholicism illustrate how the church can contribute in a beneficial manner to the American democratic experiment. I would be remiss, however, if I did not point out that there are alternatives to church lobbying for restrictive abortion laws. Rather than the Catholic church becoming a powerful political lobbyist able and willing to use political clout to ban abortion, I think the church could more effectively exemplify pastoral care and social service by supporting concrete measures to assist involuntarily pregnant women. Such measures include disability rights for pregnant employees, parental leave policies, childcare benefits, family-planning funding, and employment training programs. The idea is to promote programs and policies that will reduce the incidence of abortion without coercing women. In my judgment, the church can better witness to the transcendent by exemplifying Gospel norms of charity and compassion in assisting involuntarily pregnant women than by lobbying legislators or using church services as occasions for grassroots political mobilization.

CONCLUSION

I have shown here the difficulties attendant upon Catholic ascendancy in American public life. But any discussion of "a Catholic moment" in public affairs raises a deeper question: Does any religious perspective deserve to be privileged in the public deliberations of a democratic, pluralistic society?

Although I realize this question is important to philosophers and theologians, it may be largely irrelevant to discussion of religion and politics in the United States. At the obvious level of constitutional law, American society is committed to non-establishment and to the institutional separation of church and state. Thus no religious tradition deserves to be privileged to any degree approaching an official established church. Despite an aversion to applying economic or marketing jargon to religious experience, we may characterize America as a religious marketplace of free ideas. This means that every faith tradition offers its way of life and principles of belief and conduct for consideration and evaluation by the community. Religious ideas will be tested in the public square. If people find them persuasive, they may look to the churches for guidance as to sound public policy. If people do not find religious ideas attractive, persuasive, or compelling, then the particular church expounding such principles will not gain influence beyond the narrow province of its own committed followers.

Demographically, Roman Catholics are the largest single denomination in the United States. But this sociological fact gives American Catholics no pride of place, no privilege, no precedence. What matters in the public deliberations of a democratic, pluralistic society is the persuasiveness of Catholic ideas, principles, beliefs, and conduct. Style and manner of communication do matter in a democratic polity. I have provided here some positive and negative examples of public Catholicism. Catholicism is a rich heritage which contains many resources of potential use in American public life. When all is said and done, however, I think that the truthfulness and persuasiveness of Catholic principles and norms of conduct are best conveyed by the example of Christian witness which the Catholic church and individual Catholics display in their daily lives.

Let me conclude by returning to the basic question our project addresses: the relation between religion and democracy. If this is "a Catholic moment" in

American history, how can Catholics contribute to the understanding and practice of key democratic ideas such as human rights, justice, equality, and tolerance? What kinds of religious belief and observance would enable Catholic believers to make this sort of contribution to American public life? Without going into too much detail, let me say that the witness of the American Catholic community should, in my view, be that of a church with integrity, which practices what it preaches. It should be the witness of a church that is more tolerant, consultative, non-clerical, even quasi-democratic in structure and administration. Thirdly, it should be the witness of a church that respects and honors women. The credibility of Catholic church witness in contemporary society is at stake here, I believe. Finally, the witness of the American Catholic church must be primarily by example. I do not think the church should adopt a political quietism and refuse to address the moral dimensions of policy issues in public debate. However, if the church does not lead by example, its political pronouncements will be considerably less effective.

NOTES

1. William Lee Miller, *The First Liberty: Religion and the American Republic* (New York: A. Knopf, 1986), 280, 291. The Berger statement is reported in David O'Brien, "American Catholics and American Society," *Catholics and Nuclear War*, ed. Philip J. Murnion (New York: Crossroad, 1983), 16. The third quotation is from Richard John Neuhaus, *The Catholic Moment: The Paradox of the Church in the Postmodern World* (San Francisco: Harper & Row), 283.

2. Neuhaus, *The Catholic Moment*, acknowledgment page.

3. Neuhaus, *The Catholic Moment*, preface.

4. This self-description is from the masthead of *First Things*. Elsewhere the journal has been described as "a neoconservative bully pulpit both within Catholicism and outside it," and as "a clone of *Commentary* in style and tone." See David Toolan, "The 'Catholic Moment' under Siege," *America* 176, no. 7 (March 1, 1997).

5. Richard John Neuhaus, *The Naked Public Square: Religion and Democracy in America*, 2nd edition (Grand Rapids, MI: William B. Eerdmans Pub. Co., 1984), ix.

6. *Ibid.*

7. *Ibid.*, p. 19.

8. George Weigel, "The Neoconservative Difference: A Proposal for the Renewal of Church and Society," in R. Scott Appleby and Mary Jo Weaver, *Being Right: Conservative Catholics in America* (Bloomington: Indiana University Press, 1995), 143.

9. John Courtney Murray, Foreward to *We Hold These Truths: Catholic Reflections on the American Proposition* (Kansas City, MO: Sheed & Ward, 1960), vii. It should be noted that, in addition to neoconservative Catholics, many others, including Catholic moderates and progressives, also lay claim to Murray's legacy.

10. The Religious Equality Amendment (REA), a constitutional amendment proposed in the 104th Congress, was intended to permit greater religious expression in public places such as public schools, sports arenas, public radio stations, government

offices, school assemblies and graduation ceremonies. The REA was the result of a major effort by religious conservatives in the Republican-controlled 104th Congress to restore school prayer. However, the REA foundered because of serious divisions within the ranks of the Religious Right and was never reported out of committee for a floor vote in the House of Representatives. See Mary C. Segers, "The Religious Equality Amendment and Voluntary School Prayer," in Jo Formicola and Hubert Morken, eds., *Everson Revisited: Religion, Education, and Law at the Crossroads* (Lanham, MD: Rowman & Littlefield Publishers, Inc., 1997), 191–217.

11. Miller, *The First Liberty*, p. 280.

12. *Ibid.*, pp. 289–291.

13. *Ibid.*, pp. 290–291.

14. *Ibid.*, p. 291.

15. John F. Kennedy, "Remarks on Church and State Presented to the Greater Houston Ministerial Association," September, 1960, in *From Many, One: Readings in American Political and Social Thought*, edited by Richard C. Sinopoli (Washington, DC: Georgetown University Press, 1997), 366–369. Neuhaus notes how Kennedy reinforced the concept of a religiously empty public square, yet Neuhaus acknowledges that JFK "had little choice in taking the tack he did. Remember, this was before Vatican II and the 'Declaration on Religious Freedom.'" See Neuhaus, *The Catholic Moment*, p. 250. William Lee Miller claims that Kennedy "turned out, in effect, to be our first Southern Baptist President—one, that is, who defended a thoroughgoing separation more characteristic of that group than of his own church. . . . This was, of course, a political necessity in that time and that situation, like Jackie Robinson keeping his temper." See Miller, *The First Liberty*, p. 286.

16. Mark S. Massa, S.J., "A Catholic for President?: John F. Kennedy and the 'Secular' Theology of the Houston Speech, 1960," *Journal of Church and State* 39; no. 2 (Spring 1997), 297–317. For an interesting analysis of the context of anti-Catholicism which Kennedy faced, see John T. McGreevy, "Catholicism in the American Intellectual Imagination, 1928-1960," *The Journal of American History* 84; no. 1 (June 1997), 97–131.

17. Wilson Carey McWilliams, "Ties That Almost Bind," *Commonweal* 124; no. 14 (August 15, 1997), p. 25. This is a review of Martin Marty's *The One and the Many: America's Struggle for the Common Good* (Cambridge: Harvard University Press, 1997) and Amitai Etzioni, *The New Golden Rule: Community and Morality in Democratic Society* (New York: Basic Books, 1997).

18. Paul Weber, "Political Implications of the Changing Catholic Demographics in the United States," Paper presented at the 1997 Annual Meeting of the American Political Science Association, Washington, DC. Weber's figures are drawn from a report from the Pew Research Center, "The Diminishing Divide: . . . American Churches, American Politics," June 25, 1996, pp. 36–37.

19. Charles R. Morris, Author Reply to Correspondence, *Commonweal* 124; no. 14 (August 15, 1997), p. 4. Morris's book is *American Catholic: The Saints and Sinners Who Built America's Most Powerful Church* (New York: Times Books, 1997).

20. For example, Archbishop Theodore McCarrick of Newark, New Jersey, reported in June 1997 that 80 percent of the Catholic students in the Newark Archdiocese were being educated in public schools. Conference on Catholic schooling, Law School of Seton Hall University, Newark, New Jersey, June 14, 1997.

21. I should be clear about what I mean by democracy. In the modern world, democracy is not simply majority rule or the rule of the many poor, as Aristotle defined it. The type of democracy important to the United States is liberal democracy which seeks maximum political participation and majority rule, yet emphasizes fundamental respect for individual and minority rights. Liberal democracy as it has developed in a large, populous, diverse society such as the United States, has come to emphasize protective institutions such as representative government, periodic elections to hold representatives accountable, individual constitutional rights defended through an independent judiciary, and private ownership of property to guarantee political independence. The values essential to a liberal democratic society include personal freedom, tolerance for the rights of others, distributive justice, citizen participation in social decision making, social discipline, and respect for law. In a sense, we could say that in an ideal liberal democracy, the welfare of the individual and the common good of society (the public interest) are the ends or goals to be achieved.

22. A. James Reichley, *Religion and American Public Life* (Washington, DC: The Brookings Institute, 1985), 359. Hertzke suggests that religious lobbies promote democratic governance by providing political access to individuals and groups previously left out of the political process. Noting that more Americans join churches than any other single voluntary association, he argues that their association with such religious groups facilitates a kind of representation hitherto denied them by a political process inevitably skewed towards powerful, well-educated, monied interests. See Allen Hertzke, *Representing God in Washington* (Nashville: University of Tennessee Press, 1988). Two recent studies—sociologist John Coleman's work on paradenominational groups in American society and the massive study of political participation in the United States by Sidney Verba, Kay Schlozman and Henry Brady—show how religion promotes democratic citizenship by training people in the civic skills necessary for effective political participation. See John A. Coleman, "Under the Cross and the Flag: Reflections on Discipleship and Citizenship in America," *America* 174; no. 16 (May 11, 1996), 6–14. See also Sidney Verba, Kay Schlozman, and Henry E. Brady, *Voice and Equality: Civic Voluntarism in American Politics* (Cambridge: Harvard University Press, 1995). Finally, both A.J. Reichley and Stephen Carter have emphasized the role churches play as socializing agents and as effective barriers to political and social tyranny. Through education and socialization, religion helps to shape the moral character of citizens. Religions, according to Carter, can serve as sources of moral understanding without which any majoritarian system can degenerate into simple tyranny. See Stephen L. Carter, *The Culture of Disbelief* (New York: Basic Books, 1993).

23. The role of the Supreme Court in the American system of government was the subject of the November 1996 *First Things* symposium entitled "The End of Democracy?" in which contributors argued that a "judicial usurpation of politics" was taking crucial decisions about American life out of the hands of citizens. In his introduction to the symposium, Neuhaus declared it was time to move beyond discussions of an imperial judiciary. Asserting that judicial arrogance had undermined the separate powers and the checks and balances of the American political system, Neuhaus proclaimed the end of democracy was nigh. "The question here explored, in full awareness of its far-reaching consequences, is whether we have reached or are reaching the point where conscientious citizens can no longer give moral assent to the existing regime." Because an imperial judiciary has drained the

American "regime" of "legitimacy," civil disobedience and even outright rebellion are warranted and may even be morally required. See the Symposium, "The End of Democracy? The Judicial Usurpation of Politics," *First Things*, no. 67 (November 1996), 18–42. See also the Symposium "On the Future of Conservatism," *Commentary* 103:2 (February 1997), 14–43. Also Jacob Heilbrunn, "Neocon v. Theocon: The New Fault Line on the Right," *The New Republic,* December 30, 1996, 20–24.

24. George Weigel, "Catholicism and the American Proposition," *First Things*, no. 23 (May 1992), 42. According to Weigel, "Calls for 'taking America seriously' that confuse the deliberative processes and structures of governance appropriate to a political community with the deliberative process and structures of governance appropriate to the community of faith involve a category error of considerable proportions."

25. Eugene C. Bianchi and Rosemary Radford Reuther, eds., *A Democratic Catholic Church: The Reconstruction of Roman Catholicism* (New York: Crossroad, 1992), 12.

26. For a fuller discussion of the Catholic church's effort to shape abortion policy, see Mary C. Segers, "The Catholic Church as a Political Actor," in *Perspectives on the Politics of Abortion* edited by Ted Jelen (Westport, CT: Praeger Publishers, 1995), 87–129.

27. Address of Bishop James W. Malone, president, to the General Meeting of the National Conference of Catholic Bishops (NCCB), excerpted in the *New York Times*, November 13, 1984, p. A22. Also in *Origins* 14, no. 24 (November 29, 1984): 384–390.

28. St. Thomas Aquinas, *Summa Theologica* I-II, Q. 96, a.2 and a.3, in Anton C. Pegis, ed., *Basic Writings of Saint Thomas Aquinas*, vol. II (New York: Random House, 1945), 791–794.

7

Post-Protestant America? Some Hegelian Reflections on the History and Theology of Religious Establishment

Eldon J. Eisenach

It is commonly accepted that nineteenth-century America was "Protestant" and that America is Protestant no longer. This is a cultural and political conclusion, and not a demographic one, for it presumes that a clearly identified informal or de facto Protestant establishment dominated American national identity and major national educational, political, cultural, and economic institutions. It is also commonly accepted that, at some point in the twentieth century, this informal religious establishment—and presumably its reigning public theology—was "disestablished" and that a new "post-Protestant" establishment and theology replaced it. And, finally, it is now commonly accepted that, at some point in the recent past, this "post-Protestant" (often termed Judeo-Christian) establishment and theology was in turn disestablished and that we now inhabit a nation whose identity and major national institutions are not only post-Protestant and post-Judeo-Christian, but, with a few rapidly diminishing exceptions, wholly secular—call it "post-religious."

While this narrative of establishment/disestablishment/reestablishment/re-disestablishment was never intended to be a neat and seamless one—the power of the Protestant establishment, for example, waxed and waned throughout the nineteenth century—it does assume that neither the Constitutional provision against religious establishment in the First Amendment nor the completion of legal disestablishment in the states in the 1830s prevented the creation of a de facto national "Protestant" religious establishment. In seeking to understand this ironic result—was de jure *state dises-*

tablishment a necessary condition for de facto *national establishment*—many other ironies suddenly appear. Here is one: if disestablishment is the test of religious freedom, was there *more* religious freedom in early nineteenth-century America—when formal establishment in the states was almost dead and the informal one had not been consolidated—than in the late nineteenth and early twentieth centuries when the informal and national Protestant establishment was at the peak of its power? As a concluding preliminary, pair this larger irony with one that is immediately relevant to our perceived condition today. In 1875, James G. Blaine, then Republican Speaker of the House, proposed an amendment to the U.S. Constitution that would make the two religious clauses of the First Amendment binding on state governments, i.e., do by formal amendment what the Supreme Court did by incorporation in the *Everson* decision—but *seventy-two years earlier*. Blaine's proposal carried in the House by a vote of 180–7, but failed in the Senate. Needless to say, Blaine (and almost the entire House of Representatives) were hardly proponents of religious neutrality and strict separation—let alone a secular humanist intellectual elite. Blaine, later known for his "Rum, Romanism, and Rebellion" presidential campaign against Grover Cleveland in 1884, was in fact mobilizing Protestant religious passions by attempting to use federal authority to prevent some cities and states from accommodating Catholics in public school policy. Religious freedom has many friends.

This essay seeks to explain the ironies in our narrative of religious freedom by relating periods of religious establishment to the way political historians periodize national political orders or "regimes." By suggesting ways in which our religious establishment history can be read as parallel to and congruent with our political regime history, we can chart the creation (establishment) and destruction (disestablishment) of national authority under the assumption that political establishments and religious establishments are two aspects of a single system of national authority. This view not only permits us to see our national political life in broad perspective, it forces us to consider the ways in which the *theology* of religious establishment—and of disestablishment—is a distinctly political theology.

In the next part of the essay, I explore the form and the changing content of this political theology—also known as our "public" or "civil" religion, "the Religion of America," "a common faith," "the American idea." In every establishment period, this political theology not only legitimates national regimes by mobilizing religious and patriotic energies on behalf of national projects and purposes, it also determines what kinds of churches and what forms of religious expression and beliefs are appropriate for full inclusion in national political deliberation. And because it serves this two-sided legitimation function, ever since the rise of *informal* religious establishments, the institutional location of our political theology has rarely been the denominational churches, and most of its leading theologians have either transcended their church identity or have not even been members of the clergy. Moreover, when seeing the role that this establishment theology plays in political regime destruction and formation, it is clear that this political theology can never be as thin and derivative as suggested by such terms as "overlapping consensus" and "common denominator" or, indeed, any concept that suggests a disparate package of discounted "remainders," as if the items of real value and power have already been sold to the separate churches or, as we now say, "faith traditions." To the contrary, under the combined auspices of powerful politico-religious establishments (or disestablishment movements seeking to replace the prevailing one) American political theology has often been a stern and demanding faith, quite willing to excommunicate, define heresies, and impose ritual obedience. Another name for this is nation-building; still another is national democratic political life under conditions of religious pluralism.

In the last part of the essay I explore our present condition. The requirement of religious freedom increasingly stipulates that all institutional churches be treated as "denominations"—i.e., as legitimate units under the canopy of a national political religion—but no one denomination can be the Church. Where then is the Church location for American political theology? To say "the nation" or "America" is the Church may well be true, but that begs the question of who or what constitutes the American nation.[1] In reviewing politico-religious establishments and their political theologies from the Progressive period until today, I conclude that the American university (including its ancillary professional and disciplinary institutions) is both the central source of this theology as a system of ideas and values and the primary institution that certifies its transmission and articulation. And while it takes no powerful act of imagination to conclude that, if this remains true today, we are clearly under a condition of radical disestablishment, it takes both imagination and faith to suggest, as I do, that the university seems on the verge of reclaiming this central and formative place as reconstituted Church bearing a new national political faith. No denominational church or coalition of "faith traditions," no matter how inclusive, has either the resources or the will to take on this task, and they can continue to thrive underneath a canopy created by others. The university, however, can only thrive if it reclaims its central role as the common and national source of our highest spiritual, intellectual, and cultural ideas. Failure would not only result in isolation from national political life, but in handing over stewardship of our national identity to other institutions and organizations—perhaps to the media, perhaps to newly energized political movements and parties.

In any event, a reading of our politico-religious history in these terms suggests that informal religious establishment is our normal condition and that we might be re-entering a normal period. I confess that this reading may cast rays of sunshine on many a rainy parade of litanies bemoaning our loss of religious values in public life, our moral decay, our anarchic individualism.

IRONIC STORIES OF DISESTABLISHMENTS

For irony, start with Virginia. Statesmen like Jefferson and Madison thought that purging the statutes of Virginia of Anglicanism would result in a self-canceling religious pluralism presided over by an enlightened gentry. What resulted was pluralism of a sort, but one that multiplied centers of shared religious enthusiasm and revival. Isaac Backus was a better prophet than Thomas Jefferson. For Backus, as for Roger Williams before him, the separation of church and state was an evangelical imperative to clear the way for the creation of a holy nation. There is an added irony here: Massachusetts, which had local legal establishments until 1833, erected the more effective defense against religious enthusiasm in politics than did Virginia. But, like Connecticut and New Hampshire before it, the established churches in Massachusetts were finally destroyed in order that the new religious energies and passions unleashed in the Second Great Awakening could more readily be released into New England society and culture. In truth, legal and constitutional disestablishment in the states was the precondition for the formation of a voluntary and cultural establishment of an ecumenical and evangelical Protestantism in the nation. Its first political expression was through anti-Jacksonian party and reform movements which together coalesced into the Whigs, creating what political historians term the second party system that persisted until the eve of Southern secession. This increasingly powerful new establishment was consolidated in the Republican Party and, with Lincoln's presidency and the victory of the North in the Civil War, expressed as a new and powerful civil religion. Although weakened and depressed during the party stalemate period of 1876–1896, through Progressive intellectuals and reformers this establishment increasingly dominated our public discourse into the next century.

This history suggests two very different understandings about the kinds of ideas that power disestablishment in America. The conventional reading holds that church disestablishment in the states was a "secularization" of politics, so the ideas driving this disestablishment are, perforce, secular. Here Jefferson and Virginia are normative even if they were not at all prophetic of what happened later in the nineteenth century. On the counter-assumption that legal or "church" disestablishment was only a rest stop on the path to a new, national voluntary religious reestablishment, a quite different reading of ruling ideas is required. These ideas must themselves be both political and religious, if not to attack the old establishment then to usher in a new one, to undermine one type of politico-religious establishment and to foreshadow a new one. These differing sets of ideas also exhibit different structures. The former set are formal, static, and grounded in fixed dualisms: secular and sacred, state and church, public and private, reason and faith, science and belief, law and conscience. The latter set are dialectical and modeled on the form of biblical history: animating values and spirits are embodied in and work through differing institutional forms, migrating over time and space and changing their power and significance. Put in terms unfamiliar to most Americans, the former ideas encode a type of scholastic or formal philosophy and the latter, a type of historicist philosophy.[2] I maintain that the former ideas are a barrier to understanding our past, our present, and, therefore, our future. If this formalistic mode of self-understanding were sufficient, then America, for all practical purposes, attained full religious freedom somewhere in the 1830s—and that slavery, Indian removal and the male-only voting franchise had nothing to do with religious freedom then, and civil rights and the conduct of U.S. foreign policy now.

Difficult as it is to sustain this formal-legal reading regarding the early national period, this understanding of our history cannot begin to explain the relationship of religion and politics in the nineteenth century. If the legal/constitutional disestablishments of 1776 and 1788 and the 1830s were underwritten by secular enlightenment values and represent democratization, what ideas powered the succession of informal or "voluntary" reestablishments of religion in the nineteenth and twentieth centuries? To say that "American values" reassert themselves with every successful *disestablishment* of these regimes does little to explain whose values were responsible for each succeeding and successful *reestablishment.*

We often celebrate the political eras marked by voluntary religious establishment as the highest expressions of the American idea even as we deny the ideas that brought these eras into being. Must we hold that the anti-Jacksonian political constituencies that later came together to constitute the Republican Party and the victors in the Civil War held religiously retrograde, anti-intellectual, and politically anti-democratic values—a real irony of fate[4] given their leadership, constituencies, institutional alliances, reform programs, and policy positions? This irony would only be multiplied in the case of the Progressives after the Civil War who were also driven by national-evangelical imperatives and projects. How and why did good Americans in all of their organizational and creedal diversity put up with this religious domination and sustain for decades on end the political majorities that carried that domination into politics? Where were our political leaders seeking to win elections on the platform of religious freedom? And where were our constitutional lawyers, judges, and other men of legal principle? Calling these successive reestablishments "hegemonic" only changes the charge on our ancestors—especially our non-evangelical Protestant ones—from cowardice to that of false-consciousness or gullibility.

But there is another possibility. Take the case of the Republican Party and the Civil War. Here, the reimposition of a morally disciplined and spiritually confident politico-religious establishment was the necessary surcharge on the cost of undertaking the project of emancipation and, in a deep sense, re-founding the American nation. But if that was the case then—enlightenment philosophy powerless without the canopy of political theology—might it also have been the case earlier, placing both Jonathan Edwards and Roger Williams at the founders' table (with Hegel as a late arrival) when we both reaffirmed past covenants and created our identity as a distinct people?[5] And might this also be the case later? That is, *any* large national political and moral projects might be inconceivable without a shared faith and common creed, one that the Constitution alone could never supply.

> I. *National Republicans*: "We wish, fully and entirely, to nationalize the institutions of our land and to identity ourselves with our country; to become a single great people, separate and distinct in national character, political interest, social and civil affinities from any and all other nations, kindred and people on the earth. . . . We have all the elements of becoming a greater people, a mightier nation, and more endurable government than has ever held a place in the annals of time." (*American Republican* [Whig], November 7, 1844.)
>
> II. *Democrats*: "1. That the Federal Government is one of limited powers, derived solely from the Constitution, and . . . ought to be strictly construed. 2. That the Constitution does not confer upon the General Government the power to commence or carry on a general system of internal improvements. 3. That the Constitution does not confer authority. . . . 4. That justice and sound policy forbid. . . . 5. That it is the duty of every branch . . . to enforce and practice the most rigid economy. . . . 6. That Congress has no power to charter a United State Bank. . . . 7. That Congress has no power . . . to interfere with or control the domestic institutions of the several states. . . . 8. That the separation of the money of the government from banking institutions is indispensable for the . . . rights of the people. 9. That the liberal principles embodied by Jefferson in the Declaration of Independence, and sanctioned in the Constitution . . . makes ours the land the liberty. . . ." (*Democratic Party Platform*, 1840, repeated *verbatim*, with slight change in order, 1844, 1848, 1852, and 1856.)[6]
>
> III. *Woodrow Wilson as Democrat*: "There is no such thing as corporate liberty. Liberty belongs to the individual, or it does not exist . . . [and] liberty is the object of constitutional government. . . . Constitutional government can exist only where there is actual community of interest and of purpose, and cannot, if it be also self-government, express the life of any body of people that does not constitute a veritable community. Are the United States a community? In some things, yes; in most things, no." (*Constitutional Government in the United States* [1908].)

IV. *Woodrow Wilson as National Republican*: "Our participation in the war established our position among the nations. . . . The whole world saw at last . . . a Nation they had deemed material and now found to be compact of the spiritual forces that must free men of every nation of every unworthy bondage. . . . The stage is set, the destiny is disclosed. It has come about by no plan of our conceiving, but by the hand of God who led us into this way. We cannot turn back. We can only go forward . . . to follow the vision. It was of this that we dreamed at our birth. America shall in truth show the way." (Speech to the Senate, July 10, 1919.)

By reading the cycles of establishment and disestablishment as one national story combining religious and political authority, we can see more clearly the alternation of dominant discourses even as we must then admit that only one of them is constitutive of a national identity thick enough to yield collective purpose and action by engaging the deepest values of its citizens. This reading also shifts our attention away from "church" and "denominational" readings of our party and religious history and forces us to look more candidly at the ways in which successful religious establishments and political theologies mobilized support by articulating shared political, social and moral projects that drew from but did not impose particular "church" or creedal religion. More to the point, this approach helps us unravel some seeming paradoxes in our more recent politico-religious past that underlie our current condition. If, as is commonly written, the second (third if you count Jacksonian democracy as the second) major disestablishment was substantially completed in the 1920s[7], what were we fighting about so religiously in the late 1960s? If, instead, we date serious disestablishment in the 1970s,[8] clearly it was not a *Protestant* (or a Republican) establishment now being disestablished. But, if not, what sort of "post-Protestant" American Religion was being successfully undermined—and where, when and how did *that* informal religious establishment and political theology come into being?

Consider the following hypothesis. Call the increasing internal divisions and steep decline of ecumenical Protestantism in the 1920s the "second disestablishment" (or third, if Jackson's was the second), and call the religious-cultural era succeeding it "post-Protestant." Was this succeeding era a disestablishment or a new establishment? If only a disestablishment, it was embarrassingly brief and incomplete—running from the final collapse of Progressivism with Hoover to the dominance of liberal internationalism during World War II and the Cold War. And even in this interlude there was a rapid restructuring of the older religious establishment marked by hiving off and sending into the wilderness Protestant "fundamentalism"[9] and creating a new tripartite (and bipartisan) holding company—call it "Judeo-Christianity vs. Fascism and Communism, Inc." This new establishment held power from World War II through the civil rights revolution and the Vietnam War.[10] Its theology was both articulated and celebrated in best-selling books written by leaders from each of its constituent elements in the 1950s, the most memorable being Will Herberg's *Protestant, Catholic, Jew.*[11] Conservatives of all religious faiths today now look back on this era as a model to emulate, both constitutionally and culturally.

What is problematic is not the fact of this reestablishment and its theology, but to what extent it differed from the establishment theology it replaced. The very lack of difference suggests that earlier establishment theologies were also a kind of Protestantism without creedal Christianity.[12] This reading is confirmed when we look at the primary seminary of establishment: the national American university. To say that these institutions were disestablished of their "Protestantism" by the 1920s to become "pluralistic" and "secular" forever after is simply to ignore the religious spirit and the regime-legitimating role they embraced from the early 1940s through the early 1970s. But they were already fully prepared to play this "post-Protestant" role: in the four decades *prior* to the 1920s it is difficult to identify *any* distinctly Protestant church creeds and doctrines in the politico-religious consensus expressed in the teaching, textbooks, and scholarship in major national universities. Indeed, from the 1880s onward, Protestant churches, creeds, and clergymen were consistently subordinated and regularly attacked by the new academics and university-based modernist theologians as barriers to the achievement of both national cohesion and social Christianity.[13] And by the 1940s and 50s, Catholic universities and intellectuals were also able and eager to join the Church. Having already achieved a fusion of American nationalism and Irish Catholicism, the Cold War was the ideal project through which to gain full partnership—and in the process, free itself from defending Catholic identity through a secular and Jeffersonian ideology within the Democratic Party. By World War II and the Cold War, Catholic identity was clearly under the protective canopy of American Religion itself.[14]

Those who conflate the end of a distinctly "Protestant" establishment in the 1920s with disestablishment *per se* have a very difficult time dealing with the politico-religious consensus of the 1950s and the oppositional politico-religious fervor of the 1970s and 1980s. But if instead we call the "post-Protestantism" of the 1950s a continuation of many of the leading ideas of the nineteenth-century Protestant establishment under a new name, then we have difficulty identifying *any* extended period in American history when religious freedom defined as freedom from the cultural/rhetorical dominance of a kind of shared trans-church and non-creedal religion was achieved. This is precisely my point: voluntary national religious establishment is our norm in the same way that coherent national political regimes are our norm. Disestablishment is not only the exception, it usually marks a crisis of national identity and moral and political coherence. Disestablishments are transitional periods between national political orders.

THE POLITICAL THEOLOGY OF AMERICAN ESTABLISHMENT

The political theology of voluntary establishment in America is "nation" centered, not "government" centered, because it insists that only under conditions of religious freedom can the voice of God's spirit—the source of our democratic political authority—be heard by the whole people. Successful establishment theology, therefore, is in but not of the state and its official powers; in but not of the separate churches and their particular creeds. It is however, both in and of the American people, providing a shared moral and spiritual orientation sufficient to authorize common political and social projects and provide adhesive ties sufficient to define us as one people distinct from other nations. Our political theology is also our national history: it is the normative framework by which and through which we have understood and shared a common experience.[15]

One can see this location and these functions of American political theology quite clearly if one tries to imagine American history under very different conditions. One such condition would be that originally envisioned by many founders: separate and powerful legal establishments in many or most of the states conceived as "small republics," resulting in cultural-religious homogeneity and intense patriotism at the state level, and only a very thin Constitutional order at the national or "enlarged republican" one. Another imagined condition would be autarkic institutional religious pluralism spread across the entire country with each church existing exclusively for its own members. Each denomination would act as if it were an "ethnic" church whose overriding purpose was defense of the particular religious creed—and perhaps the language—brought from the country of immigration. There would be no American Catholic Church, for example, but only its self-enclosed ethnic parts; no Protestant evangelical popular fronts; no ecumenical institutions, including colleges and universities; no political speech integrating religious, moral, and political commitments; no general religious press or publications; no national history and literature reflecting shared spiritual struggles and commitments. There would be no religious "mission" or "outreach" activity by the churches except within their respective ethnic communities. All religious expression would be contained within the churches, consisting of religious creeds, rituals, and doctrines combined with narratives of ethnic solidarity that would be endlessly reproduced and handed down to each new generation. Because ethnic and religious identity are codependent, the decline of ethnic identity would spell the decline of the church and, therefore, religion itself. For this reason, issues of language and of education—indeed, the entire problem of "cosmopolitanism"—would be intractably and deeply religious issues as well. All attempts at national integration would be threats both to religious and to ethnic identity.

However fanciful these two scenarios, one fact is undeniable: *national religious freedom would be absolutely guaranteed*, for the national government would have nothing whatsoever to do with religion, even at the level of partisan speech or ceremonial expression. The only problem is whether the American nation could have been formed and persisted under either of these forms of national religious freedom.

Our real national history and development has been radically different from these imagined ones, and so has our understanding and experience of religious freedom. And for this reason, I want to explore further the political theology of successful voluntary establishment. I want to explore why it so often and persistently swept the field, why it prevailed not only among the most sophisticated, thoughtful, responsible and morally serious citizens but why *the available alternatives to it* were rejected by most other citizens as well. And, finally, I want to suggest why this theology was so protean, so capable of reinventing and renewing itself, carrying it over periods of both religious depression (e.g., 1870s and 80s, and 1920s and 30s) and sectarian religious conflict (e.g., 1840s—and perhaps the 1980s and 90s). And if this nineteenth-century "Protestant" theology of establishment could so readily spawn a mid-twentieth century "post-Protestant" (Judeo-Christian-Western Civilization) theology of establishment, there is reason to believe that this same theological structure is even now the stream bed for a new establishment in the next century that we are almost fated to call "post-Christian" or, God help us, "post-religious."

The three major tenets of the theology underwriting American voluntary establishment are (1) that God's revelation and spirit is continuous and progressive until the end of time, a progress marked by God's word increasingly inspiriting all social institutions and practices; (2) that God speaks to peoples or nations and that the American nation or people is the primary unit through which God now speaks in history; and (3) that the test of religious belief, both individual and social, is active participation in the achievement of goodness and justice in the larger society; conversion, righteousness, and citizenship are largely coterminous.[16]

This national theology presupposes a national covenant and therefore a standing question of performance because its tenets rest on a biblical hermeneutic grounded in the kingdom theology of the Old Testament and the Gospels in the New Testament. And because revelation is continuous, faith requires that each generation use its own best knowledge to discover God's word for them and to reinterpret past revelation accordingly. God speaks through reason and faith and, because this twin revelation is cumulative and progressive, knowledge gives to faith—especially to biblical revelation—increasing clarity and confidence. This is the core of what can be called its "Protestantism." This same core was incorporated into the shaping of American Catholicism, first in its battles against the calls for an ethnic church by German immigrants, then in its social doctrines, and finally in its understanding of religious freedom. This same political-theological core can also be read as a freestanding philosophy of history and theory of social evolution that served, variously, as the foundation for nineteenth-century American moral philosophy, historiography, and the new social sciences.

While these tenets and their underlying hermeneutic took many different forms and were subjected to continuous reinterpretation and contestation, their centrality was rarely questioned. In this theology, separation of church and state and the prohibition of creedal tests for holding public office are religiously commanded of America and for the coming age. Moreover, it should not be presumed that the standing institutional churches and ordained clergyman are the exclusive or even chosen instruments of God's contemporary revelation; they, too, might require "Christianization"—or new institutional competitors—infused by the evangelical spirit and the new knowledge of the universities. A religious life, as defined by this national theology, is not opposed to that defined by the separate churches and creeds, but requires extension into the home, the community, the school, the laboratory, the business enterprise, the political party, and the state. And unlike the nineteenth-century constitutional order, the more progressive side of establishment theology not only included women and blacks, it sometimes accorded them central roles in the achievement of American destiny.[17] According to this understanding, the "state" itself is seen not as a constitutionally created set of separate "public" institutions but, at particular times, as the highest expression of a nationally shared democratic faith. Thus, Samuel Batten, a prominent Baptist social gospel minister, declared that "in the last analysis the State is the organized faith of a people," and Mary Follett, a high priestess of Progressive political science, concluded that "[t]he state must be no external authority which restrains and regulates me, but it must be myself acting as the state in every smallest detail of life."[18] Each of these sites can serve either as a bearer of or a barrier to the coming of the kingdom. The evangelical imperative in the Progressive era to Christianize the society is equally an imperative to democratize and "Americanize" the society by infusing all of its institutions and practices with shared national values of social justice.[19]

Informing these writings explicating the theology of voluntary establishment in nineteenth-century America is a social evolutionary view of human destiny that extended biblical understandings of progressive revelation into philosophy, secular history, and the social sciences. The merging of evangelical theology, philosophy, and philosophy of history was first articulated in Germany by Hegel (1770–1831) and Schleiermacher (1768–1834) and became normative in American theology first at Unitarian Harvard and then, through Andover Seminary, Princeton, and Yale, within liberal evangelical Protestantism generally.[20] While it is common knowledge that a vast majority of the founders of the social sciences in America were trained in German historical scholarship in the 1870s and 80s, it is not so well known that their philosophical and theological mentors had preceded them in this study. Most of the early post-Civil War faculty of religion and divinity at Harvard, Andover, Yale, and Princeton, and the editors of the leading theological and philosophical journals, had studied in Germany in the 1830s through 1860s. Thus, in post-Civil War America it was difficult to distinguish theologian from philosopher from social scientist from public moralist and reform intellectual. This, in itself, is proof that a broad-based and voluntary establishment theology is in force.[21]

Granting the power of this establishment and the reach of its theology in the nineteenth and early twentieth centuries, it is often charged that its very success, especially in its more "secular" articulations and sponsorships by Progressive academics, was the cause of its decline and the reason for the 1920s "disestablishment." This argument is buttressed sociologically by chanting the now familiar mantra, "religious pluralism." Setting aside how the truth of this charge might be adjudicated, the important question to ask is *whether this constitutes its weakness or its strength*. In so far as these very features foreshadow the establishment theology in the 1950s through 1970s—one that successfully brought together not only Catholics and Protestants, but Jews and those professing no formal religion at all—this is a latent strength. So the charge of weakness and decline must really be postponed for about half a century—the 1970s—when this later liberal establishment was successfully challenged. Given the general instability and fragility of national political and cultural authority in America, to call either of these establishments (1880s–1920s and 1940s–1970s) self-subversive and weak invokes the obvious response: compared to what?

There is a serious question behind this charge, however, but it applies to the very origins and nature of political theology under conditions of religious freedom. To what extent is a reform-oriented, ethically-centered and national political theology a "religion" at all? Isn't there an inherent subversion of Christian doctrine simply because *it can serve* to inspirit and authorize national moral, social, and political reform movements and projects? Isn't this political theology as social gospel always going to end up as a secular moral, social and political program without distinctly religious foundations and therefore neither Protestant nor Christian nor Judeo-Christian?

My simple answer is no, that this reading is something of an ahistorical illusion regarding the stability of religious doctrine within the churches themselves and regarding the organizational forms through which that religious belief is expressed, articulated and understood in the larger culture. Moreover, this charge cannot begin to explain the history and practices of American churches—let alone why tens of millions of committed Christians and Jews from many differing churches and doctrinal positions could see this political theology as publicly acknowledging their more specific church and personal faiths and thus strengthening their identities as both Christians or Jews and Americans. Church and doctrinal specificity are necessary results of religious freedom, but so, perhaps, is voluntary religious establishment, for without this canopy, religion and religious freedom itself would retreat into pure subjectivity and thus be removed altogether from civic and public spheres.

There is the opposite charge of religious oppression insofar as specific creedal or ecclesiastical elements cling to this public theology as "remainders" and as reminders of its origins, thus privileging certain churches and faiths. This is of course true, and countless political and court battles have been fought to remove them. But these tags and remnants, for all their symbolic weight, are really inconsequential compared to the power (or weakness) of a shared political theology in the general culture.[22] Moreover, it is not really to the point that certain elites overrepresenting particular churches or faith traditions gain and cling to power in the founding periods of each new voluntary politico-religious establishment—this is also true in periods of disestablishment, albeit with a different church mix and distribution. Every successful translation from (religious) spirit to moral and political "common sense" (or social science and legal doctrine) makes it accessible to increasingly diverse groups and individuals who in turn become powerful by using these languages *if the invitation to join is accepted.* The very act of creating a distinct "regime" or "political order" mandates both the initial inequality and the new horizon of opportunity. *The primary issue is whether and for how long national leaders and institutions are able to mobilize the energies, spirits and resources of the larger society for constructive common purposes at all.*

John Quincy Adams exactly echoed Tocqueville's charge that unchecked democratic individualism is incompatible with sustaining nationality because "it has no forefathers, it looks to no posterity, it is swallowed up in the present, and thinks of nothing but itself." A century later, Mary Follett put this same opposition more bluntly: "To substitute for the fictitious democracy of equal rights and consent of the governed, the living democracy of a united, responsible people."[23] Follett, of course, did not seek to destroy either equal rights or consent of the governed and, Andrew Jackson to the contrary, neither did John Quincy Adams. Like all theologians of voluntary establishment, both knew that an authoritative public discourse that integrates personal, social and political roles also and necessarily ranks and measures ways of life. While this is often blandly called "civic education," it necessarily distinguishes between lower and higher forms of citizenship, thereby subordinating some ends and spheres of life to others. All significant acts of democratic political life entail these choices.

Because every national political order, its sustaining religious establishment, and its legitimating political theology has both a beginning and an end, both its formation and its later repudiation mandates some fixed narrative conventions. Just as the founders want to portray the formation of their new regime as the attainment of a higher form of religious freedom and political democracy because it exposed and repudiated the limits (i.e., injustices, inequalities) of the earlier one, so those who later succeed in destroying it need to portray its rejection/disestablishment in the same terms. In both cases, the participants (and their apologetic historians) declare to themselves and to the nation, "we have *finally* got it right and achieved a state of religious freedom"—as if religious freedom were a state and not a continuous and historically situated practice.[24] This narrative convention, however, barely hides its theological (and Hegelian) roots and, with it, a deep and important belief essential to American national identity, namely, that religious freedom and democracy are revealed at a higher level with each overcoming. What it does successfully hide, however, is the debt that each succeeding victor owes the earlier but now defeated victors. This debt is built into the very dialectical structure of political theology, serving to bind the generations and the political/religious eras into a common story.

This binding together is recognized in a second narrative convention. Inclusion in the new establishment by major participants in the rejected one requires an act of contrition: *mea culpas* must be made by them (or by their apologetic historians) for past failings, past injustices, and past exclusions. This requirement is not to be disparaged, for every national political order tends to failure and often responds to challenges in self-serving, arrogant, and even oppressive ways. This act of contrition, forgiveness, and rededication is also testament that the jeremiad—itself a dialectic—remains the dominant rhetorical form of our political discourse.

A truly distorting side effect of these and similar narratives, however, has been the conclusion that *earlier* establishments in America were more authentically Protestant, or Christian, or even religious, but that yesterday's (or tomorrow's) are not. Even this, however, serves some necessary political and religious purposes. The first is to contrast the narrowness and "elitism" of the earlier establishment to the inclusiveness of the prevailing one—indeed, to the implicit denial that the prevailing one is an "establishment" at all. But what this conclusion overlooks is that each member of the "new" establishment has, in the process of accepting the invitation, *modified its own religious self-understandings and the way it presents its beliefs to its own members and to the larger community.* The fact is that only those who want to decline the standing or future invitation (or were the most prominent members of the earlier establishment) really think it "too thin"—even as they fear its energy and power both in and through other churches and in the culture at large. Rejection, however, exacts heavy spiritual costs on churches and their theologies. To insist that one's formal or church theology defines and occupies the entire content and space of the spirit is to pay high costs in a religiously pluralistic and democratic society. Foremost is removal of that religious community and its institutions from participation in the larger spiritual and intellectual life of the nation and, through that, of one's own era. Indeed, at its best, American political theology is often the path by which particular church theologies confront the world, grapple with its new knowledge and powers, and thereby instill a greater depth and reflexivity back into their own theologies. Rather than being conceptually thin and ethically shallow, American political theology is often too demanding of these churches, so they retreat into themselves.

This is why voluntary religious establishment and a political theology are so crucial in underwriting larger conceptions of religious freedom. An obvious negative case in point is Protestant fundamentalists in the 1920s until the recent past. American Catholics are the more interesting case. When Irish Catholicism in America tried, and for a long time succeeded, to build a separate social, spiritual and intellectual world in America, it was forced to defend that world with a secular enlightenment philosophy of political life that its own theology deeply repudiated. It escaped that contradiction by *de facto* institutional assimilation and through a vibrant national patriotism. Explicit entry into the voluntary establishment in the 1940s made it possible for Catholics to be truer to their faith because they now had a *religious* basis for mediation. And while there was a price to be paid—Catholic churchmen must now share with Catholic lay persons, Protestants, and Jews the authority to define and legitimate their own teachings—these same teachings and teachers are now increasingly dispersed into the larger intellectual culture.

Thus, while the costs of exclusion are very high, those for inclusion are not inconsiderable either. Inclusion always entails a process of mutual legitimation: this happened first with the Protestant clergy and churches between 1776 and the 1830s.[25] As the church or faith tradition authorizes the new establishment theology, so the political theology legitimates the church as a fully equal but never privileged "denomination." This means that no church and no faith tradition can be both part of the voluntary establishment and remain the sole arbiter of its own theology and identity. That is a privilege and a freedom that only the Amish and similar groups enjoy without envy, bitterness and the need for revenge. And in any case, these costs of inclusion are often not even seen by new entrants because, prior to their joining, they enjoyed the sweet victory of "defeating" the previous establishment that had excluded them. Almost by definition, then, each church entrant has already modified its theological self-understanding in its struggle for recognition, just as the new political theology was being shaped to accommodate the new members. This is the very meaning and purpose of voluntary religious establishment, even if, like Minerva's owl, we usually only see this process of struggle, inclusion and assimilation in retrospect.

Thus, despite the voluminous histories of religious victimization and sellout—"getting even" retroactively is always an indicator of a current period of disestablishment—it is quite remarkable how effective voluntary establishment has been in the process of American nationality formation. While coercion is always present at some level in both the formation and dismantling of establishments, the living tradition of this political theology in our religious, intellectual and moral culture has been a standing resource by which and through which new or marginal groups in America are able to interpret themselves through this larger experience. To paraphrase Theodore Roosevelt, this is no mere "political" (external, legal) inclusion, it is an "ethnic" (moral, religious) assimilation. This same living tradition of political theology, continuously replenished and articulated, not only makes possible this wide array of self-interpretive connections, it is also the basis from which a variety of different invitations can be extended to ever more and differing religious and ethnic communities.[26] The clearest historical example is that of German Jews and Republican Progressivism from the 1880s onward. Here the invitation was social Christianity translated into the social sciences, the settlement house, and the formation of the profession of social work.[27] Somewhat later, and under late-arriving Democratic and urban progressives, Catholics and newly-arrived Jews were invited to join through the trade union movement. In this and, indeed, in all periods of successful establishment, the intellectual and religious culture was creative enough to uncover and to generate resources of sufficient power to constitute invitations to join the national covenant. Sometimes these invitations were generous and compelling and at other times they included coercion and intimidation. *But we must always remember that in no case was the coercion and intimidation ever equal to the "invitation" extended to the white South to rejoin the refounded nation in the 1860s.* This, after all, was the decisive moment in American political theology and in the story of American nation building. However tragic the Civil War, it was American political theology, and not the Constitution, that made it possible for the South to bear its loss. This was foreshadowed in the words of Lincoln, "The Union is older than the Constitution."

OUR PRESENT CONDITION

Is voluntary establishment any longer a possibility? In terms of the argument of this essay, this is equivalent to asking, in the title of a recent book forecasting a new national political identity and order, will there be a "next American nation?" Because the Constitution alone is an insufficient source of national political authority and national identity and because Americans will never adhere together for long through state worship or presidential charisma, the more appropriate question might be, from what intellectual and spiritual sources and from what institutions will a political theology be constructed to serve as the basis for the next national political order? My answer is that the only possible institution is the American university and that the intellectual and spiritual sources for this task remain the same as they have always been, namely, the master narratives in the human sciences and the humanities that serve to interpret and integrate our social and self-knowledge.

Given the politicization of knowledge and the conditions of intellectual disarray (some call it nihilism) that now prevail in the universities, this proposal might appear laughable and even perverse. Before showing that it is neither and that there are already signs that this political-theological formation is already taking place, I think it important to be reminded of the ways that the American university, from its origins more than a century ago, has almost continuously served as the seminary and even the "Church" of American political theology. Its moral-political foundations and the source of its contemporary legitimacy and power still rest on fulfilling this function. One little-recognized proof of this is that, for more than a century we have enforced a strict uniformity on national American universities and subordinated all other institutions of higher education to the values of that uniform ideal. In marked contrast to churches, for example, we have brooked little deviation from a unified norm and have been energetically—even ruthlessly—efficient in punishing deviations.[28] In functional terms, this means that the common standards and values of the university legitimate and define more diverse church and denominational discourses and identities and not vice versa. And no wonder. When, on the eve of the last millennium, Chicago's president, William Rainey Harper, speaking at the University of California at Berkeley, equated the spirit of the new research university with a "religion of democracy," this idea was perfectly understood by his audience:

> Democracy has been given a mission to the world, and it is of no uncertain character. . . . The university is the prophet of this democracy, as well, its priest and its philosopher. . . . The university is the Messiah of this democracy, its to-be-expected deliverer.

As the Church of the American religion, Harper continued, the university must be self-governing and free from interference by either state or church. Harper hardly needed to remind this audience that the political theology produced by the American university must not be distinctly Christian in creed, but must carry the spirit of Judaism, Christianity, and philosophy itself into every aspect of American life. In this sense the university is a national "evangelical" Church, instilling its vision and knowledge into the nation so that the nation might bring brotherhood and righteousness into the world. The university carries God's spirit into the nation not through doctrine but through service; its teachings are conveyed not through law and coercion but freely, through selflessness and by example. Here Harper echoed the ideas of his most famous faculty recruit, John Dewey, who also saw the fulfillment of Christianity in the achievement of a democracy "in which the distinction between the spiritual and the secular has ceased, and as in Greek theory, as in the Christian theory of the Kingdom of God, the church and the state, the divine and the human organization of society are one."[29] In the language of one of our national anthems, "freedom's holy light" can only shine when knowledge is pursued freely under the protective authority of "Great God, our King."[30]

One might want to reduce Harper's call to a mainline masculine Protestant power play—but this discounts the fact that this ideal (with some of its religious metaphors changed and its gender references altered) remains today the only worthy moral and political source of legitimacy for the American university that is on offer. To be sure, this reduction sustains the saving myth that the university was purged of religion and became "secular" in the 1920s; this was the standard line in disciplinary and university histories written in the 1950s and 60s, and nicely served to explain the start of the rapid flow of women, Catholics, Jews and non-believers into the disciplines and universities. But this understanding is false, first because it mistakes the *translation* of spirit into common sense (and science and humanist values) with the *repudiation* of spirit and second, because it cannot account for the crucial spiritual role played by the university in legitimating both domestic liberalism and liberal anti-Communism in the 1950s and 1960s—a role so central that the university became the primary site where the battle for disestablishment was fought in the 1970s.

The truth is that in both Harper's university and in ours, the search for truth and the advancement of knowledge is, first and foremost, free and "for its own sake" in order that its teachings enter and inform our personal and our common life. Without this high purpose, the fate of the university would come to rest on how well it serves whatever customers, for whatever reasons, happen to purchase its goods and services. Spirit would move elsewhere or disappear into sectarian redoubts.

If our current condition, as a nation and as a university, flows from the turmoil beginning in the late 1960s, we must examine this period with some care before deciding whether the American university as American Church can and will reclaim its originating purpose. Like establishment history generally, the most recent disestablishment of the American university is heavy with irony. The first irony is that in the 1960s, the establishment *defense* of the university against New Left disestablishmentarians was *that the American university had no soul of its own.* The modern research university was explicitly defended as a soulless "multiversity" whose neutral creed was service to all of the various values and interests of a "pluralist democracy."[31] Berkeley's Clark Kerr, lecturing at Harvard, proclaimed that the university was "value free" and morally neutral *because* it embodied and served *all* of American society in all of its diversity. Here enters the second irony: the university, without a soul of its own, defended its authority because it was the veritable dynamo of America's moral, economic, political, and spiritual virtue/power in the world, shaping and channeling the energies of America into the defense of democracy and freedom at home and abroad. The university did not need a distinct soul because *America* was the soul; the university as the seminary authorizing American political theology existed only to nourish, articulate, and preserve that soul. The virtue and power of the national government and its leaders was defended on exactly the same value-free terms as the national university: social scientists declared the end of ideology and proclaimed the birth of a new value free "pluralist" democracy in which all values become interests, all interests get a hearing, and no single interest is permitted to dominate. The "constitution" of freedom is procedural neutrality.[32]

In retrospect these twin defenses appear almost as parodies of intellectual-spiritual complacency and moral-political hypocrisy. And worse, they do not begin to do justice to the operative religious values and the moral and political accomplishments of the establishment being defended.

The ironies of establishment denial are mirrored in the ironies of disestablishment desire. The first irony is that the New Left desperately wanted the university *to regain its soul*, to become reborn as a democratic and confessional Church in order to witness against an imperialist American state and a racist and corrupt society. Their jeremiad was a call to conversion and higher service, a call that requires opposition and sacrifice and suffering. Regarding the Vietnam War and racial segregation, they were singularly successful in this call. Regarding the internal issues of ecclesiology—university governance, curricula reform, and the reconstruction of the disciplines—the critics were much less successful. In these areas many changes occurred—again and again—but the putative victors markedly failed to instill shared ideas and values on which to reconstitute the university as a common enterprise. What resulted instead was twenty-five years of incessant struggle and intense scholarship (the two go together) in the human sciences and the humanities. This is our present condition: a disestablishment that has persisted not by design but by default. During this same period, again mostly by default, the term administrative nihilism is an apt description of university priority setting.

A quarter of a century of intellectual and bureaucratic power struggles in the university, however, have not ended in mutual exhaustion. Here we need Hegel and the logic of agonistic spirits to understand what has happened. Toward the end of the day, there have been clear winners and losers in precisely those areas of intellectual life that are the intellectual and spiritual sources of what Whitman had earlier termed "a sublime and serious Religious Democracy sternly taking command, dissolving the old, sloughing off surfaces, and from its own interior and vital principles, reconstructing, democratizing society."[33]

What are the signs of this emergent spirit and what has it dissolved? Dissolved was the exhausted establishment theology that equated existing American society and practices with the achievement of social justice and democracy. At its least self-conscious extreme, this theology ended by excluding any traces of "church" religion from a serious place in the university and its disciplines, resulting in a kind of complacent "established nonbelief."[34] Against this bland and "value free" secularism, in the human sciences, history, and the humanities, the identification of objectivity and scientific method with American practice and American practice with democratic values was subjected to withering attack. Each of these disciplines are now much more self-conscious, deeper, and more interesting because they were opened up to new values and orientations drawn from cultural, religious, and philosophic traditions long ignored or forgotten. Struggles over matters of the soul (i.e., identity) and intellectual vocation demand a critical spirit and, for all its querulousness and occasional dogmatisms, require recourse to and recovery of historical and moral resources to make coherent arguments. This, in itself, signals a new receptivity for the life of the spirit in the disciplines and in the university. The most overt result is that religion—even some "church" religion—and matters of the spirit now have a much more overt and obvious presence in all of these disciplines, in the humanities generally, and in the life of the university.

I would point first to critiques starting in the 1960s in the social sciences and humanities that have now transformed the moral and political orientations of these disciplines. Not only have many areas of the social sciences jettisoned "behaviorism" and other superficial claims of value neutrality, they have come together under the rubric of the "human sciences" that draw upon the moral sources and resources of philosophy, cultural history, religion, and ethics. This shift has typically resulted in practically ignoring older "departmental" boundaries and creating entirely new communities of scholarship based on the "experiential foundations" of shared moral orientations.[35] The project for which this essay was written is itself an example. And the orientations that are driving these fields are precisely those that take seriously the role of values and commitment in human agency and in human history. Even academic philosophy—at least the academic philosophy that other intellectuals and academics now read—has rediscovered phenomenology and pragmatism. This, too, is a source of religious depth, for both phenomenology and pragmatism place spirit, experience and purpose *inside* thought and therefore inside the history of thought. Social history generally and women's studies in particular—despite their auras of *ressentiment*—have rediscovered spirit as a guide to understanding, infusing history, the humanities and the social sciences with issues of identity and directing reflection on and research into the moral and religious sources of the self.

My own field of moral and political philosophy has attained an energy, reach and attractive power far outside of political science departments even as it has drawn on resources and ideas far outside its earlier boundaries. With these resources, political theorists have launched a many-sided reconsideration of the foundations of liberalism, individualism, and rights. Entailed in this reconsideration is a rediscovery of "civic republicanism" either as an alternative to or as a deeper understanding of liberalism. In seeking to recover more civically-oriented ideas of individuality and citizenship, this enterprise has necessarily drawn upon narratives and ideas excluded from the dominant story of liberalism and modernity that ended in the ahistorical and procedural ideal of the unencumbered self. Put differently, moral and political philosophy is rediscovering the history of religion and power enabling it to write the history of and chart a future for liberalism that includes religious spirit and moral purpose. Here, the writings of Charles Taylor are both exemplary and causal.

Beyond the intellectual fruits of these new enterprises, it must be stressed that all this flowering of "spirit" is taking place in a university that now includes a racial, religious, and ethnic diversity quite inconceivable only twenty years ago. Whether all this intellectual creativity in these conditions will come to constitute the basis of a shared and authoritative political theology remains to be seen. What is the case is that there is now a lot more serious dialogue and much less shouting between and among these communities of scholarship than any time in the past two decades. This is illustrated by the ways in which we now routinely "borrow" from across disciplinary boundaries and moral or religious orientations in our teaching and research. This process, in turn, calls for the construction of common historical narratives to anchor the exchange. That is to say, as more scholars envision common projects of scholarship and study, so they construct common pasts to shape that future. These narratives, moreover, are primarily *national* constructs addressed both to American universities and to *national* audiences of political intellectuals and other opinion leaders. Alasdair MacIntyre's *After Virtue* has reminded us to pay attention to stories, because it is through personal, professional, institutional, and political narratives that one tracks and interprets the growth and decay of spirit.[36] From the 1960s onward, every deep critique of an academic discipline and every creation of new scholarly communities required at some point a story, both to unmask and to show new directions. In America, this is commonly referred to as our attachment to the "jeremiad" and many of our unmaskings take precisely this moralistic and dialectical form. Is there any doubt that these critiques are political-theological? At bottom, these narratives proclaim what *national* covenants have been broken, what *national* commitments have not been kept, what *national* errands have gone unfulfilled in our scholarship and our teaching.

This same proclamation is an invitation to reform and to reclaim the covenant on a higher level.

In the academy, as in the larger society, one might say that spiritually dead establishmentarians are routinely and rightly hoisted on their own petards because those petards were constructed from real spiritual experiences, moral choices, and political commitments now most vividly remembered by their critics. This was as true at the time of the First Great Awakening as it was in the 1960s.[37] At those moments it is the critics who seek to reclaim history because they claim the duty to call America back to its covenantal obligations. It remains a very open question whether all of the resulting spiritual and intellectual agon in the university will ultimately produce a reconstituted political theology for the nation. It is, I think, rapidly producing one in microcosm and for itself that effectively includes participants who in the larger political and cultural world are neither speaking to nor understanding each other. Whether these emerging "master narratives" uniting previously distinct moral orientations and scholarly communities in the humanities and the human sciences will achieve spiritual mastery of—and reconstitute the soul of—the university is the first question. Whether this newly inspirited university can or will reclaim its spiritual role in the larger society is the next one. The best we can do for now is to look for the signs and help call them forth.

NOTES

1. Two recent books that explore this question with historical depth and clear periodizations are Michael Lind, *The Next American Nation: The New Nationalism and the Fourth American Revolution* (New York: Free Press, 1995) and Rogers Smith, *Civic Ideals: Conflicting Ideals of Citizenship in U.S. History* (New Haven: Yale University Press, 1997).

2. Some recent studies of American political thought that recognize and use this distinction are Eldon Eisenach, *The Lost Promise of Progressivism* (Lawrence: University Press of Kansas, 1994); David Greenstone, *The Lincoln Persuasion: Remaking American Liberalism* (Princeton: Princeton University Press, 1993), 48-65; Daniel Walker Howe, *The Political Culture of the American Whigs* (Chicago: University of Chicago Press, 1979); Lawrence F. Kohl, *The Politics of Individualism: Parties and the American Character in the Jacksonian Era* (New York: Oxford University Press, 1989); and Major Wilson, *Space, Time and Freedom: The Quest for Nationality and the Irrepressible Conflict, 1815–1851* (Westport, CT: Greenwood Press, 1974).

3. Two examples illustrate this difficulty. The Jeffersonian and populist historian Vernon Parrington declared it only "a curious irony of fate" that Jonathan Edwards, "a reactionary Calvinist . . . became the intellectual leader of the revolutionaries." *Main Currents in American Thought*, vol. 1 (New York: Harcourt, Brace and Company, 1927), 164. The Catholic theologian, John Courtney Murray, dismisses the normative

status of Roger Williams as "a seventeenth-century Calvinist who somehow had got hold of certain remarkably un-Calvinist ideas on the nature of the political order in its distinction from the church." Quoted from William Lee Miller, *The First Liberty: Religion and the American Republic* (New York: Paragon House, 1988), 219. Here, secular-Jeffersonian and Catholic join hands—and not for the first time—in insisting that no "Protestant" theology, or indeed, any "church" ideas, can be taken as constitutive of American nationality by incorporating them into readings of the Declaration of Independence, the Constitution, or its Bill of Rights. On their reading, religious freedom in America is the product of a secular philosophy that provides the necessary articles of peace in a religiously pluralistic society. For some religious readings of these same documents and events, see, William Lee Miller, *First Liberty*; Sacvan Bercovitch, "How the Puritans Won the American Revolution," *The Massachusetts Review* (Winter, 1976), 597–630; Ruth Bloch, "Religion and Ideological Change in the American Revolution," in Mark Noll, ed., *Religion and American Politics* (New York: Oxford University Press, 1990), 44–61; Eldon Eisenach, "Cultural Politics and Political Thought: The American Revolution Made and Remembered," *American Studies* 20 (1979), 71-98; and John Wilson, "Religion, Government, and Power in the New American Nation," in Noll, *Religion and American Politics*, 77–91.

4. Here the issue is the widely differing perceptions of the Jacksonians and the Whigs and other anti-Jacksonian parties and movements. Because the anti-Jacksonian parties were composed primarily of evangelicals, the related issue is whether this social force and the movements it supported were progressive or reactionary. An excellent discussion of the origin and persistence of National Republican [Whig] ideology is John Gerring, "Party Ideology in America: The National Republican Chapter, 1829–1924," in *Studies in American Political Development*, vol. 11, K. Orren and S. Skowronek, eds. (New York: Cambridge University Press, 1997), 44–108; and Kohl, *Politics of Individualism.*

5. This would explain, too, the consensual language of John Jay and George Washington who seem almost deliberately misleading according to our readings of colonial religious diversity today. Jay, in Federalist Paper #2, claimed that "Providence has been pleased to give this one connected country to one united people . . . professing the same religion"; Washington, in his "Farewell Address," reminded his countrymen that, "with slight shades of difference, you have the same religion." Quoted in Miller, *First Liberty*, 322 and 244.

6. Donald B. Johnson and Kirk H. Porter, eds., *National Party Platforms, 1840-1972* (Urbana: University of Illinois Press, 1975), 1–2.

7. See Robert Handy, "The American Religious Depression, 1925–1935," *Church History* 29 (1960), 3–16 and *A Christian America: Protestant Hopes and Historical Realities* (New York: Oxford University Press, 1971)184–225; and George Marsden, *The Soul of the American University: From Protestant Establishment to Established Nonbelief* (New York: Oxford University Press, 1994) on equating disestablishment per se with the end of "mainline" Protestant hegemony in the 1920s.

8. See Sydney E. Ahlstrom, *A Religious History of the American People* (New Haven: Yale University Press, 1972); Wade Clark Roof and William McKinney, *American Mainline Religion* (New Brunswick: Rutgers University Press, 1987); and

Christopher F. Mooney, *Boundaries Dimly Perceived: Law, Religion, Education, and the Common Good* (Notre Dame: University of Notre Dame Press, 1990) on religious pluralism supplanting a common faith of Judeo-Christian ecumenicism in the 1970s.

9. Put differently, the long-standing tensions in liberal evangelicalism of nineteenth-century Protestantism became, by the 1920s, a divide between "modernism" and "fundamentalism." For the former, biblical revelation was wholly absorbed into and subordinate to social evolutionary and historicist philosophy; for the latter, all post-biblical knowledge had to be grounded in and ratified by biblical inerrancy. See William R. Hutchison, *The Modernist Impulse in American Protestantism* (Durham: Duke University Press, 1992); and George Marsden, *Fundamentalism and American Culture* (New York: Oxford University Press, 1980).

10. It was in the 1950s that God was legislated onto our coinage and into our pledge of allegiance—the same period when public school "release time" programs of religious instruction swept the country. On religious consensus in this period, see William McGuire King, "The Reform Establishment and the Ambiguities of Influence," in William R. Hutchison, ed., *Between the Times: The Travail of the Protestant Establishment in America, 1900–1960* (Cambridge: Cambridge University Press, 1989), 122–140; Martin Marty, *Modern American Religion: Under God, Indivisible, 1940–1960*, vol. 3 (Chicago: University of Chicago Press, 1996); and Mark Silk, *Spiritual Politics: Religion and America Since World War II* (New York: Simon and Schuster, 1988). We should also recall that the very term "post-Protestant" came into common use in the 1960s and was coined to denote not a disestablishment, but a *new public theology* and a new adhesive faith. Roof and McKinney, *American Mainline Religion*, 13.

11. Will Herberg, *Protestant, Catholic, Jew* (Chicago: University of Chicago Press, 1983/1955). See Silk, *Spiritual Politics*, 44–53 on these books and their common theme. This was followed by Harvey Cox, *The Secular City* (New York: MacMillan, 1965), an ambitious but ill-timed attempt to integrate this literature under the banner of a new social gospel. Although Judeo-Christian theology was strongly resisted by many Catholics, they and their most effective leaders were more than willing to accept it through its political and moral agenda, especially in foreign policy.

12. To a lesser extent, this same process was happening within Catholicism. Both the success of their common school system and the creation of the National Catholic War Council in 1917 helped to create an American Catholic identity across the many class, ethnic, regional, and racial lines on the basis of shared American moral and democratic values. This prepared Catholics to join the next religious establishment following World War II; indeed, the fusion of American nationalism and Irish Catholicism was achieved much earlier. John M. Cuddihy, *No Offense: Civil Religion and Protestant Taste* (New York: Seabury Press, 1978); Dorothy Dohen, *Nationalism and American Catholicism* (New York: Sheed and Ward, 1967); and Robert Handy, *Undermined Establishment: Church-State Relations in America, 1880–1920* (Princeton: Princeton University Press, 1991), 171–175.

13. For examples in university social science textbooks, see Eisenach, *Lost Promise of Progressivism*, 57–61 and 68–70; and see John Bascom, *Sociology* (New York: G. P. Putnam's Sons, 1898); and Josiah Strong, *The New World Religion* (New York: Doubleday, Page, and Co., 1915).

14. Dohen, *Nationalism and American Catholicism*; Charles Morris, *American Catholic* (New York: Times Books, Random House, 1997).

15. See Sacvan Bercovitch, "How the Puritans Won the American Revolution," on the theological structure in George Bancroft's histories of America.

16. Good examples of these three tenets are found in Josiah Strong, *New World Religion*; and Bascom, *Sociology*. Both books draw heavily on other writers and summarize the liberal and modernist movements in Protestant theology generally. And see Eisenach, *Lost Promise of Progressivism*, on Samuel Zane Batten, *The New Citizenship: Christian Character in its Biblical Ideals, Sources, and Relations* (Philadelphia: Union Press, 1898) and other clergymen. The definitive work here is Hutchison, *The Modernist Impulse*. A summary similar to mine is found in John E. Smylie, "National Ethos and the Church," *Theology Today* 20 (1963), 313–14, and used by Sidney E. Mead, *The Nation with the Soul of a Church* (New York: Harper and Row, 1975), 73. These tenets were not the sole preserve of liberal evangelicalism. In the words of Archbishop John Ireland at the turn of the century, "We cannot but believe that a singular mission is assigned to America, glorious for itself and beneficent to the whole race. . . . With our hopes are bound up the hopes of the millions of the earth. The Church triumphing in America, Catholic truth will travel on the wings of American influence, and encircle the universe." Quoted in Dohen, *Nationalism and American Catholicism*, 109. The definitive hermeneutical analysis of political theology is Oliver O'Donovan, *The Desire of the Nations: Rediscovering the Roots of Political Theology* (New York: Cambridge University Press, 1996).

17. Ronald G. Walters, *The Antislavery Appeal: American Abolitionism after 1830* (Baltimore: Johns Hopkins University Press, 1977).

18. Quoted in Eisenach, *Lost Promise of Progressivism*, 130–131. Earlier, Batten echoed John Dewey and most other Progressive intellectuals of this time in holding that democracy "is less a form of government than a confession of faith; it is the confession of human brotherhood" (Batten, 1898, *The New Citizenship*, 253). See also Eisenach, *Lost Promise*, 62, for others making this same argument.

19. There are many deep differences between pre- and post-Civil War establishment theology. Compare, for example, Daniel Walker Howe, "Religion and Politics in the Antebellum North," 121–145, to Robert Handy, "Protestant Theological Tensions and Political Styles in the Progressive Period," 281–301, both in Noll, ed., *Religion and American Politics*; and Gerring, "Party Ideology in America."

20. Hutchison, *Modernist Impulse*, is the definitive work in this area, but also see Eisenach, *Lost Promise*; Daniel Walker Howe, *The Unitarian Conscience: Harvard Moral Philosophy, 1805–1861* (Cambridge: Harvard University Press, 1970); Bruce Kuklick, *Churchmen and Philosophers: From Jonathan Edwards to John Dewey* (New Haven: Yale University Press); and Louise Stevenson, *Scholarly Means to Evangelical Ends: The New Haven Scholars and the Transformation of Higher Learning in America, 1830–1890* (Baltimore: Johns Hopkins University Press, 1986) for the role of this theology in broader reaches of American intellectual life. For these same features in English theology and philosophy in the nineteenth century, see Howard Murphy, "The Ethical Revolt against Christian Orthodoxy in Early Victorian England," 60 *American Historical Review* (1955), 800–817; and the splendid collection in Richard Helmstadter and Bernard Lightman, eds., *Victorian Faith in Crisis: Essays on*

Continuity and Change in Nineteenth-Century Religious Belief (Stanford: Stanford University Press, 1990).

21. For biographical sketches of nineteen such Progressive academics and reform intellectuals, see Eisenach, *Lost Promise of Progressivism*, 31–47. Yale was the center of liberal evangelical theology in the mid-nineteenth century and produced the founding presidents of three major new national universities: Andrew Dickson White of Cornell, Daniel Coit Gilman of Johns Hopkins, and William Rainey Harper of Chicago. John Bascom, who straddles the transition from churchman to academic philosopher and social scientist, illustrates this integrative reach; G.P. Putnam's Sons published 14 of his books, whose titles include, aesthetics, rhetoric, comparative psychology, English literature, philosophy of religion, natural theology, political economy, ethics, sociology, evolution and religion, historical interpretation of philosophy, and, inspiriting them all, *The Words of Christ as Principles of Personal and Social Growth*. A graduate of Andover Seminary (a center of German historical scholarship), Bascom was president of the University of Wisconsin, 1874–87, and professor at Williams College, 1891–1903.

22. Jews, for example, were still fighting Sunday closing laws in the 1950s—as if this were of major communal importance in the face of a combined liberal and conservative anti-communism that had far deeper and more permanent effects on Jewish identity and standing in America. On the explanatory contradictions and resort to ad hoc argument in trying to measure Jewish religious freedom and equality on these formal-legal scales across time, see Naomi Cohen, *Jews in Christian America: The Pursuit of Religious Equality* (New York: Oxford University Press, 1992).

23. Quoted in Eldon Eisenach, "Reconstituting the Study of American Political Thought in a Regime Perspective," in *Studies in American Political Development*, vol.4, K. Orren and S. Skowronek, eds. (New Haven: Yale University Press, 1990), 186 and 210. Tocqueville's oft-repeated quotation reads, "the woof of time is every instant broken and the track of generations effaced. Those who went before are soon forgotten; of those who will come after, no one has any idea: the interest of man is confined to those in close propinquity to himself" (ibid., 186n.).

24. This is convincingly argued by Steven D. Smith, *Foreordained Failure: The Quest for a Constitutional Principle of Religious Freedom* (New York: Oxford University Press, 1995).

25. There is no better example of this than Ann Douglas, *The Feminization of American Culture* (New York: Doubleday, 1988).

26. Perhaps the best example, at all levels of national life, is American Mormonism.

27. The head of the Department of Applied Christianity at Grinnell [Iowa] College from 1903–1941 was George Steiner, a Slovakian Jew with a Ph.D. from Heidelberg and a divinity degree from Oberlin. His core belief was the social gospel interpreted to mean that only when Christ is freed from historic Christianity to become truly universal will the messiah have finally come: "When he emerges from the tangle of Greek philosophy, Roman legalism and Byzantine traditionalism—when 'in deed and in truth' he becomes the Gentile's Messiah, He will also become the Messiah of the Jew." Discussed in Eldon Eisenach, "Bookends: Seven Stories Excised from the *Lost Promise of Progressivism*, in *Studies in American Political Development*, vol. 10, K. Orren and S. Skowronek, eds., (New York: Cambridge University Press, 1996), 175–176.

28. Marsden, *Soul of the American University*, 429–440.

29. Quoted in Marsden, *Soul of the American University*, 249–250. Both Dewey and Harper were democratic Fichte's, and rightly so, for both had been steeped in Fichtean and Hegelian ideas of the university by their many German-trained teachers.

30. "My Country, Tis of Thee," fourth stanza, Samuel F. Smith (1808–1895).

31. Clark Kerr, *The Uses of the University* (Cambridge: Harvard University Press, 1963).

32. Robert Dahl, *Pluralist Democracy in the United States* (Chicago: Rand McNally, 1967); and see Richard Neustadt, *Presidential Power: The Politics of Leadership with Reflections on Johnson and Nixon* (New York: Wiley, 1976), on the modern presidency as a morally neutral integrator of all major social interests.

33. Walt Whitman, "Democratic Vistas," in *Leaves of Grass* (New York: Holt, Rinehart and Winston, 1955), 531.

34. Marsden, subtitle of *Soul of the American University.*

35. A good discussion of this dynamic is William Scott Green, "Religion Within the Limits," in *Academe* 82, no. 6 (Bulletin of the American Association of University Professors, 1996), 24-28.

36. Alasdair MacIntyre, *After Virtue* (South Bend: University of Notre Dame Press, 1984). And see the excellent collection of writings on this theme in Lewis P. Hinchman and Sandra K. Hinchman, eds., *Memory, Identity, Community: The Idea of Narrative in the Human Sciences* (Albany: State University of New York Press, 1997).

37. Contrast, for example, the tone and spirit of Clark Kerr's *The Uses of the University* to Robert Paul Wolff's rejoinder, *The Ideal of the University* (Boston: Beacon Press, 1969).

8

How Should We Talk?

Jean Bethke Elshtain

This is America. So we needn't worry about theocracy—this despite the hyperbole one encounters from time to time in the mainstream media that sees us advancing steadily toward our own version of such, usually spearheaded by that ever-present monolithic threat, "the Christian right." Although there is no realistic chance of anything remotely approaching the establishment of religion as an enshrined constitutional order in America, this possibility, skulking somehow in the interstices of the order (if we are to believe the alarmists) often frames the discussion that follows. That is, the threat from religion, or perhaps more accurately, from a religion, cannot be dismissed lightly, we are told. It follows that we are all in danger of having Pat Robertson or Jerry Falwell or someone else tell us how we are to live our lives. It follows further that we must remain forever vigilant against the encroachment of this threat. So we effect, in constitutional terms, a bright line that separates church and state. But even more, that bright line now extends to encompass *religion* all-encompassingly and *politics*, similarly represented as the embodiment of everything religion somehow threatens if the chasm between the two is not vigilantly maintained.

Given the construction of this threat, the political solution increasingly got posed, in our (relatively) recent past, as a legal one tied to various theoretical propositions. The details of the legal situation I leave to constitutional lawyers. Suffice it to say that the ardent separationists held sway for a sustained period of time. The Supreme Court, in *Agostini v. Felton* (June 23,

1997), appeared to signal a mild turning away from such peculiar holdings as the one that prompted the challenge and which dictated that federally funded programs providing supplemental, remedial instruction to disadvantaged children could not be administered by "sectarian schools" without violating the establishment clause. This had led to the spectacle of mobile units perched outside parochial and other religious schools as children, even children with severe disabilities, in weather fair or foul, were hauled out of the school building and into these units in order to receive instruction.[1] The Court (5-4) no longer believes that the mere physical placement of public employees on parochial school grounds "inevitably results in the impermissible effect of state-sponsored indoctrination or constitutions a symbolic union between government and religion."[2]

Is this a shot across the bow signaling a new day in church-state adjudication? Hard to say. But it does invite critical reflection on the emergence of a kind of *liberal monism*, by which I mean the view that all institutions internal to a democratic society must conform to a single authority principle, a single standard of what counts as reason and deliberation, and a single vocabulary of political discussion. Democracy is defined in such a way that religion must be kept marginalized. Reason is defined in such a way that faith is automatically discounted as something else, whether irrationalism or a peculiar atavism, or a form of private solace that should be utterly privatized. Authority is defined in such a way that only something akin to "one person, one vote" models of representation and acquiescence in the outcome of such representation passes muster as a legitimate, hence allowable, form of authority in a democratic society. Those who adhere to this position, or some version of it, begin with the menace of establishment and the spectre of advancing hordes of priests or televangelists as backdrop. Then they go on to construct their bright line forms of defense. This powerful school, associated with the work of John Rawls but not he alone, holds that when persons religious enter the public sphere they are obliged to do so in a specifically secular civic idiom shorn of any explicit reference to religious commitment and belief. I will not rehearse this position yet again. It has been done over and over again, to my mind to the point of tedium. I will, instead, simply assume this *liberal monist* position as backdrop and move on.

There have been several religious responses to *liberal monism*, positions much underrepresented in the academy but quite visible in the civic world at large. The first holds that the fullness of religious belief, commitment, and witness must enter the public sphere and precisely on religious terms. This has nothing to do with the legal establishment of religion. It has to do, rather, with the conviction that religion is undermined if persons with religious commitment are compelled to engage in *any translation* of these commitments into a civic idiom. Let us call this *full bore* Christian politics. The Christian Right would enter here, in part, although there are many distinctions between fundamentalists, pentecostalists, and evangelicals that I cannot now spell out. But I would like to put one distinction on the table before moving on. It is altogether meet and right for persons of faith to speak from that faith at its fullest in moments of unusual challenge or crisis. In other words, while those who push for an undiluted "Christian politics" seek Christian saturation of ordinary, everyday political discourse and action, the figures I have in mind responded to extraordinary situations from the fullness of religious commitment. Thus: No one demanded that Martin Luther King drop any and all references to the Prophet Amos in his "I Have a Dream" speech. No one demanded that the Berrigan brothers refuse to cite Scripture in advancing their pacifist anti-Vietnam war cause. (Those who disagreed with the Berrigans did so on political grounds or because they did not believe Scripture called everyone who claimed to take Scripture seriously to a Berrigan-like witness.) No one told John Brown he was a whacked-out extremist *because* he cited Scripture: he was an extremist who also cited Scripture. The problem was not the Scripture, it was Brown's extreme response to slavery, a response supported (so he claimed) in Scripture.

Note that none of these prophetic positions and witnesses constitute (as liberal monists seem to claim or to believe) critically unassailable positions. Neither King nor Berrigan (I am less sure about Brown) wanted to envelop the entire universe of a pluralistic democratic society with a strong, doctrinal blanket of normativity. Discussion always remains open when people turn to religion with a prophetic intent in mind. Denunciation of a given intolerable situation begins the argument; it doesn't end it, as the liberal monists seem to believe. What Abraham Lincoln drew from Scripture was not the same as John Brown's message. What a religiously based defense of race separation drew from Scripture was *certainly* not what Dr. King did.[3]

Thus we find that even the ostensibly simple case of religion being represented fully and on religion's terms in the public square does not create a situation beyond discourse and dispute. There are some in our midst whose sense of Christian politics is that the positions they advance from a doctrinal stance are, or ought to be seen as, nigh unassailable civically because these are directly Biblically enjoined and inspired. But this is not possible in a pluralistic civic world, in part because many other persons of religious commitment, speaking from the fullness of *their* beliefs, will offer challenge. The prophetic citizen-activists I have noted, then, do not advance a position of epistemological incorrigibility. As well, they tacitly retreat from the conviction that Christian politics at its fullest is everyday, garden variety politics: that the full force of Christian witness must be brought to bear on *every public policy question*. Thus, there should be a Christian view of the balanced budget as there is a Christian view of euthanasia or of war. This is not the position of democratic prophets who reserve their Christian witness at its most intense and uncompromising to situations of unusual civic moment and moral challenge, like slavery, unjust wars, segregation. But it is the view of many lumped together as Christian Right or, less frequently, as Christian Left.[4]

As if this weren't already complicated enough, a strong alternative both to *liberal monism* and to *full bore Christian politics* is that most ably represented by the work of Stanley Hauerwas. Here the critical worry is that when religion—specifically, Christianity—engages politics it is bound to do so on the world's terms, especially in a liberal age. Having accepted a lousy deal by signing on with the liberal social contract and accepting civic peace *on the world's terms*, the Church ceases to be Church. The central worry is not what happens to politics but what happens to Christianity. If one version of Christian politics veers towards a kind of *integralist* posture in which church and politics are drawn into a very tight relationship, not theocracy but a kissing cousin, the version here sketched is a kind of *radical dualism*: the church must, above all, be church. And if the world wants to come to religion's understanding, fine, but that isn't religion's primary concern. The danger with liberal monism is presented by Hauerwas and others as a nigh-overweening danger, one that has yielded an odd kind of liberationist posture in which what is liberated is not persons but politics, wrenched free from any and all religious authority, argument, and constraint. The deep, and it seems to me, correct insight of the dualist posture that effects a strong severance of Christian from rights-based liberalism, is that much of the story of mainline Protestantism in America this century has been that of churches veering more and more toward the monist position, thereby embracing the world on its terms rather than the Church's terms. That Christian thinkers must present a strong ecclesiological understanding also seems to me essential and this is an important dimension of the dualist position.

But does insisting on a strong ecclesiology mean that one is by definition drawn into the orbit of the dualist position? I shall argue no. Nonetheless, we should be wary, as Hauerwas has so often and so eloquently insisted, of the threats posed to the practice of religion and the religion of practitioners from the side of an all-encompassing social or civic ideology (liberalism, Americanism, etc.) If the two are merged, what will give way in cases of dispute is most often religious belief or moral command rather than political interest. So we are forewarned. How can we best forearm ourselves? The remainder of the paper will be devoted to a discursive exploration of this matter. Let me put my cards on the table in a rough and ready way before moving to complexify matters considerably. What I shall be aiming for is not so much an amalgam of the integralist or dualist postures (as I have tagged them, borrowing vocabulary in general use) but, rather, a third position that draws insights from the other positions or tendencies without seeking a compromise between them. I am interested in another way to situate the discussion, one that isn't framed by advancing as the peril an extreme version of the position one aims to counter. What I propose, in brief, is a way to distinguish between different dimensions of the public sphere so that we can offer a nuanced assessment of the way religion enters civic discourse depending upon the nature of the issues involved—What are the stakes?—and depending on what arenas or spheres of human social existence are affected and how—Who are the key players? How should those implicated in any given instance address the issues at stake and express their concerns to their co-religionists and, as well, to their fellow citizens?

Tertullian put the philosophical matter in the second century when he queried: "What has Jerusalem to do with Athens, the Church with the Academy?" But the more salient question, also posed by early Christian fathers, was "What has Christ to do with Caesar?" One response was to "spoil the Egyptians," that is, to cull from the mixed glories of the ancient world those contributions, ideas, and cultural artifacts that could best serve the new Christian dispensation. This was not so easy, whether philosophically or politically. Given that Christ would have us live in the world but not be of it, it follows, on this view, that an engagement with the Empire (and we are always in the Empire), poses as least as much threat as promise. The threat is that marked by the camp I tagged dualist, namely, that in most engagements with the world, if the intent is to reshape the world at large in some fundamental way, the world wins. Better by far, then, to be truly the Church and in that way to offer what the current Pope calls a "sign of contradiction."[5]

There is no easy tag or name for the position I will sketch and that I hinted at above in my discussion of King, the Berrigans, and John Brown. Please note that a *fully* fleshed out position requires what I am in no position to provide here, namely, an explicit ecclesiology that begins with an anthropology, an understanding of the human person and of what it means to live *in communio.* The anthropology I can articulate briefly; the ecclesiology must await another day. This anthropology is Christologically centered and analogically driven and it exists in tension with, if not outright opposition to, the anthropological presuppositions that underwrite liberal contractarianism. I don't want to overdo this. There is a *social liberalism* that can be drawn into a much closer relationship with Christian anthropology than the one I am about to sketch. But the dominant anthropology sees us as essentially free standing, self-possessing, self-defining, self-naming creatures. We relate to others to the extent it seems expedient, prudential, part of self-interest rightly understood. Of course, there is love and family commitment but the tendency is either to bracket this as the exception that proves the rule or to bring the family, too, under the wings of an anthropology that distorts it profoundly. And does the same to friendship and many other, if not all, human relations.[6]

What are the stakes? Who are the players? Is the heart of Christian anthropology at issue? Are the players a small group of contesting elites or is the entire society, including its most defenseless members, also implicated? Most often the engagement of Christianity with power is not so sharp edged as, for example, was the Catholic Church's contestation against authoritarian communism in pre-1989 Poland, certainly not in a democratic society. Most of the time the engagement of Christianity with politics is a series of half-advances and half-retreats. In the American democracy, the process of assessing "what Christ has to do with Caesar" is even trickier than in other modern industrial societies, for several reasons. An extraordinary number of Americans profess belief in God and in personal immortality; indeed, the figures on America's religious enthusiasm stagger observers from other societies as well as our most strenuous secularists with some 95 percent of Americans professing belief in God and 70 percent claiming membership in a church or synagogue. Second, the American democracy from the beginning was premised on the enactment of projects that were a complex intermingling of religious and political imperatives. The majority of Americans were religious seekers and believers who saw in communal liberty the freedom to *be* religious, rather than freedom from religion. It is, therefore, not surprising that such a huge chunk of American juridical life has been devoted to sorting out the inaptly named church-state debate. In a less "churched" society this would be a far less salient issue.

Let us assume that Christianity's task is not primarily to underwrite a politics external to itself, including democratic politics.[7] That having been said, it seems to me undeniably the case that Christians, and the Church, unavoidably *must* engage politics. The question, as I've already indicated, is the nature of that encounter. Certainly, there is no single right way to do this. It is important, at times, for Christian identity to be made manifest in as clear-cut a manner as possible so that there can be little doubt about where the Christian stands, or ought to, if he or she is to be called by the name "Christian." But such moments will likely be rare in a democratic society, one in which the good, the bad, and the ugly are often commingled in dizzyingly complex ways. For example: is it good to stop people from consuming huge amounts of liquor? Certainly. Excessive alcohol intake violates the integrity of the body; it wounds others and breaks relationships; it even threatens the lives of persons if driving is involved, and so on. Does this mean one must follow the Women's Christian Temperance Union of late nineteenth and early twentieth century fame and demand a constitutional amendment to compel prohibition? Not necessarily, although the good ladies of the WCTU believed it did. But prudential considerations must enter as well. Will such a political intervention likely do more harm than good? What is the good it will do by contrast to the harm it might engender? In the case of prohibition, we have a historic case study ready-to-hand and it undermines the strict prohibitionist case.

When and where the issues calling for a sharp, decisive break of Christianity with secular power appear, politics as usual is likely to have already disappeared. This was the claim of the Confessing Church at the time of the Barmen Declaration, for example. The Nazi state had overstepped its legitimate mandate. The time had come, in Dietrich Bonhoeffer's words, to put a spoke in the wheel. That Christian voice should emerge clearly and decisively. Here one is reminded of Albert Camus's powerful essay, "The Unbeliever and the Christian," a statement made at the Dominican Monastery of Latour-maubourg in 1948. Camus insisted that the Christian has many obligations and that, in fact, what the world needs most today is "Christians who remain Christians."[8] Camus continues that he does not like priests "who are anticlerical" any more than philosophies that are "ashamed of themselves. . . . What the world expects of Christians is that Christians should voice their condemnation in such a way that never a doubt, never the slightest doubt, could rise in the heart of the simplest man. That they should get away from abstraction and confront the blood-stained face history has taken on today."[9] After Camus poses the question—What can Christians do for us?—the us in this case being unbelievers, the answer emerges. First, to abandon pronouncing maledictions and, second, to "reduce the number of tortured children. Perhaps we cannot prevent this world from being a world in which children are tortured." But, he asks his audience of monks, "If you don't help us, who else in the world can help us do this?"[10] Interestingly, then, Camus would have Christians be Christians, but he derives from this the insistence that Christians must engage a world in which children will always be tortured. Their task—their political task—must be to work to lessen the frequency and the acceptance of this horror.

Surely the assessment that American society faces such a horror lies behind much of the "extreme" rhetoric from the pro-life side in the abortion debate. The state at its highest level having thrown all its weight to one side only, that tagged "pro-choice," those called to anti-abortion witness, or at least many thus called, believe they are dealing with an issue absent any moral ambiguity, one that indeed presents a harsh and terrible "choice" that should not even be dignified with the language of "choice." (Or the view is that the language of choice is by now so deeply corrupt it can be accorded no automatic legitimacy, this despite the fact that the notion of agentic, choosing persons—the free will question—is radically inexplicable minus a Christian backdrop. But that is another discussion.) I think there is considerable merit in stressing the moral weightiness of the stakes involved in the abortion debate and a cluster of others, among them euthanasia, cloning, some aspects of reproductive technology and the like. But, unlike at least some on the pro-life side, I do not believe this dictates a series of political interventions so clearly: the marching orders are not attached to the moral mandate with the political equivalent of super-glue. Abortion would certainly be a candidate—likely the *only* candidate in American society at present—for an issue of the moral moment of the sort that makes defensible and intelligible an unequivocal position.[11] Still, the "abortion option" is not the same as fighting Nazism, so even here Camus's hope, one that calls for Christians to be Christians, that is, faithful to their own identity and, from that identity, to reach out to the world in a way that promotes clarity rather than opacity on moral questions; in a way that is open-hearted and compassionate yet, if needs be, severe, gets tangled up in a series of ethical and pragmatic considerations.

Let's explore this a bit further by assuming that, in a democratic society, Christians are obliged to continue the argument, to engage in dialogue even with those with whom they differ radically. Let us further assume that one has assessed a situation and determined that the heart of the matter—persons *in communio*, Christian anthropology—is at stake in the most dramatic way: Who is worthy of moral consideration? Who is inside or outside the boundary of moral concern? Further, one has determined that it is a *common good* question, that the well-being of the entire society is up for grabs—this is not a contest to divvy up goodies between a small number of already powerful groups. How does one proceed? How should we talk? First, we should avoid maledictions. We are dealing with fellow citizens, not enemies. That many of our fellow citizens may be deeply misguided and a few actually pernicious is certainly possible. But the space for disputation remains open; hence, one must assume that even those one finds most resistant to the message one is advancing must be considered candidates for persuasion. This leads to the second clear task: to offer reasons from clear religious commitment to those who claim no such commitment and who may even be hostile to Christian reason-giving if this is done in and through what gets called "doctrinal" language. One's reason-giving might take the form of pointing out, for starters, that the commitment we all share to democracy rests, in large part, on Biblically grounded norms and, moreover, that the entire human rights armamentarium of modernity is simply inexplicable, nigh unthinkable, minus Christianity's commitment to the dignity and worth of human persons. If Christians are committed to ontological equality and dignity, human rights is the political face that equality and dignity present to us in late modernity.

An irony, then, in how we should talk in *this* democratic society is that a society most solidly associated with both equality and liberty may invest itself in flawed interpretations of an order of magnitude that undermine these commitments over the long run. But this is a case that must be made and not merely assumed. It begins by refusing to grant sacral status to democracy itself. The voice of the people is not necessarily the voice of God. As John Paul II argues in the recent encyclical, "Evangelium Vitae,"

> democracy cannot be idolized to the point of making it a substitute for morality or a panacea for immorality. Fundamentally, democracy is a "system" and, as such, is a means and not an end. Its "moral value" is not automatic, but depends on conformity to the moral law to which it, like every form of human behavior, must be subject: In other words, its morality depends on the morality of the ends

which it pursues and of the means which it employs. . . . The value of democracy stands or falls with the values which it embodies and promotes. Of course, values such as the dignity of every human person, respect for inviolable and inalienable human rights, and the adoption of the "common good" as the end and criterion regulating political life are certainly fundamental and not to be ignored.[12]

John Paul continues that these values—the common good, or a version of egalitarianism, inviolable human rights, human dignity—"cannot be provisional and changeable . . . opinions," but derive from the "acknowledgment of an objective moral law . . . written in the human heart, the obligatory reference point for civil law itself."[13] Without this grounding, he continues, "not even democracy is capable of ensuring a stable peace, especially since peace which is not built on the values of the dignity of every individual, and of solidarity between all people, frequently proves to be illusory."[14]

So: in giving reasons for opposing the current regime of abortion on demand, one would begin with the anthropological issues, including an affirmation of a notion of human rights as the way in which modernity expresses a commitment to human dignity. It follows that, to the extent that we translate everything we want into a right, we vulgarize rights. We are obliged not to conflate rights with mere wants and preferences, as our dominant politics currently does. This is a point that should be made ongoingly and routinely. But the full display of this point, including the underlying anthropological presuppositions, itself comes into play *only* in the most strenuous circumstances and where the toughest—the highest stake—cases are concerned. So the way one talks in, say, a debate about welfare reform should bring a portion of the full panoply to bear. But when the matter at hand is abortion or euthanasia or cloning or other matters going to the heart of what it means to affirm the dignity of persons, then fuller reason-giving is required. And note that it will and must be reason-giving of the sort liberal monism would rule out of court (or have a court rule out of court!) and, as well, that a full bore Christian politics would render supererogatory as politics in all its aspects and features, on this view, must reflect, on each and every issue, a set of authoritative religious commitments. Thus, in Christian politics (whether of the right or the left) the distinctions between the high stakes issues and those subject to far more pragmatic considerations—workfare is not the same issue as abortion or euthanasia—are hopelessly muddled.

The position I am working toward, even as it frames *all* political discussion with Christian anthropological presuppositions, can advance or retreat from full-fledged reason-giving depending on an assessment of the stakes and the nature of the players: is this a common good issue undeniably? My position also clears the way for some strong language but used sparingly.[15] Some might counter that the strong reactions, responses, and judgments I am clearing space for—couched precisely in a full display of religious reason-giving—fails the test of democratic dialogue or conversation. Let's drop conversation as too tepid for starters. Democracy is not about conversation: that is what happens at cocktail parties. But democracy *is* about dialogue and debate. What I aim for is a restoration of authentic dialogue rather than generic, low-grade substitutes. We have lost a robust understanding of dialogue in the present moment. Thus, we have come to think of dialogue in quasi-therapeutic terms, meaning that people should never disagree fundamentally with one another but should, instead, "feel" one another's pain to the point of terminal and indiscriminate empathy. Authentic dialogue, however, is far more than interpersonal exchange. It requires, at the outset, a belief that there is some *truth to the matter*; that better and worse arguments can be assessed; that while all persons are of equal dignity not all positions and ideas are equally compelling, justifiable, or decent. "Being real" or sincere is not the same as having good reasons. So dialogue does not disallow strenuous argument that involves strong discernments, *pace* the sublimination of dialogue into therapeutic "validation" or mere conversation.

Let me add a final, few points based upon a reading of Oliver O'Donovan's extraordinary book, *The Desire of the Nations. Rediscovering the Roots of Political Theology.*[16] O'Donovan's is a project best encompassed under the rubric of *ressourcement*, or a return to the wellsprings of the present, a rediscovery and reappropriation of the full history of wisdom, Judaeo-Christian wisdom specifically. This return, if it is sufficiently nuanced, actually promotes what is usually counterposed to it, namely, *aggiornamento*, opening the windows to fresh breezes. Although the two go together we, in late modernity, strive mightily to drive them apart. In returning to the wellsprings, O'Donovan shows the expansive view we are then afforded.

O'Donovan reminds us of just "how striking" the political vocabulary of the Scriptures is, dotted with words like king, kingdom, judge, power, and so on. There are rulers, peoples, narratives of collective deliverance or, as we would now say, liberation. As he puts it: "The question is, what does this paradoxical redeployment of political description, with a Virgin at its centre and heaven at its perimeter, intend to achieve? Is it meant to be the start of a new mode of political thinking? Or is it, on the contrary, a stratagem for overwhelming politics with religion, shrewdly converting the language of politics into a grand religious metaphor?"[17] He opts for the former—the new mode of thinking—rather than the latter, although it isn't so easy to tease the two apart. Political theology, on O'Donovan's view, "does not suppose a literal synonymy between the political vocabulary of salvation and the secular use of the same political terms. It postulates an analogy . . . between the acts of God and human acts, both of them taking place within one public history which is the theatre of God's saving purposes and mankind's social undertakings."[18] O'Donovan reinstates the essential "politicalness" of Scripture, including Jesus's ministry, demonstrating convincingly that one cannot effect a bright line between religion and politics: too much of the same territory has been claimed by each and in an analogous vocabulary.

Going against the currents of the time which see in the presence of authority itself an unacceptable imposition, O'Donovan demonstrates that legitimate political authority "confers freedom" rather than "taking it away."[19] This is a point made eloquently by a number of vital thinkers, including the late Hannah Arendt, but it bears repeating to counter the antinomianism of our age. Another example of the challenge O'Donovan presents lies in his resolute deconstruction of a perduring, even foundational, pair of terms structuring the tradition of political thought, namely, the dilemma of the "one and the many." O'Donovan argues that this is a misunderstanding, plain and simple, born of a "Neoplatonic conception of metaphysical tension." But "unity and diversity," he argues, are not locked in ineradicable tension *if* we follow Scripture; indeed, plurality, "so far from being a diminution of the divine autarky, is its fullest demonstration."[20] This, of course, throws many of the presuppositions from which liberal monism begins into complete disarray by seeing unity and diversity, plurality and commonality, not as opposites but as constituent features of one another—thereby resituating the religion-politics debate and church-state conundrum.

By the time O'Donovan gets to the sixteenth century and the emergence of legal-constitutionalism, he finds, not a move away from Christendom, but the expression of its very "essence" in many respects. The difference between the Christendom understanding and that of social-contractarian popular-will construals, is that absolutism in the latter instance grows ever more unchecked by any other sovereignty. The idea of "universal Natural Law" collapses and is replaced by "nationalistic positivism."[21] The results of this collapse we know all-too-well. So when we say, as we are wont to do these days, that Christendom has ended, that, indeed, we live in a "post-Christian" society, what are we talking about? "Our contemporaries no longer think that the rulers of the earth owe service to the rule of Christ," undeniably so.[22] But to whom, then, is service owed? The usual formulae—like separation of church and state—don't take us very far. What we wind up with is an amorphous, headless entity called "society," an entity shorn increasingly of a political vocabulary—not just the political vocabulary of "the Kingdom" but a political vocabulary strong enough in its own right and clear enough about its ontological indebtedness to sustain a politics of human respect and decency. O'Donovan reminds us that much of what we most cherish about our society at its best is deeply indebted to the Hebrew and Christian traditions and he raises an unsettling question: How long before the stream runs dry and we are left only with a dry bed, all pebbles, dirt and debris absent the clear running waters of replenishment and renewal?

NOTES

1. Having tried to describe this phenomenon, and others, to audiences in South Africa recently, I encountered utter bewilderment. What on earth did the Court and the disestablishment extremists think they were accomplishing by this sort of thing? Good question.

2. *Agonistini vs. Felton, Origins* (CNS Documentary Service, July 3, 1997, vol. 27, no. 7), p. 97.

3. Need I add that I think those who defend racial segregation on Scriptural grounds are committing a hermeneutic travesty, to put it mildly. My point here is not to separate better from worse interpretations but, rather, to make the simple point that interpretation is *always* at issue.

4. Just a note to the reader. I am here laying down a marker that will be taken up more fully when I sketch out an alternative to "Christian politics."

5. Mind you, I am not here associating the Pope with the dualist position as it isn't one he shares. Indeed, I will draw him in as one vital proponent of the view I shall endorse.

6. My book, *Public Man, Private Woman: Women in Social and Political Thought* (2nd Edition; Princeton: Princeton University Press, 1994,) goes over this terrain although I talk about contrasting accounts of "human nature" rather than "anthropology." But it is basically the same topic.

7. This, of course, assumes that the Church itself constitutes a politics. I have tended to be somewhat wary of this argument given the reigning definition of politics among us as a interest-maximizing process of power aggregation. But I am now persuaded that the Church does indeed embody a politics—it is just that it is a politics much at odds with the constitutive proceduralisms of constitutional republics and even more jarring if what is at stake is twentieth century totalitarian or authoritarian societies—with these the Church can or ought not "make any peace."

8. This essay appears in the collection *Resistance, Rebellion and Death* (New York: Alfred A. Knopf, 1961, pp. 69–74), p. 70.

9. *Ibid.*, pp. 70–71.

10. *Ibid.*, p. 73.

11. I say the "only" candidate because the state, as embodied in the rule of law at its very highest level, has sanctioned the nearly unrestricted reign of a practice that involves a "solemn affirmation of human rights and their tragic denial in practice," in the words of John Paul II. Or it does so if one accords the fetus a human status. Actually, "accords" isn't the right word here. Better: if one acknowledges the fetus's human status. It is pressing that acknowledgment that should lie at the heart of prolife politics.

12. *Origins* (April 6, 1995, vol. 24, no. 42), p. 714.

13. *Ibid.*

14. *Ibid.*

15. To claim that strong language—e.g., "judicial usurpation"—is defensible in argumentation about first and last things doesn't mean that I find it the best way to proceed. It does seem to me an entirely legitimate way to proceed as it leaves open space for counter-argument.

16. Cambridge: Cambridge University Press, 1996.

17. *Ibid.*, p. 1.

18. *Ibid.*, p. 2.

19. *Ibid.*, p. 127.

20. *Ibid.*, p. 177.

21. *Ibid.*, p. 241.

22. *Ibid.*, p. 244

9

Christians and Political Self-Restraint: The Controversy over Same-Sex Marriage

Michael J. Perry

Imagine a legislator who must decide whether to vote to outlaw, or otherwise disfavor, particular conduct. She wonders whether she should put any weight on her religiously based belief that the conduct is immoral; indeed, she worries that it might not be appropriate for her to rely on her religiously based moral belief. Elsewhere I have asked whether either the morality of liberal democracy counsels her, in deciding whether to disfavor the conduct, not to rely on her religiously based belief that the conduct is immoral.[1] In this essay, I pursue a different but complementary inquiry; I explore the possibility that her own religious tradition counsels her to be wary, in some if not all circumstances, about relying on her religiously based belief that the conduct is immoral. For purposes of the inquiry to which I referred in the sentence before last, the morality of liberal democracy was paramount. But for purposes of the inquiry in this essay, a believer's own religious tradition is paramount. In deciding whether she should forgo or at least limit reliance on her religiously based belief that (particular) conduct is immoral, a citizen of a liberal democracy who is a religious believer will want to consult the wisdom of her own religious tradition at least as much as she will want to consult either the morality of liberal democracy or, if she is a citizen of the United States, the American constitutional morality of religious freedom.

I

In the United States today, many persons, including many religious believers, hold that same-sex marriage is not immoral and that the law should recognize same-sex marriage by extending to same-sex marriage the legal benefits it grants to heterosexual marriage. (Same-sex marriages already exist; they exist in spite of the fact that the law does not recognize them. The question is whether the law should recognize them. Even though, for now, the law does not recognize them, they exist: "[C]ertain same-sex unions already are functioning in their communities as marriages. These gay and lesbian couples support and are supported by the community's practices of marriage and family as a whole. With these unions already in place, the task is not to reformulate marriage so that gays and lesbians might enter. Instead, the task is to understand how and why these same-sex unions fit so well, given that so many good arguments are made against them."[2]) But many other persons hold that homosexual sexual conduct, including same-sex marriage, is always immoral and that the law should not recognize same-sex marriage; for the law to do so, they argue, would be for the law both to affirm and, thereby, to encourage the spread of immorality. The argument about whether homosexual sexual conduct is always immoral is at bottom an argument about the requirements of human well-being. Those who believe that homosexual sexual conduct is always immoral do so mainly because they believe that engaging in homosexual sexual conduct is always hostile to the authentic well-being of those who do so and is never, therefore, a fitting way for human beings to act. Thus, the argument about whether homosexual sexual conduct is always immoral exemplifies something I explained elsewhere,[3] namely, that "moral" argument is often about this.

What is good—truly good—for those we should care about (including ourselves)? And what is bad for them? In particular: What are the requirements of one's well-being? (Again, the "one" may be, at one extreme, a particular human being or, at the other, each and every human being.) What is friendly to (the achievement of) one's well-being, and what is hostile to it? What is conducive to or even constitutive of one's human well-being, and what impedes or even destroys it?

Many homosexual persons and others hold that same-sex marriage is (or would be) truly good for many homosexual persons. But many others hold that same-sex marriage is always truly bad for all homosexual persons. Moreover, many persons who hold that same-sex marriage is always truly bad—that is, is always hostile to (authentic) human well-being—do so because they accept a biblically based belief that homosexual sexual conduct is always hostile to human well-being. (By a biblically based belief, I mean a belief based on the Bible understood as a God-inspired text. A biblically based belief is, of course, one kind of religiously based belief.) I have argued elsewhere that nothing in the morality of liberal democracy counsels religious believers, in deciding whether to ban or otherwise disfavor conduct, to forgo reliance on religiously based belief that the conduct is immoral *just in virtue of the fact that the belief is religiously based.* This does not mean, however, that religious believers, in deciding whether to disfavor conduct, have no reason to forgo reliance on a religiously based belief that the conduct is immoral. I explain, in this essay, why some religious believers—namely, Christians who accept a biblically based belief that homosexual sexual conduct is always immoral, in the sense that the conduct is always hostile to human well-being—should be wary, in some circumstances, about relying on that belief as a ground for opposing the legal recognition of same-sex marriage.

In my book, *Love and Power*, I presented several reasons why citizens and their political representatives should be cautious about outlawing or otherwise disfavoring conduct they believe to be immoral—reasons why they should sometimes tolerate conduct they believe to be immoral.[4] Those reasons counsel citizens and their representatives to be cautious about disfavoring same-sex marriage even if they believe that homosexual sexual conduct is always immoral—that is, always hostile to human well-being. (That one should be cautious or wary about doing something does not entail that at the end of the day one should not do it.) Here my focus is more narrow: I explain why Christians should be wary about disfavoring, by opposing the legal recognition of, same-sex marriage on the basis of a biblically grounded belief that homosexual sexual conduct is always hostile to human well-being.

Of course, not every religious tradition is the same; not every religious tradition offers the same counsel. The particular religious tradition that informs my argument in this essay is the one that has been formative for me: Roman Catholicism. My argument here is rooted in Catholic Christianity. My argument is meant to speak, however, not just to Catholics, but to all Christians. (As the twenty-first century begins, Christians still constitute the largest group, by far, of religious believers in the United States.[5]) I hope that my argument also speaks, even if only partially and indirectly, to religious believers who are not Christian.

II

Many persons who accept the Bible as a God-inspired text—in particular, as a text that, *inter alia,* reveals the will of God—believe that the Bible indicates that homosexual sexual conduct is always contrary to God's will, that it is always, in that fundamental sense, immoral. This belief about God's will is best understood as a belief about the requirements of human well-being. A religious believer might object that for him or her, this belief is not about (the requirements of) human well-being but only about God's will. It is implausible, however, to believe that a loving God—indeed, a God who *is* love (1 John 4:8 and 4:16)—has both fashioned human nature—has defined the requirements of human well-being—in such a way that same-sex marriage can be, for some, a truly and deeply fulfilling relationship for them as human beings, and at the same time willed that no human being ever enter into such a relationship.[6] Therefore, to believe that same-sex marriage is always contrary to God's will is to believe that same-sex marriage can never be truly fulfilling for anyone, that it is always hostile to authentic human well-being.

Charles Curran, the eminent Catholic moral theologian, has raised a helpful question, in correspondence, about my "emphasis on human well-being and human nature. Some people might criticize that [emphasis] as being too anthropocentric and not theocentric enough for a truly Protestant position. . . . The primary question perhaps even in the reformed tradition is what is the will of God and not what is human flourishing or human nature."[7] However, given two assumptions that few if any Christians would want to deny, the distinction between doing "what God wills or commands us to do" and doing "what fulfills our nature" is quite false. The two assumptions are, first, that human beings have a nature—indeed, a nature fashioned by God—and, second, that it is God's will that human beings act so as to fulfill or perfect their nature. As Bernard Williams has observed, "[preferred ethical categories] may be said to be given by divine command or revelation; in this form, if it is not combined with a grounding in human nature, the explanation will not lead us anywhere except into what Spinoza called 'the asylum of ignorance.'"[8] The biblically based belief that homosexual sexual conduct, including same-sex marriage, is always contrary to God's will is, therefore, the belief that the Bible teaches—that God reveals in the Bible—that homosexual sexual conduct is always hostile to human well-being. Some religious believers hold that according to the inerrant teaching of the Bible, no kind of homosexual sexual relationship can be, for anyone, truly fulfilling.

Let me now explain why, in my judgment, Christians who believe that the Bible teaches that homosexual sexual conduct is always hostile to human well-being should be wary about relying on that belief as a ground for opposing the legal recognition of same-sex marriage.

I said that many Christians believe that the Bible teaches that homosexual sexual conduct is always hostile to human well-being; they believe that the Bible teaches that no kind of homosexual sexual relationship can be, for anyone, truly fulfilling. The most relevant Old Testament passages are thought to be Genesis 19:1–29 and Leviticus 18:22 and 20:13; the most relevant New Testament passages, each from one of St. Paul's letters, are Romans 1:18–32, 1 Corinthians 6:9, and 1 Timothy 1:10. (According to Richard Hays, who believes that the Bible teaches that homosexual sexual conduct is always immoral, "[t]he most crucial text for Christian ethics concerning homosexuality remains Romans 1, because this is the only passage in the New Testament that places the condemnation of homosexual behavior in an explicitly theological context."[9]) However, many other Christians have come to believe that, properly interpreted, the Bible does *not* teach that homosexual sexual conduct is always hostile to human well-being; they have come to believe that it is a mistake to conclude that the Bible teaches that no kind of homosexual sexual relationship can be, for anyone, truly fulfilling. There is now widespread and growing disagreement among Christians about what the Bible does or does not teach about homosexual sexual relationships. Moreover, this disagreement is less interdenominational than intradenominational; it is less a disagreement that divides some Christian denominations from other Christian denominations than one that divides many members of several denominations from many other members of the same denominations. (Keith Hartman provides an informative report in his book, *Congregations in Conflict: The Battle over Homosexuality* [1996].) That the disagreement is more intradenominational than interdenominational is significant: The dissenting position that the Bible does not teach that homosexual sexual conduct is always hostile to human well-being cannot be dismissed by the members of one denomination as just one more lamentable example of the false (heretical) beliefs of the members of one or more other denominations. The dissenting position that the Bible does not teach that no kind of homosexual sexual relationship can be, for anyone, truly fulfilling is a belief that grips growing numbers of Christians largely without regard to their denominational affiliation. This datum will give pause—indeed, should give pause—to any reflective Christian.

The literature participating in this increasingly widespread, intradenominational disagreement is large. Recent pieces defending the traditional belief that the Bible teaches that homosexual sexual conduct is always immoral include:

- Richard B. Hays, "Awaiting the Redemption of Our Bodies: The Witness of Scripture Concerning Homosexuality"[10]
- Thomas E. Schmidt, "Romans 1:26–27 and Biblical Sexuality"[11]

Recent pieces dissenting from the traditional belief include:

- Victor Paul Furnish, "The Bible and Homosexuality: Reading the Texts in Context"[12]
- Daniel A. Helminiak, "The Bible on Homosexuality: Ethically Neutral"[13]
- Patricia Beattie Jung and Ralph F. Smith, "The Bible and Heterosexism"[14]
- Jeffrey S. Siker, "Homosexual Christians, the Bible, and Gentile Inclusion"[15]

The interested reader can consult these (and kindred) pieces for herself. My professional expertise does not qualify me to pass judgment here on the competing scriptural arguments—arguments about the true meaning of the relevant biblical passages. Not that I don't find some of the arguments more persuasive than others. Still, I have no professional expertise in the matter; the interested reader should consult the relevant pieces, which are easily obtainable, and decide for herself. I want simply to note that there is, and that it is *undeniable* that there is, a growing, intradenominational disagreement among Christians about whether, according to the Bible, homosexual sexual conduct is invariably immoral—immoral without regard to any particularities of context. Indeed, some Christian ministers and communities are already "blessing" same-sex marriages;[16] many more are welcoming and affirming same-sex couples as *faithful* members of their congregations. It bears mention here that as I was drafting this essay, the *New York Times* reported that "[a]n effort to repeal a law that effectively bars ordination of [noncelibate] gay men and lesbians in the Presbyterian Church (U.S.A.) was defeated by a 3-to-2 ratio yesterday by the church's General Assembly, the top policymaking body." What is remarkable is not that the effort was defeated but that so many "commissioners," as the assembly's delegates are called, voted to support the effort. The tally was 319 to 198.[17]

Of course, such disagreement among Christians about what the Bible teaches about morality is not a new phenomenon. In the past there was such disagreement about, for example, the morality of slavery. Precisely because such disagreement is not a new thing, and because the historical experience of Christians discloses that Christians can be radically mistaken about what the Bible teaches about morality, such disagreement—increasingly widespread disagreement among Christians, disagreement that is less interdenominational than intradenominational—should be an occasion for Christians to subject the traditional belief to careful, critical scrutiny. (Of course, doing so necessitates subjecting the emergent belief that challenges the traditional belief to such scrutiny too.) Indeed, for Christians faced with such disagreement, to fail to subject the traditional belief to serious reexamination would be, not an act of humble fidelity, but an act of prideful infidelity. Two passages are relevant here, one from John Mahoney's magisterial book, *The Making of Moral Theology: A Study of the Roman Catholic Tradition* (1987), the other from John Noonan's illuminating essay, *Development in Moral Doctrine* (1993). First, Mahoney:

> At any stage in history all that is available to the Church is its continual meditation on the Word of God in the light of contemporary experience and of the knowledge and insights into reality which it possesses at the time. To be faithful to that set of circumstances . . . is the charge and the challenge which Christ has given to his Church. But if there is a historical shift, through improvement in scholarship or knowledge, or through an entry of society into a significantly different age, then what that same fidelity requires of the Church is that it respond to the historical shift, such that it might be not only mistaken *but also unfaithful* in declining to do so.[18]

Now, Noonan:

> One cannot predict future changes; one can only follow present light and in that light be morally certain that some obligations will never alter. The great commandments of love of God and of neighbor, the great principles of justice and charity continue to govern all development. God is unchanging, but the demands of the New Testament are different from those of the Old, and while no other revelation supplements the New, it is evident from the case of slavery alone that it has taken time to ascertain what the demands of the New really are. All will be judged by the demands of the day in which they live. It is not within human competence to say with certainty who was or will be saved; all will be judged as they have conscientiously acted. In new conditions, with new insight, an old rule need not be preserved in order to honor a past discipline. . . . In the Church there can always be fresh appeal to Christ, there is always the possibility of probing new depths of insight. . . . Must we not, then, frankly admit that change is something that plays a role in [Christian] moral teaching? . . . Yes, if the principle of change is the person of Christ.[19]

Again, such disagreement over what the Bible teaches about morality—increasingly widespread, intradenominational disagreement—should be an occasion for Christians to subject the traditional belief to careful, critical scrutiny. In particular, the increasingly widespread, intradenominational disagreement among Christians over whether the Bible teaches that no kind of homosexual sexual relationship can be, for anyone, truly fulfilling should be an occasion for Christians to subject to serious reexamination the traditional belief that homosexual sexual conduct is always contrary to the teaching of the Bible. How might a Christian do that? One obvious way is to carefully examine the emergent, dissident scriptural arguments that the Bible, properly interpreted, does not teach that homosexual sexual conduct is always hostile to human well-being.

But that is not the only way. There is another.

III

Mahoney refers, in the passage quoted above, to the Church's "continual meditation on the Word of God in the light of contemporary experience and of the knowledge and insights into reality which it possesses at the time." Noonan refers to "new conditions" and "new depths of insight." In her essay, *An Ethic for Same-Sex Relations* (1983), Margaret Farley writes:

> The final source for Christian ethical insight is [contemporary human experience]. Scripture, tradition, and secular disciplines must all reflect on experiences, past and present. What differentiates the source I am calling "contemporary experience" is the unsystematic way we have access to it. In this context, I

am referring primarily to the testimony of women and men whose sexual preference is for others of the same sex.[20]

There is a another, complementary way for Christians to subject the traditional belief—the belief that, according the the Bible, homosexual sexual conduct is always hostile to human well-being—to careful, critical scrutiny. It is for Christians to inquire whether any persuasive argument based, not on the Bible, but on contemporary human experience supports the belief that homosexual sexual conduct is always hostile to human well-being—the belief that no kind of homosexual sexual relationship can be truly fulfilling for any human being. (By "persuasive," I mean persuasive to the Christian inquirer herself.) Why is contemporary experience relevant? Authentic well-being is something that, in normal circumstances, human beings can be expected to experience. With respect to questions about the conditions of human well-being, human experience is, to say the least, probative. "Ethics will never be like physics, chemistry, or certain types of sociology, because it understands the moral reality to be about an interaction between persons and the world which can only be known from the reports of those who experience that interaction."[21] Farley acknowledges, in her essay, that "we have as yet no univocal voice putting to rest all of our questions regarding the status of same-sex relations." But, she continues,

> [w]e do . . . have some clear and profound testimonies to the life-enhancing possibilities of same-sex relations and the integrating possibilities of sexual activity within these relations. We have the witness that homosexual activity can be a way of embodying responsible human love and sustaining Christian friendship. Without grounds in scripture, tradition, or any other source of human knowledge for an absolute prohibition of same-sex relations, this witness alone is enough to demand of the Christian community that it reflect anew on the norms for homosexual love.[22]

This, then, is the path I am proposing here: that Christians, faced with a widespread, intradenominational controversy among Christians over what the Bible teaches about the requirements of human well-being, inquire whether any persuasive argument based, not on the Bible, but on contemporary human experience, supports the traditional belief about human well-being that is now being challenged. This path—this way of subjecting to serious reexamination the challenged traditional belief (here, the belief that homosexual sexual conduct is always hostile to human well-being)—should be an attractive option for Christians who accept what Thomas Aquinas taught:

> Aquinas remained . . . convinced that morality is essentially rational conduct, and as such it must be accessible, at least in principle, to human reason and wis-

> dom. . . . In the teaching of Aquinas, the purpose of revelation, so far as morality is concerned, appears to be essentially remedial, not absolutely necessary for man . . . [T]he Christian revelation contains in its moral teaching no substantial element over and above what is accessible to human reason without revelation. . . . Revelation as such has nothing in matters of moral behaviour to add to the best of human thinking.[23]

The Roman Catholic religious-moral tradition follows Thomas Aquinas in embracing this position. But Aquinas's enormous influence on the Christian religious-moral tradition extends far beyond just Catholic Christianity. Christians generally, and not just Catholics, would "want to argue (at least, many of them would) that the Christian revelation does not require us to interpret the nature of man in ways for which there is otherwise no warrant but rather affords a deeper understanding of man as he essentially is."[24]

For Christians who accept the Thomist understanding of the relation between "revelation" and "reason," any biblically based belief about (the requirements of) human well-being should be a highly suspect ground for banning or otherwise disfavoring conduct if (a) the belief is the object of widespread, intradenominational disagreement among Christians themselves and (b) no persuasive argument based on contemporary human experience supports the biblically based belief. Given the demonstrated, ubiquitious human propensity to be mistaken and even to deceive oneself about what God has revealed, including what God has revealed in the Bible, the absence of a persuasive argument based on human experience in support of a biblically based claim about human well-being warrants suspicion that the claim might be false, that it might be the defective yield of that demonstrated human propensity. In particular, it warrants wariness about relying on the biblically based claim as a ground for a political choice banning or otherwise disfavoring conduct. At least, the absence of a persuasive argument based on human experience in support of a biblically based claim about human well-being warrants such suspicion and wariness if, as I said, the claim is the object of widespread, intradenominational dissensus among Christians themselves.

Now, some Christians might try to repress dissensus among the members of their community of faith and insulate themselves from such suspicion and wariness by means of one or more doctrines about their or their religious leaders' privileged (e.g., infallible) insight into God's revelation, including God's revelation about human well-being. But any such doctrine, which will likely seem to many other Christians (and others) as an understandable but nonetheless prideful and self-serving stratagem,[25] is conspicuously ill suited to the politics of a religiously pluralistic democracy like the United States. As Richard John Neuhaus has warned: "So long as Christian teaching claims to be a privileged form of discourse that is exempt from the scrutiny of critical reason, it will understandably be denied a place in discussions that are authentically public."[26] Listen, too, to J. Bryan Hehir, who, as the principal drafter of the U.S. Catholic bishops' 1983 letter on nuclear deterrence,[27] has some experience in the matter:

> [R]eligiously based insights, values and arguments at some point must be rendered persuasive to the wider civil public. There is legitimacy to proposing a sectarian argument within the confines of a religious community, but it does violence to the fabric of pluralism to expect acceptance of such an argument in the wider public arena. When a religious moral claim will affect the wider public, it should be proposed in a fashion which that public can evaluate, accept or reject on its own terms. The [point] . . . is not to banish religious insight and argument from public life[, but only to establish] a test for the religious communities to meet: to probe our commitments deeply and broadly enough that we can translate their best insights to others.[28]

In 1988, the drafters of the Williamsburg Charter, a group that included many prominent religious believers, articulated a similar contention: "Arguments for public policy should be more than private convictions shouted out loud. For persuasion to be principled, private convictions should be translated into publicly accessible claims. Such public claims should be made publicly accessible . . . because they must engage those who do not share the same private convictions."[29] Richard Neuhaus, who was instrumental in the drafting of the Williamsburg Charter, has cautioned that "publicly assertive religious forces will have to learn that the remedy for the naked public square is not naked religion in public. They will have to develop a mediating language by which ultimate truths can be related to the penultimate and prepenultimate questions of political and legal contest."[30]

Insisting on a persuasive argument based on human experience in support of a claim about human well-being is obviously one way for Christians to abide the counsel of Neuhaus, Hehir, and the drafters of the Williamsburg Charter, *especially if many Christians are themselves deeply skeptical about the biblical argument for the claim.* Even more importantly, it is an important way—and, moreover, a relatively ecumenical way—for the citizens of a religiously pluralistic democracy, including Christians and other religious believers, to seek the truth by testing the various statements about what God has revealed that are sometimes articulated in public political debate—for example, statements that certain biblical passages "'prove' that heterosexuality is God's exclusive intention for human sexuality and that homosexuality is an abomination before God."[31] Only a historically naive religious (or other) tradition would doubt the value of such ecumenical dialogue, which is an essential way of correcting error and broadening and deepening one's apprehension of truth.[32] "There is, of course, much to gain by sharpening our understanding in dialogue with those who share a common heritage and common experience with us. . . . Critical understanding of the [religious] tradition and a critical awareness of our own relationship to it, however, is sharpened by contact with those who differ from us. Indeed, for these purposes, the less they are like us, the better."[33] Defending the moderate style of his participation in public discourse about abortion and other issues implicating what he famously called "the consistent ethic of life," the late Joseph Cardinal Bernardin, archbishop of Chicago, said,

> The substance of the consistent ethic yields a style of teaching it and witnessing to it. The style should . . . not [be] sectarian. . . . [W]e should resist the sectarian tendency to retreat into a closed circle, convinced of our truth and the impossibility of sharing it with others. . . . The style should be persuasive, not preachy. . . . We should be convinced we have much to learn from the world and much to teach it. A confident church will speak its mind, seek as a community to live its convictions, but leave space for others to speak to us, to help us grow from their perspective.[34]

In various addresses, John Paul II has expressed concern about the marginalization of religious wisdom in public political deliberations about fundamental moral questions.[35] It bears emphasis that the principle of political self-restraint I am proposing here, if widely embraced, would not lead to such marginalization. The insight into the requirements of human well-being achieved over time by the Christian tradition is, whatever else it may be, *the yield of the lived experience of a historically extended human community.* Therefore, that insight has a resonance and indeed an authority that extends far beyond just those who accept the tradition's religious claims—in particular, the claim that the Bible is the revealed word of God. Put another way, many of the most basic claims about human well-being made by Christians are often made, and in any event can be made, without invoking biblical authority. What Catholic moral theologian James Burtchaell says about the nature of moral inquiry or discernment in the Catholic religious tradition is true of any Christian tradition:

> The Catholic tradition embraces a long effort to uncover the truth about human behavior and experience. Our judgments of good and evil focus on whether a certain course of action will make a human being grow and mature and flourish, or whether it will make a person withered, estranged and indifferent. In making our evaluations, we have little to draw on except our own and our forebears' experience, and whatever wisdom we can wring from our debate with others. . . . Nothing is specifically Christian about this method of making judgments about human experience. That is why it is strange to call any of our moral convictions "religious," let alone sectarian, since they arise from a dialogue that ranges through so many communities and draws from so many sources.[36]

Many religious believers and nonbelievers alike seem to overlook the overwhelming extent to which both the development of insight into human well-being and the debate that attends such development is, inside religious traditions as much as outside them, nonrevelational. Because the insight into human well-being achieved over time by the various religious traditions is substantially nonrevelational, bringing that insight to bear in a politics in which religious believers' participation is self-restrained in the way I am recommending here is not the problem some religious believers and nonbelievers might imagine it to be. As Jesuit sociologist John Coleman has observed: "[M]any elements and aspects of a religious ethic . . . can be presented in public discussion in ways that do not presume assent to them on the specific premises of a faith grounded in revelation. Without being believing Hindus, many Westerners, after all, find in Gandhi's social thought a superior vision of the human than that of ordinary liberal premises."[37] Martin Marty has commented, in much the same spirit, that "religionists who do not invoke the privileged insights of their revelation or magisterium can enhance and qualify rationality with community experience, intuition, attention to symbol, ritual, and narrative."[38]

If, as the comments by Burtchaell, Coleman, and Marty suggest, religious insight into the requirements of human well-being can speak with a powerful resonance even to nonbelievers, and thereby play a central role even in a thoroughly secularized politics, then such insight can certainly play a central role in American politics, which is far from being thoroughly secularized.[39]

IV

Again, there is now widespread and growing disagreement among Christians about what the Bible does or does not teach about homosexual sexual relationships; moreover, this disagreement is intradenominational: It divides many members of several denominations from many other members of the same denominations. According to the principle of political self-restraint I have proposed in this essay, a faithful Christian, confronted both by this disagreement about what the Bible teaches and also by the necessity of choosing whether or not to oppose the legal recognition of same-sex marriage, should make the following judgment: Does contemporary human experience support the claim that homosexual sexual conduct is always hostile to human well-being and that therefore same-sex marriage can never be truly fulfilling for anyone? Or, instead, does human experience belie that claim?

The aim, of course, is informed judgment, not ignorant judgment. Happily, in deciding whether human experience supports or, instead, belies the claim that same-sex marriage is always hostile to human well-being, the faithful Christian—and, indeed, anyone, Christian or not, believer or not—will be aided enormously by a large literature that has emerged in recent years, a literature that addresses the question whether, as a matter of human experience, same-sex marriage can be truly fulfilling for some persons. I refer the reader to some of that voluminous literature both in the note accompanying this sentence and in the text of the next two paragraphs.[40]

I mentioned earlier in this essay that the particular religious tradition that has been formative for me is Roman Catholicism. The *Catechism of the Catholic Church* holds (in paragraph 2357) that "homosexual acts are intrinsically disordered" and "[u]nder no circumstances can they be approved." Nonetheless, in recent years, some of the most powerful arguments to the effect that same-sex marriage can be truly and deeply fulfilling for some persons have been made by Roman Catholic thinkers. One of the most acclaimed such works is Kevin T. Kelly, *New Directions in Sexual Ethics* (1998).[41] (Kelly, a Catholic priest in England with broad pastoral experience, is a moral theologian.) Other such contributions by Catholic writers include:

- Jack A. Bonsor, "Homosexual Sexual Orientation and Anthropology: Reflections on the Category 'Objective Disorder.'"[42] Bonsor teaches theology at Santa Clara University, a Jesuit institution.
- Margaret A. Farley, "An Ethic for Same-Sex Relations."[43] Farley, a member of the Sisters of Mercy, is the Gilbert L. Stark Professor of Christian Ethics at Yale University and a former president of the Society of Christian Ethics.
- Patricia Beattie Jung and Ralph F. Smith, *Heterosexism: An Ethical Challenge* (1993). Jung teaches theology at Loyola University of Chicago; Smith, now deceased, was an ordained Lutheran pastor who taught at Wartburg Theological Seminary (Dubuque, Iowa).
- David McCarthy Matzko, "Homosexuality and the Practices of Marriage."[44] Matzko teaches theology at the College of Saint Rose (Albany, New York).
- Paul J. Weithman, "Natural Law, Morality, and Sexual Complementarity."[45] Weithman teaches philosophy at the University of Notre Dame.

Catholic writers who have recently defended the Vatican's position that homosexual sexual conduct is always hostile to human well-being include:

- John Finnis: "Law, Morality, and 'Sexual Orientation'" and "The Good of Marriage and the Morality of Sexual Relations: Some Philosophical and Historical Observations."[46] Finnis teaches law both at Oxford and at Notre Dame.
- James P. Hanigan, "Sexual Orientation and Human Rights: A Roman Catholic View."[47] Hanigan teaches theology at Duquesne University (Pittsburgh, Pennsylvania).
- Patrick Lee and Robert P. George, "What Sex Can Be: Self-Alienation, Illusion, or One-Flesh Union."[48] Lee teaches philosophy at the Franciscan University of Steubenville (Ohio); George is a member of the Department of Politics at Princeton.

It is not surprising that so many theologians, philosophers, and others in the Roman Catholic tradition are addressing the issue of same-sex marriage not, or not principally, as a question about what the Bible teaches but rather as a question about what human experience discloses to be the conditions of authentic human well-being. Again, the Roman Catholic religious-moral tradition, under the influence of Thomas Aquinas,[49] is committed to position "that the Christian revelation does not require us to interpret the nature of man in ways for which there is otherwise no warrant but rather affords a deeper understanding of man as he essentially is."[50] So, when John Finnis (for example) sets out to defend the traditional Roman Catholic teaching that homosexual sexual conduct is always antithetical to true human well-being, he does not present an argument about what the Bible teaches or even about what the Pope teaches; instead, he tries to construct an argument that is, in Finnis' own words, "reflective, critical, publicly intelligible, and rational."[51]

I said, a few paragraphs back, that in deciding whether human experience supports or belies the claim that same-sex marriage is always hostile to human well-being, the faithful Christian (and indeed anyone) will be aided enormously by a large literature that has emerged in recent years. As the citations I have provided illustrate, much of the recent literature is moral-theological in character. It bears emphasis that the principle of political self-restraint I have proposed here does not privilege "secular" argument over moral-theological argument. In my judgment, some of the most impressive arguments about what human experience discloses about same-sex marriage and human well-being—the arguments, for example, of Farley, Jung and Smith, Kelly, and Matzko—are moral-theological. That an argument about human well-being—i.e., an argument based on human experience—is moral-theological rather than secular is irrelevant to the principle.

It is no part of my aim in this essay to adjudicate the controversy about same-sex marriage. I do want to acknowledge, however, that in my judgment, contemporary human experience belies the claim that homosexual sexual conduct is always hostile to authentic human well-being; in particular, it belies the claim that same-sex marriage can never be truly fulfilling for anyone. Not that the principle of political self-restraint I have proposed here entails this judgment about human experience. It does not. Even if she accepts the proposed principle of political self-restraint, the faithful Christian must reach her own judgment about what human experience discloses about same-sex marriage and human well-being. In any event, given the careful, thorough, and, in my view, persuasive arguments recently offered by the Catholic thinkers I have cited,[52] and others,[53] it would be otiose for me to argue here that human experience discloses that same-sex marriage can be truly, deeply fulfilling for some persons.

* * * * *

A growing number of Christians do not oppose the legal recognition of same-sex marriage, because they no longer believe that human experience discloses, or perhaps even that the Bible teaches, that homosexual sexual conduct is always hostile to human well-being. Many Christians, however, continue to believe that the Bible teaches, and that human experience discloses, that homosexual sexual conduct, including same-sex marriage, is invariably—that it is always and everywhere—hostile to human well-being. But what is a faithful Christian to do who falls between these two groups—who comes to find herself, perhaps in consequence of consulting some of the work I have cited here, in the grip of serious doubt about whether human experience discloses, and perhaps even about whether the Bible teaches, that homosexual sexual conduct is always hostile to human well-being? The principle of political self-restraint I have defended in this essay counsels her to be wary about opposing the legal recognition of same-sex marriage. The principle—which is perhaps better described as an attitude—is not an algorithm; how wary she should be depends on how serious is her doubt about whether same-sex marriage is invariably hostile to human well-being. Of course, if she has moved beyond doubt to disbelief—if she disbelieves that same-sex marriage is hostile to human well-being—she no longer accepts the principal reason some Christians do not want the law to recognize same-sex marriage. The principle/attitude of political self-restraint defended here is for Christians who have not moved beyond doubt to disbelief and who may therefore be inclined to remain opposed to the legal recognition of same-sex marriage. As a response to doubt about what human experience discloses about same-sex marriage and human well-being, wariness about continuing to oppose the legal recognition of same-sex marriage seems especially fitting for any Christian who affirms—as many persons, perhaps most, in our society do—that, as a general matter, a competent adult is, if not always the best judge, then one of the best judges of what way of life is best for her.[54]

V

Many Christians will be skeptical about the principle (or attitude) of political self-restraint I have proposed in this essay, because they are skeptical about—indeed, many Christians reject—the understanding of the proper relation between "faith" (here, reliance on the Bible, understood as "revelation") and "reason" (here, reliance on human experience) on which the principle rests. I now want to speak mainly to such Christians.

As I noted earlier, Christians still constitute, at the beginning of the twenty-first century, the largest group by far of religious believers in the United States.[55] For many Christians in the United States—including Catholics,

Lutherans, Presbyterians, Episcopalians, Methodists, and others—the purported opposition between "faith" (or "revelation") and "reason" is a false opposition. Many Christians understand that they do not have to choose between "faith" and "reason;" for them, faith and reason are not in tension, they are not incompatible. To the contrary, faith and reason are, for such Christians, mutually enriching. David Hollenbach explains:

> Faith and understanding go hand in hand in both the Catholic and Calvinist views of the matter. They are not adversarial but reciprocally illuminating. As [David] Tracy puts it, Catholic social thought seeks to correlate arguments drawn from the distinctively religious symbols of Christianity with arguments based on shared public experience. This effort at correlation moves back and forth on a two-way street. It rests on a conviction that the classic symbols of Christianity can uncover meaning in personal and social existence that common sense and uncontroversial science fail to see. So it invites those outside the church to place their self-understanding at risk by what Tracy calls conversation with such "classics."[56]

Hollenbach then adds, following Tracy: "At the same time, the believer's self-understanding is also placed at risk because it can be challenged to development or even fundamental change by dialogue with the other—whether this be a secular agnostic, a Christian from another tradition, or a Jew, Muslim, or Buddhist."[57]

Or, we may add, even if this be a homosexual man or woman living in a same-sex marriage. Recall, here, Margaret Farley's reference to "the testimony of women and men whose sexual preference is for others of the same sex." It is, she writes, "clear and profound testimon[y] to the life-enhancing possibilities of same-sex relations and the integrating possibilities of sexual activity within these relations." In what Hollenbach calls "dialogue with the other," Christian believers may come to concur in Farley's judgment that "[w]e have the witness that homosexual activity can be a way of embodying responsible human love and sustaining Christian friendship" and that "this witness alone is enough to demand of the Christian community that it reflect anew on the norms for homosexual love."[58]

Some Christians, however, are skeptical of the kind of "dialogue with the other" to which Hollenbach refers; in particular, some are skeptical of relying on human experience, including what Hollenbach calls "shared public experience:" morally conservative Christians who embrace "revelation," but who marginalize if not reject "human reason," as a source of moral understanding.[59] There are such Christians in many denominations, but the most prominent examples of such Christians in the United States today are fundamentalist Christians, Mormons, and some evangelical Christians. As Hollenbach says, "[f]aith and understanding go hand in hand in both the Catholic and Calvinist views of the matter." But for some Christians faith and understanding do not go hand in hand but are often incompatible; in their view, human reason is often too corrupted to be trusted. For example, David Smolin, a law professor who identifies himself as an evangelical Christian, has written that

> even our intellectual capacities have been distorted by the effects of sin. The pervasive effects of sin suggest that creation, human nature, and human reason are often unreliable means for knowing the law of God. . . . Thus, scripture and Christian tradition have come to have a priority among the sources of knowledge of God's will. Indeed, these sources of revelation are considered a means of measuring and testing claims made on behalf of reason, nature, or creation, in order to purify these now subsidiary means of the distortive effect of sin.[60]

However, Christians like Smolin overlook that, as the history of Christianity discloses, sin can distort, and indeed often has distorted, what human beings believe about "scripture and Christian tradition."[61] Given their belief in the "fallenness" of human nature—which is, after all, *their* nature, too—Christians should be especially alert to this dark possibility.

Christians skeptical of arguments based on contemporary human experience—including arguments about human well-being—would do well to reflect on Mark Noll's powerful, eloquent book, *The Scandal of the Evangelical Mind* (1994). Noll—the McManis Professor of Christian Thought at Wheaton College (Illinois), one of the foremost evangelical Christian colleges in the United States—is himself a committed evangelical Christian. Noll comments critically, in one chapter of his book, on the emergence of "creation science" in evangelical Christianity: "[I]f the consensus of modern scientists, who devote their lives to looking at the data of the physical world, is that humans have existed on the planet for a very long time, it is foolish for biblical interpreters to say that 'the Bible teaches' the recent creation of human beings." Noll explains:

> This does not mean that at some future time, the procedures of science may shift in such a way as to alter the contemporary consensus. It means that, for people today to say they are being loyal to the Bible and to demand belief in a recent creation of humanity as a sign of obedience to Scripture is in fact being unfaithful to the Bible, which, in Psalm 19 and elsewhere, calls upon followers of God to listen to the speech that God has caused the natural world to speak. It is the same for the age of the earth and for all other questions regarding the constitution of the human race. Charles Hodges's words from the middle of the nineteenth century are still pertinent: "Nature is as truly a revelation of God as the Bible, and we only interpret the Word of God by the Word of God when we interpret the Bible by science."[62]

Consider, too, these observations by the historian George Marsden (who, like Noll, identifies himself as an evangelical Christian):

> Some [historical] knowledge cuts across all theories and paradigms, and it provides all people of good sense a solid reality basis for testing some aspects of theories. So in practice there is a common ground of historical inquiry. When we look at the past, if we do it right, what we find will in large measure correspond to what other historians find.
>
> From a Christian perspective, we may explain this phenomenon simply by observing that God in his grace seems to have created human minds with some ability to experience and know something of the real world, including the past. Furthermore, these structures are substantially common to all normal people so that, despite the notorious theoretical problems of subjectivism and point of view, we can in fact communicate remarkably well and be assured that we are talking about the same things. It may be difficult to explain, except as a matter of faith, what basis we have for reliance on these common abilities; but the fact remains that only philosophers and crackpots can long deny that often they are reliable.[63]

Why should we believe that what Noll says about the proper relation between faith and inquiry into the origins of human beings is not also true about the proper relation between faith and inquiry into the conditions of human well-being? Why should we believe that what Marsden says about historical inquiry is not also true about inquiry into the conditions of human well-being? Why should we not say, with Anthony of the Desert, a fourth-century Christian monk: "My book, O philosopher, is the nature of created things, and any time I wish to read the words of God, the book is before me."[64]

The principle of political self-restraint I have recommended in this essay does not presuppose that in making political choices about the morality of conduct, Christians should forget that they are Christians, it does not presuppose that they should "bracket" their Christian identity, that they should act as if they are persons who do not have the religious beliefs that they in fact do have. (I have contended against such "bracketing" elsewhere: "One's basic moral/religious convictions are [partly] self-constitutive and are therefore a principal ground—indeed, the principal ground—of political deliberation and choice. To 'bracket' such convictions is therefore to bracket—to annihilate—essential aspects of one's very self. To participate in politics and law . . . with such convictions bracketed is not to participate as the self one is but as [someone else]."[65]) Rather, it is *because* they are Christians—it is because they are, *as Christians*, painfully aware of the fallenness, the brokenness, of human beings—that they should be extremely wary about making a political choice banning or otherwise disfavoring conduct on the ground of a biblically based belief about human well-being if (a) the belief is the object of widespread, intradenominational disagreement among Christians themselves and (b) no persuasive argument based on human experience supports the biblically based belief. Christians have *their own* reasons—reasons *internal both to their own religious (theological) tradition and to their own historical experience*—to accept this modest principle of political self-restraint. It scarcely seems radical, or unfaithful, to suggest that Christians, too, no less than other religious believers, must be alert to the possibility that a scripture-based belief about morality is mistaken—and worse. Scripture-based arguments for the moral permissibility of slavery were mistaken,[66] but they were also worse than mistaken. They were rationalizations for a fundamentally sinful state of affairs—a state of affairs centrally constituted by an existential repudiation of the fundamental Christian commandment to "love one another just as I have loved you" (John 13:34). The principle of political self-restraint proposed here is rooted in the realization that even some contemporary scripture-based arguments about moral permissibility or impermissibility may be mistaken. In particular, biblically based arguments that same-sex marriage is morally impermissible may be mistaken; indeed, they may be worse than mistaken; like biblically based arguments against interracial marriage, they may be rationalizations for sinful prejudice. Listen, in that regard, to Robert Bellah:

> A principled rejection of gay sexuality, whether put forward by the church or any other sector of society, is morally indefensible. It has the same status today as arguments for the inferiority of women. To remain stuck in that position, as the church for the time being seems likely to do, is not only unfortunate: it makes the church collaborate in continuing forms of domination. To put it even more strongly: it makes the church collaborate in sin.[67]

In circumstances in which Christians disagree deeply among themselves about what the Bible teaches about the requirements of human well-being, especially when that disagreement is intradenominational, Christians have good reason to probe contemporary human experience in their effort to discern the truth about (the requirements of) human well-being. (Their effort to discern the truth about human well-being is also, if indirectly, an effort to discern what the Bible does not teach about human well-being, since, for Christians, the Bible does not teach about human well-being something that is contrary to the truth about human well-being. Of course, few Christians believe that the Bible's teaching about human well-being is exhaustive: The Bible does not teach every truth about human well-being; it does not address every question about human well-being that might arise.) They also have good reason, in such circumstances, to forgo making a political choice against conduct on the ground that the conduct is always hostile to the well-being of those who engage in the conduct if the reflective yield of contemporary human experience seems increasingly to put into serious question the claim that the conduct is always hostile to human well-being (and also the claim, therefore, that the Bible teaches that the conduct is always hostile to human well-being).[68]

NOTES

This essay is drawn from a work in progress—a book—that I don't expect to finish before the spring of 2001. The tentative title of the book is *One Nation, Under God: Democracy, Morality, and Religion.*

1. Cf. Perry, *One Nation Under God.*

2. David McCarthy Matzko, "Homosexuality and the Practices of Marriage," *Modern Theology* 13 (1997), 371, 372. Cf. Mae Kuykendall, "Resistance to Same-Sex Marriage as a Story about Language: Linguistic Failure and the Priority of a Living Language," *Harvard Civil Rights-Civil Liberties Law Review* 34 (1999), 385.

3. Cf. Michael J. Perry, "What Is 'Morality' Anyway?" *Villanova Law Review* (forthcoming, 2000).

4. Cf. Michael J. Perry, *Love and Power: The Role of Religion and Morality in American Politics* (New York: Oxford University Press, 1991), 132–38.

5. According to the 1998 edition of the *Statistical Abstract of the United States* (p. 72), 84 percent of the "civilian noninstitutional population, 18 years old and over," identify themselves as Christian: 58 percent identify themselves as Protestant, 26 percent as Catholic.

6. Cf. Peter Cicchino, Letter to Michael Perry, 2 September 1998: "Consider the question of whether God's commands are intrinsically related to the flourishing of human life. If God's commands are only accidentally related to human flourishing, then God is a capricious tyrant. If God's commands inhibit or prevent human flourishing, then God is a sadistic tyrant. If God's commands are intrinsically related to human flourishing, then presumably we have a reason for obeying those commands independent of whether God commands them: namely, our own good."

7. Letter to Michael Perry, 7 August 1995.

8. Bernard Williams, *Ethics and the Limits of Philosophy* (Cambridge, MA: Harvard University Press, 1985), 96.

9. Richard B. Hays, "Awaiting the Redemption of Our Bodies: The Witness of Scripture Concerning Homosexuality," in *Homosexuality in the Church: Both Sides of the Debate*, ed. Jeffrey S. Siker (Louisville, KY: Westminster John Knox Press, 1994), 3, 7.

10. Cf. Siker, *Homosexuality in the Church*, 3.

11. In *Same Sex: Debating the Ethics, Science, and Culture of Homosexuality*, ed. John Corvino (Lanham, MD: Rowman & Littlefield, 1997), 93.

12. Cf. Siker, *Homosexuality in the Church*, 18.

13. Cf. Corvino, *Same Sex*, 81.

14. In Patricia Beattie Jung and Ralph F. Smith, *Heterosexism: An Ethical Challenge* (New York: State University of New York Press, 1993), 61.

15. Cf. Siker, *Homosexuality in the Church*, 178.

16. Cf. Gustav Niebuhr, "Laws Aside, Some in Clergy Quietly Bless Gay 'Marriage,'" *New York Times*, 17 April 1998, A1.

17. Gustav Niebuhr, "Presbyterian Church Upholds Ban on Ordaining Homosexuals," *New York Times*, 26 June 1999, A26.

18. John Mahoney S.J., *The Making of Moral Theology: A Study of the Roman Catholic Tradition* (Oxford: Oxford University Press, 1987), 327 (emphasis added).

19. John T. Noonan, Jr., "Development in Moral Doctrine," *Theological Studies* 54 (1993), 662, 676–77.

20. Margaret A. Farley, "An Ethic for Same-Sex Relations," in *A Challenge to Love: Gay and Lesbian Catholics in the Church*, ed. Robert Nugent (New York: Crossroad, 1983), 93, 99–100.

21. Robin W. Lovin, "Empiricism and Christian Social Thought," *Annual of Society of Christian Ethics* (1982), 25, 41.

22. *Id.*

23. Cf. Mahoney, *The Making of Moral Theology*, 106, 107, 108. Mahoney then adds: "[B]ut such human thinking is not always or invariably at its best." *Id.* 109. Cf. *id.* 105–06: "[In principle, because t]he participation by man in God's eternal law through knowledge . . . can be corrupted and depraved in such a way that the natural knowledge of good is darkened by passions and the habits of sin. For Aquinas, then, not all the conclusions of natural law are universally known, and the more one descends from the general to the particular, the more possible it is for reason to be unduly influenced by the emotions, or by customs, or by fallen nature."

The American philosopher Robert Audi (who identifies himself as a Christian) seems to me naive about the vulnerability of "secular" argument relative to religious argument in suggesting that "good secular arguments for moral principles may be *better* reasons to believe those principles to be divinely enjoined than theological arguments for the principles, based on scripture or tradition. For the latter arguments seem (even) more subject than the former to cultural influences that may distort scripture or tradition or both; more vulnerable to misinterpretation of religious or other texts or to their sheer corruption across time and translation; and more liable to bias stemming from political or other non-religious aims. Granting, then, that theology and religious inspiration can be sources of ethical insight, we can also reverse this traditional idea: one may sometimes be better off trying to understand God through ethics than ethics through theology." Robert Audi, "Liberal Democracy and the Place of Religion in Politics," in Robert Audi & Nicholas Wolterstorff, *Religion in the Public Square* (Lanham, MD: Rowman & Littlefield, 1997), 1, 20–21. Secular moral argument can be no less vulnerable to distorting "cultural influences" than religious argument. Cf. Paul F. Campos, "Secular Fundamentalism," *Columbia Law Review* 94 (1994), 1814.

24. Basil Mitchell, "Should Law Be Christian?" *Law & Justice* 96/97 (1988), 12, 21.

25. Discussing usury, marriage, slavery, and religious freedom, John Noonan has demonstrated:

> Wide shifts in the teaching of moral duties, once presented as part of Christian doctrine by the magisterium, have occurred. In each case one can see the displacement of a principle or principles that had been taken as dispositive—in the case of usury, that a loan confers no right to profit; in the case of marriage, that all marriages are indissoluble; in the case of slavery, that war gives a right to enslave and that ownership of a slave gives title to the slave's offspring; in the case of religious liberty, that error has no rights and that fidelity to the Christian faith

> may be physically enforced. . . . In the course of this displacement of one set of principles, what was forbidden became lawful (the cases of usury and marriage); what was permissible became unlawful (the case of slavery); and what was required became forbidden (the persecution of heretics).

Cf. Noonan, "Development in Moral Doctrine," 669. See also Seán Fagan, SM, "Interpreting the Catechism," *Doctrine & Life* 44 (1994), 412, 416–17:

> A catechism is supposed to "explain," but this one does not say why Catholics have to take such a rigid, absolutist stand against artificial contraception because it is papal teaching, but there is no reference to the explicit centuries-long papal teaching that Jews and heretics go to hell unless they convert to the Catholic faith, or to Pope Leo X, who declared that the burning of heretics is in accord with the will of the Holy Spirit. Six different popes justified and authorised the use of slavery. Pius XI, in an encyclical at least as important as *Humanae Vitae*, insisted that co-education is erroneous and pernicious, indeed against nature. The Catechism's presentation of natural law gives the impression that specific moral precepts can be read off from physical human nature, without any awareness of the fact that our very understanding of "nature" and what is "natural" can be coloured by our culture.

26. Richard John Neuhaus, "Reason Public and Private: The Pannenberg Project," *First Things* (March 1992), 55, 57.

27. Cf. National Conference of Catholic Bishops, *Challenge of Peace: God's Promise and Our Response* (1983).

28. Bryan Hehir, "Responsibilities and Temptations of Power: A Catholic View," unpublished manuscript (1988). The Dutch theologian, Edward Schillebeeckx, who is Catholic, has written: "Even when their fundamental inspiration comes from a religious belief in God, ethical norms . . . must be rationally grounded. None of the participants in [religiously based moral discourse] can hide behind an 'I can see what you don't see' and then require [the] others to accept this norm straight out." Edward Schillebeeckx, *The Schillebeeckx Reader*, ed. Robert Schreiter (New York: Crossroad, 1984), 263. Even if we assume for the sake of argument that Schillebeeckx's principle should not govern moral discourse in *all* contexts—for example, in the context of a small, monistic, charismatic religious community—the principle should certainly govern moral discourse in *some* contexts, especially in the context of a large, pluralistic, democratic political community like the United States.

29. *The Williamsburg Charter: A National Celebration and Reaffirmation of the First Amendment Religious Liberty Clauses* (1988), 22.

30. Richard John Neuhaus, "Nihilism Without the Abyss: Law, Rights, and Transcendent Good," *Journal of Law & Religion* 5 (1987), 53, 62. In commenting on this passage, Stanley Hauerwas has said that "[r]ather than condemning the Moral Majority, Neuhaus seeks to help them enter the public debate by basing their appeals on principles that are accessible to the public." Stanley Hauerwas, "A Christian Critique of Christian America," in *Religion, Morality, and the Law*, ed. J. Roland Pennock & John W. Chapman (New York: New York University Press, 1988), 110, 118.

31. Jeffrey S. Siker, "Homosexual Christians, the Bible, and Gentile Inclusion: Confessions of a Repenting Heterosexist," in *Homosexuality in the Church*, 184. For Siker's criticism of such interpretations, cf. *id.* 184–91.

32. I have discussed the value of ecumenical political dialogue elsewhere Cf. Perry, *Love and Power*, chapter 6. Cf. also David Lochhead, *The Dialogical Imperative: A Christian Reflection on Interfaith Encounter* (Maryknoll, NY: Orbis Books, 1988), 79: "In more biblical terms, the choice between monologue and dialogue is the choice between death and life. If to be human is to live in community with fellow human beings, then to alienate ourselves from community, in monologue, is to cut ourselves off from our own humanity. To choose monologue is to choose death. Dialogue is its own justification."

33. Robin W. Lovin, "Why the Church Needs the World: Faith, Realism, and the Public Life," unpublished manuscript (1988 Sorenson Lecture, Yale Divinity School).

34. Joseph Cardinal Bernardin, "The Consistent Ethic of Life After *Webster*," *Origins* 19 (1990), 741, 748.

35. In October 1995, for example, during a homily delivered at a mass in Baltimore, John Paul asked:

> Can the biblical wisdom which played such a formative part in the very founding of your country be excluded from the [political] debate [about the morality of particular conduct]? Would not doing so mean that America's founding documents no longer have any defining content, but are only the formal dressing of changing opinion? Would not doing so mean that tens of millions of Americans could no longer offer the contribution of their deepest convictions to the formation of public policy?

John Paul II, "Faith and Freedom: Text of the Homily Delivered at Mass in Baltimore," *New York Times*, 9 October 1995, B15. Two months later, in the Vatican newspaper *L'Osservatore Romano*, the Pope recurred to the same theme:

> I am thinking here of the claim that a democratic society should delegate to the realm of private opinion its members' religious beliefs and the moral convictions which derive from faith. At first glance, this appears to be an attitude of necessary impartiality and "neutrality" on the part of society in relation to those of its members who follow different religious traditions or none at all. Indeed, it is widely held that this is the only enlightened approach possible in a modern pluralistic state.
>
> But if citizens are expected to leave aside their religious convictions when they take part in public life, does this not mean that society not only excludes the contribution of religion to its institutional life, but also promotes *a culture which redefines man as less than he is?* In particular, there are moral questions at the heart of every great public issue. Should critics whose moral judgments are informed by their religious beliefs be less welcome to express their most deeply held convictions? When that happens, is not democracy itself emptied of real meaning? Should not genuine pluralism imply that firmly held convictions can be expressed in vigorous and respectful dialogue?

John Paul II, "Man Is Bound by Nature to Seek the Truth," *L'Osservatore Romano* (Weekly ed.), December 1995, 1, 7.

36. James Tunstead Burtchaell, "The Sources of Conscience," *Notre Dame Magazine* 13 (Winter 1984–85), 20–21 (emphasis added). (On our neighbor always turning out to be the most unlikely person, cf. Luke 10:29–37, the parable of the good Samaritan.)

37. John A. Coleman, S.J., *An American Strategic Theology* (Mahwah, NJ: Paulist Press, 1982), 196.

38. Martin E. Marty, "When My Virtue Doesn't Match Your Virtue," *Christian Century* 105 (1988), 1094, 1096. "Of course, these communities and their spokespersons argue with one another. But so do philosophical rationalists." *Id.*

Indeed, to embrace a biblical premise about what it means to be human, about how it is good or fitting for human beings to live their lives, and then to rely on the premise in public discourse, is not even *necessarily* to count oneself a participant in the religious tradition that has yielded the premise; it is not even necessarily to count oneself a religious believer. One certainly doesn't have to be Jewish to recognize that the prophetic vision of the Jewish Bible is profound and compelling, any more than one has to be Catholic or Presbyterian or Baptist or even Christian to recognize that the Gospel vision of what it means to be human is profound and compelling. Gandhi was not a Christian, but he recognized the Gospel vision as profound and compelling. As the eminent Catholic theologian David Tracy has emphasized: "Some interpret the religious classics not as testimonies to a revelation from Ultimate Reality . . . but as testimonies to possibility itself. As Ernst Bloch's interpretations of all those daydreams and Utopian and eschatological visions that Westerners have ever dared to dream argue, the religious classics can also become for nonbelieving interpreters testimonies to resistance and hope. As Mircea Eliade's interpretations of the power of the archaic religions show, the historian of religions can help create a new humanism which retrieves forgotten classic religious symbols, rituals, and myths." David Tracy, *Plurality and Ambiguity: Hermeneutics, Religion, Hope* (San Francisco: Harper & Row, 1987), 88. Tracy continues: "If the work of Bloch and [Walter] Benjamin on the classic texts and symbols of the eschatological religions and the work of Eliade and others on the primal religions were allowed to enter into the contemporary conversation, then the range of possibilities we ordinarily afford ourselves would be exponentially expanded beyond reigning Epicurean, Stoic, and nihilistic visions." *Id.* 88–89.

39. "But, the objection may be pressed," writes Basil Mitchell,

> can a religious body argue its case in a secular forum (ie., one that is not already antecedently committed to the religion in question)? Either, it may be said, it will rely on Christian premises, which *ex hypothesi* opponents will not accept; or it will employ purely secular premises, in which case the ensuing law will not be Christian. In neither case will any genuine debate have taken place between Christians and non-Christians. The dichotomy, however, is altogether too neat to be convincing. It presupposes that there is and always must be a complete discontinuity between Christian and secular reasoning. Certainly this can occur—if, for example, the Christian is an extreme fundamentalist and the secular thinker regards individual preferences as the sole

> basis for morality. . . . But . . . Christians would presumably want to argue (at least, many of them would) that the Christian revelation does not require us to interpret the nature of man in ways for which there is otherwise no warrant but rather affords a deeper understanding of man as he essentially is. If that is so, there is room for a genuine exchange of ideas.

Cf. Mitchell, "Should Law Be Christian?" 21.

40. Cf., e.g., Corvino, *Same Sex; Sex, Preference, and Family: Essays on Law and Nature*, ed. David M. Estlund and Martha C. Nussbaum (New York: Oxford University Press, 1997); "Forum: Sexual Morality and the Possibility of 'Same-Sex Marriage,'" *American Journal of Jurisprudence* 1997, 51–157; *Sexual Orientation and Human Rights in American Religious Discourse*, ed. Saul M. Olyan and Martha C. Nussbaum (New York: Oxford University Press, 1998); Siker, *Homosexuality in the Church; Same-Sex Marriage: Pro and Con*, ed. Andrew Sullivan (New York: Vintage Books, 1997); *Homosexuality and American Public Life*, ed. Christopher Wolfe (Dallas, TX: Spence Publishing, 1999).

41. For a laudatory review of Kelly's book, cf. James F. Keenan, S.J., *The [London] Tablet*, 6 July 1998, 878–79.

42. *Theological Studies* 59 (1998), 60–83. Compare Janet E. Smith, "Thomas Aquinas on Homosexuality," in Wolfe, *Homosexuality and American Public Life*, 129.

43. In *A Challenge to Love: Gay and Lesbian Catholics in the Church*, ed. Robert Nugent (New York: Crossroad, 1983), 93–106. Cf. also Margaret A. Farley, "Response to James Hanigan and Charles Curran," in Olyan, *Sexual Orientation and Human Rights in American Religious Discourse*, 101.

44. *Modern Theology* 13 (1997), 371–397.

45. In Estlund, *Same Sex, Preference, and Family*, 227–246.

46. The first essay (re)appears in *Notre Dame Journal of Law, Ethics & Public Policy* 9 (1995), 11, 16; the second appears in *American Journal of Jurisprudence* (1997), 97–134.

47. In Olyan, *Sexual Orientation and Human Rights in American Religious Discourse*, 63–84 Cf. also James P. Hanigan, *Homosexuality: The Test Case for Christian Sexual Ethics* (Mahwah, NJ: Paulist Press, 1988).

48. *American Journal of Jurisprudence* (1997), 135–157.

49. Cf. Mahoney, *The Making of Moral Theology*, 105–106.

50. Cf. Mitchell, "Should Law be Christian?" 12, 21.

51. John M. Finnis, "Law, Morality, and 'Sexual Orientation'," *Notre Dame Journal of Law, Ethics & Public Policy* 9 (1995), 11, 16.

52. In particular, Kelly, Jung & Smith, and Matzko.

53. Cf., e.g., Siker, "Homosexual Christians, the Bible, and Gentile Inclusion;" Andrew Koppelman, "Is Marriage Inherently Heterosexual?" *American Journal of Jurisprudence* (1997), 51. Koppelman's careful essay is especially important for those who want to evaluate the argument of the "new natural lawyers:" John Finnis, Robert George, and others.

54. See introduction.

55. See note 6, above.

56. See David Hollenbach, S.J., "Contexts of the Political Role of Religion: Civil Society and Culture," *San Diego Law Review* 30 (1993), 877, 894.

57. *Id.*, 894–95.

58. Farley, "An Ethic for Same-Sex Relations," 93, 99–100.

59. Not all morally conservative Christians reject or even marginalize "human reason" as a source of moral understanding. Many Catholics, for example, defend morally conservative positions on issues like contraception and homosexuality not by rejecting "human reason" but by exercising it (or by purporting to exercise it). John Finnis is a prominent example. Cf., e.g., John M. Finnis, "Law, Morality, and 'Sexual Orientation'," *Notre Dame Journal of Law, Ethics & Public Policy* 9 (1995), 11, 16.

60. David M. Smolin, "The Enforcement of Natural Law by the State: A Response to Professor Calhoun," *University of Dayton Law Review* 16 (1991), 318, 391–92.

61. *Id.*

62. Mark Noll, *The Scandal of the Evangelical Mind* (Grand Rapids, MI: W. B. Eerdmans Pub. Co., 1994), 207–08.

63. George Marsden, "Common Sense and the Spiritual Vision of History," in *History and Historical Understanding*, ed. C.T. McIntire & Ronald A. Wells (Grand Rapids, MI: W. B. Eerdmans Pub. Co., 1984), 55, 59.

64. Quoted in *The Wisdom of the Desert*, ed. Thomas Merton (New York: New Directions, 1960), 62.

65. Perry, *Morality, Politics, and Law* (New York: Oxford University Press, 1988), 181–82. Cf. also Perry, *Love and Power*, 4.

66. Cf. Noonan, "Development in Moral Doctrine."

67. Robert N. Bellah, "Foreword" to Richard L. Smith, *AIDS, Gays and the American Catholic Church* (Cleveland, OH: Pilgrim Press, 1994), xii–xiii.

68. Of course, many Christians will and do conclude that the reflective yield of human experience, including contemporary human experience, does *not* put that traditional Christian belief into serious question. But there seems to me little reason to doubt that, in the United States and kindred societies, the number of such Christians will continue to diminish sharply over time.

10

The King's Torah: The Role of Judaism in Shaping Jews' Input in National Policy

Elliot N. Dorff

> If, after you have entered the land that the Lord your God has assigned to you, and taken possession of it and settled in it, you decide, "I will set a king over me, as do all the nations about me," you shall be free to set a king over yourself, one chosen by the Lord your God. Be sure to set as king over yourself one of your own people; you must not set a foreigner over you, one who is not your kinsman. Moreover, he shall not keep many horses . . . and he shall not have many wives, lest his heart go astray; nor shall he amass silver and gold to excess.
>
> When he is seated on his royal throne, he shall have a copy of this Torah (Teaching) written for him on a scroll by the levitical priests. Let it remain with him and let him read in it all his life, so that he may learn to revere the Lord his God, to observe faithfully every word of this Teaching as well as these laws. Thus he will not act haughtily toward his fellows or deviate from the Instruction to the right or to the left, to the end that he and his descendants may reign long in the midst of Israel (Deuteronomy 17:14–20).

In these verses, the Torah describes the biblical view of religion and state. The Torah's ideal state is not, strictly speaking, a theocracy, for it is not religious leaders who rule. Nevertheless, religion was to have a dominant role in the biblical state, determining the criteria of eligibility for the rulers and much of the content of their decrees. Thus the king must be an Israelite and therefore presumably committed to the Torah. Moreover, he must possess and repeatedly read his own copy of the Torah so that God's laws are fresh in his mind. In the end, his own decrees may not "deviate . . . to the right or to the left" from God's Instruction (Torah). The Bible's historical accounts of Israel's and Judah's rulers in the books of Judges, I and II Samuel, and I and II Kings indicate that that ideal was not often achieved, but the biblical authors had a clear conception of the proper role of religion in government and used that theory to judge Israel's rulers.

However much contemporary American Jews are committed to Judaism, they certainly cannot apply the Torah's theory straightforwardly to American government. For one thing, the vast majority of American citizens are not Jewish. For another, the founding documents of the government of the United States proclaim both religious freedom and, as interpreted by the Supreme Court, "a wall of separation" between church and state.[1] These are clearly vastly different circumstances than the ones the Torah contemplated and completely different assumptions from the ones that it made.

For over 80 percent of the nearly four-thousand-year history of the Jewish people, though, Jews have not lived under the conditions that the Torah describes. Until the creation of the modern State of Israel in 1948, Jews ruled themselves only during the First Temple period (c. 950 B.C.E.-586 B.C.E.) and the Maccabean period (165 B.C.E.-63 B.C.E.). In all other times and places, Jews have been a minority population living under some other group's sovereignty. Babylonians, Persians, Greeks, Romans, Muslims, and Christians have all ruled the places where Jews dwelled. Jews were sometimes granted the right to govern the internal matters of their own community, but in the broader scheme of things, they were second-class citizens at best, and a persecuted minority at worst, all too often subject to expulsion or death.

As a result of this precarious, minority status, one can readily understand why the Rabbis would say on the one hand, "Pray for the welfare of the government, for without respect for it people would swallow each other alive,"[2] while, on the other hand, they would also say, "Love work, hate lordship, and seek no intimacy with the ruling power," and "Be on your guard against the ruling power, for they who exercise it draw no man near to them except for their own interests; appearing as friends when it is to their own advantage, they do not stand by a man in his hour of need."[3] The respect for authority but the simultaneous wariness of it, as embodied in these early rabbinic comments, shaped the attitude of Jews toward government in most times and places throughout the last two thousand years, articulated perhaps most famously by the Rabbi's comment in the opening number of *Fiddler on the Roof*: "May God bless and keep the czar—far away from us!"

The Enlightenment was a breath of fresh air for Jews. For the first time since the time of the Maccabees, they were to be accepted as full citizens, eligible for voting, university education, government service, residence anywhere in the realm, and equal treatment in the courts. This was, indeed, a new world.

That equal status, though, would come with some troubling consequences. These were already evident in the questions Napoleon posed to the

Sanhedrin of Jewish leaders he convened in 1807. Would French Jews marry French non-Jews? In what areas would French law govern Jews, and in what areas would the Rabbis insist on their own authority?[4]

These questions of intermarriage and assimilation in an open society plague American Jews to this day. Jews worry openly about the continuity of Judaism and the Jewish people. After all, while Christians make up a full third of the world's population, Jews constitute 0.2 percent, and so defections from the Jewish people threaten its very existence. While we have managed to survive persecution for all these centuries, it is thus not clear that we can survive the conditions of freedom.

ARGUMENTS FOR SEPARATION OF CHURCH AND STATE

In response to these realities, some religiously and politically conservative Jews argue that a strong Christian hand in government and in society generally would ultimately be good for the Jews, for it would strengthen the Jewish resolve to remain Jewish. People, after all, define themselves, in part, by what others are doing. If everyone is (or appears) the same, nobody will have a strong sense of separate, unique identity. A strong Christian voice in government and society, then, might produce a strong Jewish response. Those who argue this also maintain that, in any case, many of the policies backed by the Christian right parallel Jewish values, and so we should support a strong Christian presence in government for that reason as well.

My own view differs substantially from that. With all of its pitfalls, the separation of church and state in this country is, for me, one of its most important assets. The great experiment in pluralism that the United States embodies is, in no small measure, a product of that separation, and so I value it as an American.

My Jewish roots, too, prompt me to support the separation of church and state. My people's historical experience makes me wary of living under a government ruled by one religion. I cannot trust that such a government would, in the end, preserve my right to adhere to my own religion. That would be especially true of a fundamentalist religion, for adherents of such groups tend to be completely sure that they are right and all others are wrong. While Judaism certainly champions strong families, communities, educational institutions, and the like, Jewish methods for arriving at those stances are definitely not fundamentalist, and most Jews, who consistently vote in overwhelming percentages for liberal candidates, are considerably less judgmental than fundamentalist Christians are of those who do not achieve such ideals.

Finally, my philosophical background motivates me to support a strong separation of church and state. Epistemologically, I believe in Mill's model for attaining social wisdom, based ultimately on Aristotle's moral epistemology—namely, that all views should be aired in the marketplace of ideas, with none given *a priori* authority (parallel to the "Establishment" clause of the First Amendment). Rather than deductively basing the definition of American concepts and values on a particular religious view, then, I would seek to determine America's commonalities in thought and values *inductively*, testing for agreement amid the diversity of traditions and attitudes brought to the table. This Aristotelian method of arriving at a decision is ultimately based on an acknowledgment that no human being is omniscient, that nobody has grounds to claim absolute knowledge, and that therefore the best that we can do is to pool our views in an attempt to arrive at the best policy. It also, coincidentally, parallels both the method and "the sound and the fury" of each page of the Talmud, where multiple opinions must be heard and evaluated before a decision is made, and where some arguments are left standing for lack of sufficient human wisdom to make a decision.

COHERENCE AND CONTINUITY AMID FREEDOM AND DIVERSITY

How, though, can agreement be reached if so many disparate voices are to be heard and somehow accommodated? When using this inductive model of decision-making, consensus is most probable, of course, when the people participating in the discussion come from similar backgrounds in the first place. Since they share common assumptions, they are more likely to agree on specific policies. Colonial America, where Madison and Jefferson created their ground-breaking provisions for religious freedom, was much less diverse than modern America is, and so America's Founding Fathers could more easily be assured that tolerance of religious differences would not undermine a coherent American society.

While consensus may be harder to achieve when the participants come from diverse backgrounds, I am convinced that substantial agreement is possible and that, moreover, the ultimate result will most likely be all the wiser for the variety of the experiences and views that were aired while shaping it. Liberty in America need not amount to anarchy; a core set of concepts and values can still define America as a coherent society.

Some examples will make this clear. In the two major national discussions on health care—that of the President's Commission on Health Care in the early 1980s, and that of the Clinton Task Force on Health Care of 1993—a remarkable degree of agreement prevailed. In reflecting on the essays produced during and for the President's Commission, Daniel Wikler noted this:

> It is true that each essay provides a different account of equity in access to health care and insists that rival accounts are mistaken. Yet there is one policy recommendation supported by each of these essays: Every person ought to be assured

> of access to some decent minimum of health care services. This conclusion cannot be said to have been "proved" by this collection of arguments, but the fact that a recommendation of universal access to (at least some) health care follows from such disparate sets of premises suggests that the recommendation is "insensitive" to choice of moral theory. Even if we do not know which moral theory is correct, then, and thus cannot provide a ground-level-up proof that all should have access to a minimum of health care, such a belief has been rendered reasonable and perhaps even compelling. In this sense, this diverse and inconsistent collection of theories of justice in health care delivery supports the consensus reached by members of the President's Commission concerning the moral obligation of our society to ensure access to health care for all its people.[5]

As a member of the Ethics Committee of President Clinton's Health Care Task Force, I can report that its experience was similar. The theoretical debates were many and, in some instances, heated. For example, in formulating the underlying moral principles that argued for universal health care guaranteed by the government, all of us agreed that the moral grounds for such a system included principles enshrined in the nation's constitutive documents, specifically, equality, justice, and the government's duty to "provide for the general welfare." The religious among us, though, wanted to include what Protestants call "our obligations of stewardship"—that is, our duty to take care of God's property, including our bodies. Even though the draft specified that the values held by all Americans would argue for universal health care and that religious Americans have yet other reasons to support the same policy, the secularists on the committee argued strenuously and heatedly to drop any and all religious language. Despite that controversy about its theoretical underpinnings, the policy advocated by both sides was the same—namely, that all Americans should be guaranteed health care.

Another example in a completely different arena will shed further light on both the strengths and weaknesses of this point. In light of a perceived failure of America's families and religious institutions to inculcate fundamental moral values, some school districts are now in the process of formulating a list of such values and curricular approaches to teach them. Clearly, these school districts have to be careful of running afoul of America's diversity in moral perspective. Indeed, these efforts are usually associated with the right wing in American politics that advocates "character education" to teach morality rather than the "values clarification" techniques favored by the more liberal elements. Values clarification assumes that each of us has his/her own unique list of values and/or interpretation of them, thus emphasizing individual freedom, while character education assumes that there is a core of objective values, regardless of background. Values clarification was popular in the 1960s, 1970s, and for part of the 1980s, but character education has more recently taken hold. Thus the Character Counts! Coalition, whose advisory council includes individuals from a variety of religious backgrounds and whose member organizations include 61 institutions, including such national educational groups as the American Association of School Administrators, the American Federation of Teachers, and the National Education Association, formulated the Aspen Declaration:

1. The next generation will be the stewards of our communities, nation, and planet in extraordinarily critical times.
2. The present and future well-being of our society requires an involved, caring citizenry with good moral character.
3. People do not automatically develop good moral character; therefore, conscientious efforts must be made to help young people develop the values and abilities necessary for moral decision making and conduct.
4. Effective character education is based on core ethical values which form the foundation of democratic society—in particular, respect, responsibility, trustworthiness, caring, justice and fairness, and civic virtue and citizenship.
5. These core ethical values transcend cultural, religious, and socio-economic differences.
6. Character education is, first and foremost, an obligation of families; it is also an important obligation of faith communities, schools, youth and other human service organizations.
7. These obligations to develop character are best achieved when these groups work in concert.
8. The character and conduct of our youth reflect the character and conduct of society; therefore, every adult has the responsibility to teach and model the core ethical values and every social institution has the responsibility to promote the development of good character.

Along with this declaration the Josephson Institute, which coordinated the effort to formulate the Aspen Declaration and to have it approved by a wide variety of national bodies, has produced a series of educational materials for children and adults to explain these values in greater detail and to apply them to issues in daily living.[6]

While the liberal side of me, nurtured by my minority status as a Jew and by the feisty argumentativeness of the Jewish tradition, worries about such sweeping statements that confidently assure unanimity in moral viewpoint, I must admit that I have no quarrel with the six values articulated in Plank 4 of the Aspen Statement and in the educational materials produced by the Josephson Institute to inculcate them in a cross-cultural setting. Indeed, as I shall develop below, I think that the proper moral view is relativity, not relativism. These educational developments, then, as well as the policy examples on health care described above, illustrate that diversity need not amount to incoherence, that liberty need not produce license for lack of any unity of vision. Instead, America's wide variety of cultures and religions—Eastern as well as Western—can all be plumbed cooperatively to produce coherent social policy.

AREAS OF MORAL DISAGREEMENT

Sometimes, of course, religious differences make for differences in policy as well. The most obvious example is abortion. Since the Supreme Court's decision in *Roe v. Wade* (1973), Americans have had the Constitutional right to have an abortion during the first two trimesters of gestation, without any requirement to justify that decision to the doctor or government. Thomas Jefferson understood the matter this way: "The practice of morality [is] necessary for the well-being of society . . . . The interests of society require observation of those moral principles only in which all religions agree."[7] What does such freedom of religion entail when a particular medical procedure is required by some religions under at least some circumstances, permitted by others, and forbidden by others?

The Jewish tradition takes an intermediate stance on abortion between that of the Catholic Church and other right-to-life advocates, on the one hand, and the secularist/feminist view that it should always be a woman's own choice, on the other. For Judaism, the human body belongs to God; God therefore can and does make demands as to how we are to care for our bodies. This includes positive obligations, such as proper diet, sleep, hygiene, and exercise, and negative duties such as refraining from harming, let alone destroying, our body. Thus, contrary to secularist views, Judaism holds that a pregnant woman does not have free reign to determine the fate of her fetus, any more than any man or woman has ultimate authority over their bodies; God's rules governing how we are to treat our bodies must be followed.

On the other hand, Judaism takes a developmental view of the growth of the fetus into a human being, classifying the embryo up to forty days of gestation as "simply water," as the "thigh of its mother" from the forty-first day until birth, and as a full human being only upon birth. Normally, neither men nor women have the right to amputate their own thigh; that would be injuring one's body, which belongs to God. If one's thigh turns gangrenous, though, one has not only the right, but the duty to amputate the thigh in an effort to save one's life. Similarly, according to Jewish law, most of the time abortion is prohibited, but in some cases it is required, and in some cases it is optional. Specifically, if the fetus seriously imperils the life or health of the mother, she has the positive duty to abort the fetus, even if, as in the movie *Steel Magnolias*, she does not want to do so. In cases, though, where the fetus poses a risk to the life or health of the mother more than that of normal pregnancy, but not so much as to constitute a clear threat to her life or health, abortion is optional; the mother, in consultation with her doctor, must decide whether or not to assume the risk of going through with the pregnancy, taking whatever steps can minimize that risk. More recent rabbinic opinions would also permit an abortion, but not require it, when the fetus is, on the basis of testing, found to be grossly malformed or afflicted with a genetic disease like Tay-Sachs. In most cases, though, abortion is prohibited.[8]

Given that stance and the contrary positions of Catholics, on the one hand, and secularists, on the other, how should Jews—and, for that matter, all Americans—handle the issue legally? My own view, like Jefferson's, is that we should all argue for governmental noninterference. That is, when there is substantial moral agreement among Americans, the government should enact that moral standard. That clearly holds, for example, for laws against murder, theft, and even more recently accepted moral positions such as bans on smoking in public, closed places. Then policies can be enacted on an *ad hoc* basis, through the legislatures or the courts, as to the degree of deviance that will be tolerated from the general agreement in the name of respecting freedom of religion and conscience. That is precisely what the United States has already done, with differing results, in, for example, the cases of Mormons practicing polygamy, Jehovah's Witnesses refusing blood transfusions, and pacifists from a variety of backgrounds refusing to register for the draft or participate in a war.

Where Americans of good conscience differ widely on a given issue, though, as in the case of abortion, the government should remain neutral, refusing either to require or to criminalize any particular response and thus sanctioning whatever individual citizens think is right. It is then up to the leaders of each group to explain their position on abortion to their fellow members. As a Rabbi, then, I would urge Jews to refrain from abortion, even though it is legal in the United States, except under the circumstances mandated or permitted by Jewish law. Individuals, after all, decide not to do many legal things, whether out of personal preference or on religious or ideological grounds.[9] This would simply be another such case.

Another good example of this form of reasoning, but with a different result, is the debate on assisted suicide. Some people ask for assistance in committing suicide to stop their pain. Judaism permits (or, on some readings, demands) the use of as much medication as necessary to quell pain. Other people ask for help in dying because it seems to them that nobody cares whether they live or die. To counteract the feelings of abandonment and loneliness that often produce such requests, the Jewish duty to visit the sick (*biqqur holim*) becomes all the more important in our time of broken and far-flung families. Supplying pain medication and visiting sick people are appropriate Jewish responses to a person's serious illness; assisting in a suicide is not. My rabbinic ruling stating these positions was approved overwhelmingly by the Conservative Movement's Committee on Jewish Law and Standards on March 12, 1997.

Even though the Jewish position on assisted suicide is thus unambiguous, at least for Conservative Jews, that did not, in advance of the Supreme Court's ruling, automatically justify our submitting *amicus curiae* briefs to the Court asking it to adopt our view, and, now that the Court has ruled, our stance for Jews does not automatically justify strongly lobbying against state initiatives to permit rendering assistance in suicides. After all, some of our opposition to assisted suicide stems from distinctly Jewish conceptions of the value of life and of the role of God in it, and those arguments would be inappropriate grounds for court rulings or state legislation. Moreover, serious moral arguments have been adduced by two appellate courts and by others in favor of allowing such assistance. These factors would make me consider carefully whether I have sufficiently strong, non-religious reasons to oppose assisted suicide in addition to my religious grounds.

As it happens, I do have such reasons. Specifically, requests for assistance in suicide almost never arise in a morally pure context, where sufficient pain medication has been afforded, the patient is supported socially, psychologically, and spiritually by the presence of family and friends, and psychological depression has been treated; those approaches must be tried before assisted suicide would ever approach being justifiable. Moreover, in an era of managed care, the right to assistance in committing suicide can all too easily become the duty to accept such assistance. These reasons independent of religious perspectives would make me willing to lobby against initiatives permitting assisted suicide.

Jewish religious beliefs may assuredly influence my own view of any matter and hopefully that of other Jews, but in the pluralistic environment that is America I must learn to separate those concerns from arguments that apply to all Americans, regardless of their religious affiliation or lack thereof. While I am not happy with the number of abortions performed in this country or the reasons for many of them, I cannot formulate good, secular grounds for opposing other people's rights to have them, and hence it would be wrong for me to lobby for legislation to forbid them. In contrast, I can articulate grounds for Americans of all religious persuasions to oppose assisted suicide. Therefore, on the latter issue I am willing to take a more assertive stand in arguing for my position's adoption into law.

THEOLOGICAL GROUNDS FOR RELIGIOUS PLURALISM

If I have a clear position on abortion, though, why should I advocate it in public forums and among my own co-religionists but hesitate to push for its adoption as law? That reluctance comes from my views about, and my commitment to, pluralism.

Some Orthodox Rabbis reject pluralism completely, both within the Jewish community and between Jews and non-Jews. So, for example, Rabbi Walter Wurzburger, past editor of the modern Orthodox journal, *Tradition*, and hardly among the hardliners within the Orthodox world, has said that: "Religious pluralism borders on religious relativism, if not outright nihilism. It rests on the assumption that no religion can be true and that it does not really matter what kind of myth we invoke in order to provide us with a sense of meaning and purpose."[10] Other Orthodox Rabbis, including Rabbis Joseph

Soloveitchik, Irving Greenberg, and David Hartman, have suggested ways in which Orthodox Jews can understand other Jews more appreciatively,[11] but none of their models would open the door to dialogue with non-Jews on national issues except on the most pragmatic of bases. However, Rabbi Simon Greenberg (1901–1993), a Conservative Rabbi who served in a variety of leadership capacities within the Conservative movement, has pointed out some features of Jewish theology that warrant pluralism not only among Jews, but between Jews and non-Jews, and I will mention some others. My goal is to explore the *theological* grounding for Jewish involvement in national policy formation but for Jewish restraint where serious moral disagreement exists among the subgroups of American society.

Rabbi Greenberg defines pluralism as "the ability to say that 'your ideas are spiritually and ethically as valid—that is, as capable of being justified, supported, and defended—as mine' and yet remain firmly committed to your own ideas and practices."[12] But what bestows legitimacy upon varying views such that a person should be pluralistic in outlook? Political pluralism, as mandated in the American Bill of Rights, can be justified by pragmatic considerations—namely, as of means to promote the peace and welfare of its citizens. What, however, legitimizes a spiritual or ethical pluralism?

Greenberg says that he knows of no philosophic justification for pluralism, for that would entail the legitimation of accepting a position and its contrary or contradictory. There is, however, a religious justification: God *intended* that we all think differently.

Greenberg learns this from, among other sources, the Mishnah, the most authoritative collection of rabbinic law from the first and second centuries. Why, the Mishnah asks, did God initiate the human species by creating only one man? One reason, the Mishnah suggests, is to impress upon us the greatness of the Holy One, for when human beings mint coins, they all come out the same, but God made one mold (Adam) and yet no human being looks exactly like another. This physical pluralism is matched by an intellectual pluralism for which, the Rabbis say, God is to be blessed: "When one sees a crowd of people, one is to say, 'Blessed is the Master of mysteries,' for just as their faces are not alike, so are their thoughts not alike."

The Midrash, the written record of rabbinic lore, supports this further. It says that when Moses was about to die, he said to the Lord: "Master of the Universe, You know the opinions of everyone, and that there are no two among Your children who think alike. I beg of You that after I die, when You appoint a leader for them, appoint one who will bear with (accept, *sovel*) each one of them as he thinks (*lefi da'ato*)." We know that Moses said this, the Rabbis claim, because Moses describes God as "God of the *ruhot* (spirits [in the plural]) of all flesh" (Numbers 24:16).[13] Thus God created us to be pluralistic, and that feature of human beings reminds us of the grandeur of God.

In addition to these sources mentioned by Greenberg, other elements of the Jewish tradition would support a pluralistic attitude. God intentionally, according to the Rabbis, reveals only a part of His truth in the Torah, and the rest must come from study and debate.[14] Study, though, can never remove the ultimate limits of human knowledge, for, as the medieval Jewish philosopher, Joseph Albo, said, "If I knew Him, I would be He."[15] Moses himself could not see God directly but only through a lens, and the other biblical prophets, although accepted as true by the tradition, saw God only through nine lenses, and cloudy ones at that: "What was the distinction between Moses and the other prophets? The latter looked through nine lenses, whereas Moses looked only through one. They looked through a cloudy lens, but Moses through one that was clear."[16]

Even those who stood at Sinai, according to the Rabbis, understood the revelation given there through their own individual abilities and perspectives.[17] "Every way of man is right in his own eyes, but the Lord weighs the hearts" (Proverbs 21:2); as Rashi (1035–1104) explains, this means that God judges each of us by our intentions precisely because a human being cannot be expected to know the truth or the right as God knows them.

God as understood in the Jewish tradition thus wants pluralism not only to demonstrate His grandeur in creating humanity with diversity, but also to force human beings to realize their epistemological creatureliness, the limits of human knowledge in comparison to that of God. One is commanded to study; one *is* supposed to be committed to learning as much of God, His world, and His will as possible. One must recognize, though, that a passion for truth does not mean that one has full or exclusive possession of it; indeed, both of the latter are humanly impossible.

Moreover, one should understand that everyone's quest for religious knowledge is aided by discussion with others, for different views force all concerned to refine and evaluate their own positions. Thus, according to the Talmud, the law is generally according to the School of Hillel rather than the School of Shammai. The School of Hillel reversed their position a number of times in response to their rivals' arguments, whereas the School of Shammai did so at most once. The Hillelites understood the epistemological and theological value of plural views and the need to learn from others.

Thus an appropriate degree of religious humility would lead one to engage in spirited, spiritual argumentation; one would not assume that one knows the truth and attempt to exclude others by fiat or by social pressure. One can and must take stands, but one should do so while remaining open to being convinced to the contrary. One should also recognize that others may intelligently, morally, and theologically both think and act differently. From the standpoint of piety, pluralism emerges not from relativism, but from a deeply held and aptly humble monotheism.

These sources indicate that pluralism is a divine creation; as such, human beings should try to adopt it, but they have difficulty doing so. To achieve the ability to be pluralistic is, in fact, the ultimate ethical and spiritual challenge, according to Greenberg. Just as "love your neighbor as yourself"—

which, for Rabbi Akiba, is the underlying principle of all the commandments[18]—requires a person to go beyond biologically rooted self-love, pluralism requires a person to escape egocentricity. It is not possible for human beings totally to love their neighbors as themselves, and neither is it possible to be totally pluralistic. We are, by nature, too self-centered fully to achieve either goal. The tradition, however, prescribes methods to bring us closer to these aims. Many of the biblical directions to gain love of one's neighbor appear in that same Chapter 19 of Leviticus in which the commandment itself appears. The Rabbis' instructions as to how to become pluralistic are contained, in part, in a famous talmudic source describing the debates of Hillel and Shammai: one must, like Hillel, be affable and humble and teach opinions opposed to one's own, citing them first.[19]

APPLYING THESE FACTORS TO PUBLIC POLICY DISCUSSIONS

It is difficult to convince some Jews of these theological reasons to tolerate and, indeed, rejoice in plural views *within* the Jewish community. One can readily understand, then, that such Jews—largely within the Orthodox camp—would have even more difficulty applying this mentality to non-Jews. Moreover, most of the above sources were clearly intended only for intra-Jewish dialogue. Nevertheless, it seems to me that some of these same considerations can form the foundation for a mutually respectful interaction among Americans of all faiths and none.

History

Historically, Christianity, to take the faith of America's majority, has been subject to change and redefinition at least as much as Judaism has, if not more so. There are, after all, over 150 denominations within American Protestantism, each with its own version of Christian faith and practice. Even within the same denomination, creeds created centuries ago are continually revised, sometimes through outright amendment and sometimes through new interpretations, emphases, and/or applications. This constantly evolving nature of both Judaism and Christianity makes some of the faithful uneasy; they long for certainty and stability. At the same time, though, each religion retains its relevance and its dynamism only by opening itself to change.

Whatever the pluses and minuses, the historical fact is that both religions *have* changed and continue to do so. The certainties of today, *even within the boundaries of one's own faith*, are not necessarily the convictions of tomorrow. Sometimes those changes are the product of internal development, and sometimes they come in reaction to external influences. History does not undermine one's ability to take a strong stand on what one believes. The historically evolutionary nature of both faiths should, however, help contemporary Jews and Christians get beyond the feeling that the present articulation of their faith is the only one possible for a decent person to have, and it should teach them that people of intelligence, morality, and sensitivity most likely exist in other faiths too—faiths that just might influence one's own.

Philosophy

This realization is only reinforced when one turns from historical considerations to philosophical ones. All human beings, whatever their background or creed, suffer from the same limitations on human knowledge. Many of us have sacred texts and traditions which, for us, reveal God's nature and will as clearly and fully as we think possible. Others, like Hindus and Buddhists, who do not worship the God of the Western faiths, nevertheless have documents that, in their view, articulate ultimate truth, goodness, and wisdom. When we recognize that other peoples make the same claim as our own group does for ultimate truth and goodness, we must either resort to vacuous and disingenuous debates like those of the Middle Ages as to which is correct, or we must confront the fact that none of us can know God's nature or will—or ultimate truth, goodness, or wisdom—with absolute certainty.

At the same time, just as the historical considerations do not make it rationally impossible or inadvisable to affirm a specific faith, so the philosophical factors do not. To see this, Van Harvey's distinction between "non-perspectivists," "hard-perspectivists," and "soft-perspectivists" will be helpful. Non-perspectivists claim that we look at the world through epistemologically transparent eyeglasses; all of us, then, would see the world in the same way if we only were sufficiently intelligent and attentive. On the other end of the spectrum, hard perspectivists claim that one's own specific view of the world is so entrenched in one's thinking and acting that no person can understand, let alone learn from, the views of others. In between these approaches to knowledge is soft perspectivism, which claims that we each have a perspective that influences how we think and act, but it is not so hard and fast that it blinds us to the views of others or makes it impossible to learn from them.[20]

If we take a non-perspectivist or hard-perspectivist approach to human knowledge, we will likely affirm our own view of things and think that alternative views are simply incorrect. Since non-perspectivists think that we should all see the same truth, they would likely advance a number of arguments in an attempt to convince those who disagree with them. Hard-perspectivists, on the other hand, might give up on such a project fairly early, convinced that those who disagree are simply too blind to see the truth and that no rational argument will help (although force may). As long as we acknowledge ahead of time, though, that no human argument on these matters can be conclusive, and as long as we assert that our particular understanding of God (and/or truth, goodness, wisdom) is the correct one for all people *as far as we can tell*, we may still leave room for a kind of pluralism in which we appreciate the intelligence and sensitivity of others, even if we disagree with their views on specific issues. One need not deny cognitive meaning to religion to take such a position, as A. J. Ayer, R. B. Braithwaite, and others did in the middle of this century;[21] one need only be humble enough to recognize that none of us is omniscient and that we are all trying to articulate the truth, the good, and the wise.

Alternatively, we may take the more "live and let live" approach embodied in soft-perspectivism. That is, we would recognize that part of the reason that the arguments for my faith seem most persuasive to me is because it is, after all, *my* faith and that of my family and my people. This view has the advantage of recognizing not only that none of us is omniscient, but also that none of us is an objective observer, that we all view the world from one or another vantage point, and that our autobiographical backgrounds inevitably do, and perhaps should, play a role in determining the content of our particular viewpoint.

Such soft perspectivism, aside from being, in my view, philosophically most astute, affords the strongest foundation for mutually respectful relations among peoples of varying faith communities and secularists, for it acknowledges the critical role our particular viewpoint has in shaping our knowledge and yet our continuing ability to learn from others who come from other traditions and who hold other views. That is, soft-perspectivism constitutes the philosophical justification and motivation for dialogue: we can and should learn from others, including the civility that comes from such discussions. At the same time, soft-perspectivism enables us to affirm what we believe as our view *of the truth*—whether that be understood as God's will or in non-theological terms—and so knowledge and values do not dissolve into whatever I, or a group, thinks is true or right. That is, soft-perspectivism does not amount to solipsism or relativism, either epistemologically or ethically. It is rather a form of relativity, where there is an objective truth to be known, but we recognize that we can only know it through the lenses of our own vantage point.

Theology

If all the Israelites at Sinai heard God according to their individual abilities and perspectives, those who came after Sinai—Jews, Christians, Muslims, and even those who adhere to Oriental religions—must surely have heard God in different ways as well. This should open us to listen to other people's understanding of God's will.

And yet there are inevitably limitations to such openness. It may be the case that God wants us to think independently and to listen to those who hold differing beliefs, but ultimately the biblical prophets assert that Judaism's Torah is God's true teaching, the one that all nations will ultimately learn. Micah, a younger contemporary of Isaiah, copies the latter's messianic vision of universal adherence to the God of Israel but then adds a line of his own which effectively changes it: "Though all the peoples walk each in the names of its gods, we will walk in the name of the Lord our God forever and ever."[22] This is a decidedly pluralistic vision of Messianic times: every people shall continue to follow its own god. Even so, Micah added this line *after* quoting Isaiah's vision that "the many peoples shall go and say: 'Come, let us go up to the Mount of the Lord, to the House of the God of Jacob, that He may instruct us in His ways, and that we may walk in His paths.' For instruction shall come forth from Zion, the word of the Lord from Jerusalem" (Isaiah 2:3; Micah 4:2). Thus even for Micah, apparently, other gods and other visions of the good life might exist, but it is only Israel that has the true understanding of God's will.

It is only natural that Jewish sources should reflect a tension between nationalism and universalism.[23] God is, according to Jewish belief, the God of all creatures, but, at the same time, God chose the Jews to exemplify ideal standards for human life. This is how *Jews* understand God's will, the reason why Jews commit all their energies and, indeed, their very lives to Jewish belief and practice.

Despite this nationalistic side of the Jewish tradition, however, what ultimately rings through it is the Rabbis' assertion that non-Jews fully meet God's expectations by abiding by the Seven Noahide Laws and the Rabbis' statement that "The pious and virtuous of all nations participate in eternal bliss."[24] Jewish sources that speak about God wanting plural approaches to the Eternal within the Jewish community can thus apparently be applied, without too much tampering, to inter-communal relations as well. Of course, the same segments of the Jewish community that have difficulty with the former would undoubtedly have difficulty with the latter, but even some pluralists within the Jewish community would need to stretch their understanding and sensitivity to apply Jewish theology in this way. Nevertheless, a firm basis for this kind of theology exists within the Jewish tradition.

Morality

Finally, moral concerns argue for respectful, but fully articulated dialogue, including the religious elements in people's positions. Even when such discussions do not directly affect a given policy decision, they can lead to understanding, tolerance, and even confession. These, in and of themselves, are beneficial to society, moral qualities that we want to promote in everyone.

Often, though, such discussions can indeed contribute recommendations for the issues at hand or suggest approaches that people would not otherwise have considered. So, for example, only Vermont and Wisconsin have established a positive duty to help someone in distress; indeed, until the recent passage of "Good Samaritan laws," in many states a person who tried to help someone else might be sued if anything untoward happened. Even in Vermont and Wisconsin, failure to come to the aid of another results in minimal fines, a legal "slap on the wrist." Jewish law, though, establishes a firm duty to come to the aid of another based on the biblical command, "Do not stand idly by the blood of your neighbor" (Leviticus 19:16). This means, to take the Talmud's example, that if you see someone drowning, you may not ignore him or her but must do what you can to save that person's life.[25] The moral character of American society has not been formed, and will not be, by laws and judicial rulings alone; much of our own sense of self comes from our moral ideals, the kind of people we would like to be. Thus, even if this Jewish ideal does not take the form of law, it can, if expressed in open discussions, motivate others to rethink their own sense of the level of responsibility we should have toward others, thus contributing to how Americans feel about each other and treat each other.

BRINGING RELIGION AND NATION CLOSER TOGETHER

I grew up in the 1950s and 1960s, when Jews roundly applauded each new brick being added by the Supreme Court to the wall of separation between church and state. The position that I have taken in this paper thus represents somewhat of a change for me. Instead of advocating all efforts to keep the public square as naked of religious views as possible, I now find myself instead arguing for religious Americans to come to the public debate as the religious people they are, contributing their distinctive religious perspectives to the discussion about, and creation of, national policy. I am not arguing here for governmental *economic* support for religious groups, even nonpreferential sponsorship such as that in Canada; whether that should happen in the United States would require another paper. In this essay, I am only arguing that American *policy* discussions and decisions should be enriched by the unself-conscious expression of religious views.

Jefferson and Madison had good reason to fear the entanglement of religion in national matters. The European experience had demonstrated beyond all reasonable doubt that that is not good either for religion or for the state. Moreover, the Jewish historical experience might suggest the same, for Jews have been badly burned when governments have done anything but let them be. In America, though, we do ourselves, religion, and the nation a disservice if we think that religion should have no role in shaping national policy. No religion should determine national policy as a matter of right, but each religion must enter the fray of public debate if that discussion is to reflect the nation as a whole and if it is to attain the richness and wisdom that only multiple parties with differing views can give it. In that sense, religion should not be stuck behind a "wall of separation," but should rather be integrally involved in our attempts to achieve the American dream of pluralism.

NOTES

In the following notes, M. = Mishnah (edited c. 200 C.E.); J. = Jerusalem (Palestinian) Talmud (edited c. 400 C.E.); B. = Babylonian Talmud (edited c. 500 C.E.); M.T. = Maimonides' *Mishneh Torah* (1177); and S.A. = Joseph Karo's *Shulhan Arukh* (1565).

1. *Everson v. Board of Education of Ewing Township* (1947).

2. M. *Avot* 3:2; B. *Avodah Zarah* 4a; B. *Zevahim* 102a. One was even supposed to pray for the welfare for non-Jewish (as well as Jewish) kings: B. *Berakhot* 58a.

3. M. *Avot* 1:10; 2:3.

4. For a thorough treatment of this episode from the point of view of Jewish sources, see Gil Graff, *Separation of Church and State: Dina de-Malkhuta Dina in Jewish Law, 1750–1848* (Birmingham: University of Alabama Press, 1985).

5. Daniel Wikler, "Philosophical Perspectives on Access to Health Care: An Introduction," in *Securing Access to Health Care* (Washington, D.C.: U.S. Government Printing Office, 1983), Vol. 2, p. 48.

6. The Aspen Declaration was formulated in the Summer, 1992 Aspen Summit Conference on Character Education. According to the Josephson Institute publicity materials, the member organizations include, as of July 1, 1997, fifty-five educational individual schools and regional school boards (e.g., Toledo, Ohio Public Schools), and the Institute has conducted ethics seminars for government groups and the staffs of a number of corporations as well as training the personnel of these schools to educate their students in the six values delineated in the Aspen Declaration. Books on character education include Thomas Likona, *Educating for Character*, and Michael Josephson, *Teaching Ethics in the 90s.* I would like to thank Dr. Michael Zeldin, Professor of Education at Hebrew Union College in Los Angeles, for his help with this educational example of my point here.

7. Cited by E. Raab, untitled essay, in *American Jews and the Separationist Faith*, David G. Dalin, ed. (Washington, D.C.: Ethics and Public Policy Center, 1993), pp. 110–111.

8. For a thorough treatment of this matter, see David M. Feldman, *Birth Control in Jewish Law* (New York: New York University Press, 1968) (reprinted as *Marital Relations, Birth Control, and Abortion in Jewish Law* [New York: Schocken, 1975]), chs. 14 and 15.

9. The religious grounds may include fear of punishment by God or exclusion from one's own religious community. Thus, even though the government may not enforce a particular religious view of what is true or right, other human agencies may, and some individuals or groups may believe that ultimately God will punish or reward specific forms of belief or behavior.

10. Walter Wurzburger, in *A CAJE Symposium: Division, Pluralism, and Unity Among Jews* (New York: Conference for Alternatives in Jewish Education, 1986), p. 11.

11. For a discussion of these various approaches, see Elliot N. Dorff, "Pluralism," in *Frontiers of Jewish Thought*, Steven T. Katz, ed. (Washington, D.C.: B'nai B'rith Books, 1992), pp. 219–229.

12. Simon Greenberg, "Pluralism and Jewish Education," *Religious Education* 81:1 (1986), p. 23. Cf. also p. 27, where he links pluralism to the absence of violence in transforming another person's opinion.

13. *Ibid.*, pp. 24, 26. The Mishnah cited is M. *Sanhedrin* 4:5; the blessing cited is in B. *Berakhot* 58a; and the Midrash cited is in *Midrash Tanhuma* on Numbers 24:16.

14. J. *Sanhedrin* 22a; *Midrash Tanhuma*, ed. Buber, Devarim, 1a; *Numbers Rabbah* 19:6. These sources are reprinted in their original Hebrew form and translated in Elliot N. Dorff, *Conservative Judaism: Our Ancestors to Our Descendants* (New York: United Synagogue of Conservative Judaism, 1996), pp. 75–76, 85–86.

15. Joseph Albo, *Sefer Ha-Ikkarim*, Part II, Chapter 30; trans. Isaac Husik (Philadelphia: Jewish Publication Society, 1946), Vol. II, p. 206.

16. *Leviticus Rabbah* 1:14.

17. *Exodus Rabbah* 29:1; see also 5:1; *Mekhilta*, "Yitro," Chapter 9; *Pesikta d'Rav Kahana*, "Bahodesh Hashlishi," end of Chapter 12, on Exodus 20:2 (Mandelbaum edition, Vol. 1, p. 224); *Tanhuma*, "Shemot," no. 22 (Buber edition, p. 7b); "Yitro," no. 17 (Buber edition, p. 40b).

18. *Sifra* to Leviticus 19:18. Ben Azzai instead cites "This is the book of the generations of Adam . . . in the likeness of God He made him" (Genesis 5:1)—a principle which extends love beyond Jews ("your neighbor") and ties it directly to God, whose image should be appreciated in every person.

19. B. *Eruvin* 13b.

20. Van A. Harvey, *The Historian and the Believer* (New York: Macmillan, 1966), pp. 205–230; cf. also James W. McClendon, Jr., and James M. Smith, *Understanding Religious Convictions* (Notre Dame, Indiana: University of Notre Dame Press, 1975), pp. 6–8.

It is interesting to note that even a medieval, hard-line anti-rationalist like Judah Halevi was open to considering the claims of other faiths and recognized that part of his inability to accept them stemmed from the fact that they were not *his* faith, that he had not had personal experience with them; cf. his *Kuzari*, Book I, Sections 5, 6, 25, 63–65, 80–91 (trans. by Heinemann, pp. 31–32, 35, 37–38, 41–45).

21. The two non-perspectivists mentioned, A. J. Ayer and R. B. Braithwaite, share the view that religion does not make true or false assertions but rather motivates one emotionally. Ayer, though, sees this as a major limitation on religion, while Braithwaite thinks that this description is both accurate and laudatory of religion's role in life. Cf. A. J. Ayer, *Language, Truth, and Logic* (London: Dover, 1936), pp. 114–120. R. B. Braithwaite, *An Empiricist's View of the Nature of Religious Belief: The Eddington Memorial Lecture for 1955* (Cambridge: Cambridge University Press, 1955); reprinted in *Christian Ethics and Contemporary Philosophy*, Ian T. Ramsey, ed. (New York: Macmillan, 1966), pp. 53–73.

22. Micah 4:5. Compare Micah 4:1–3 with Isaiah 2:2–4.

23. See Elliot N. Dorff, "The Covenant: How the Jews Understand Themselves and Others," *Anglican Theological Review* 64:4 (1982), pp. 482–484; reprinted in *Toward a Theological Encounter: Jewish Understandings of Christianity*, Leon Klenicki, ed. (New York: Paulist Press, 1991), pp. 45–48.

24. The doctrine of the Seven Noahide Laws appears in T. *Avodah Zarah* 8:4 and B. *Sanhedrin* 56a-b; it is thoroughly discussed in David Novak, *The Image of the Non-Jew in Judaism: An Historical and Constructive Study of the Noachide Laws* (New York: Edwin Mellon Press, 1983). The doctrine that righteous non-Jews inherit a place in the World to Come appears in the *Sifra* on Leviticus 19:18.

25. For the talmudic principle: B. *Sanhedrin* 73a. For this principle in American law, see, for example, Samuel Freeman, "Criminal Liability and the Duty to Aid the Distressed." *University of Pennsylvania Law Review* 142:5 (May, 1994), pp. 1455–1492; and Mitchell McInnes, "Protecting the Good Samaritan: Defences for the Rescuer in Anglo-Canadian Criminal Law," *Criminal Law Quarterly* 36:3 (May, 1994), pp. 331–371.

In Wisconsin the law requires that "anyone who knows that a crime is being committed and that a victim is exposed to bodily harm shall summon law enforcement officers or other assistance or provide assistance to the victim" unless compliance would put the potential rescuer in danger or would interfere with duties the person owes to others or assistance has already been summoned or provided by others (Wisconsin Criminal Statutes 940.34, "Duty to Aid Victim or Report Crime"). In Vermont, the law states that "a person who knows that another is exposed to grave physical harm shall, to the extent that the same can be rendered without danger or peril to himself or without interference with important duties owed to others, give reasonable assistance to the exposed person unless that assistance or care is being provided by others" (Vermont Statutes, Title 12, par. 519). Even in those two states, though, failing to save someone's life is a misdemeanor, punishable by a small fine (in Vermont the fine cannot be more than $100). Typical for American legal theory, this positive obligation, limited as it is, is justified as a protection against an abuse of the rights of the person in distress (since s/he has a right to life), not a moral duty which now has legal consequences. See Lon T. McClintock, "Duty to Aid the Endangered Act: The Impact and Potential of the Vermont Approach," *Vermont Law Review* 7:1 (Spring, 1982), pp. 143–183

On this duty in Jewish law generally, together with some comparisons to Western law, see Anne Cucchiara Besser and Kalman J. Kaplan, "The Good Samaritan: Jewish and American Legal Perspectives," *The Journal of Law and Religion* 10:1 (Winter, 1994), pp. 193–219; Ben Zion Eliash, "To Leave or Not to Leave: The Good Samaritan in Jewish Law," *Saint Louis University Law Journal* 38:3 (Spring, 1994), pp. 619–628; and Aaron Kirschenbaum, "The Bystander's Duty to Rescue in Jewish Law," *Journal of Religious Ethics* 8 (1980), pp. 204–226. I would like to thank professors Martin Golding and Arthur Rosett for these references.

11

Faith, Doubt, and Public Dialogue

Glenn Tinder

It is no longer easy to think seriously about dialogue. The term (now a verb, as well as a noun) is applied indiscriminately to all kinds of talk and negotiation, and has become so common it is tiresome. This is a kind of tribute to the idea, however, for until it was trivialized by carelessness and overuse it was one of the most appealing concepts current in social and political thought. It is at once warmly personal and coolly intellectual. Its provenance is both Jewish and Greek, having been worked out imaginatively in our own time by Martin Buber—presumably inspired by his knowledge of the listening and speaking God of Jewish Scripture—yet having at the same time a clear Socratic tone. It is celestial, one might say, since it denotes a search for ultimate realities, such as the idea of the Good in the Platonic dialogues; it is also earthly, for it is nothing more than serious conversation, carried on here and now, among concrete human beings.

The thesis of this essay is that the idea of dialogue possesses not merely faded charms but lasting worth. I shall try to uphold this thesis by showing how the idea can help us resolve one of the most intractable dilemmas facing liberal societies today: the proper role of religion in public life. Liberalism prescribes a public realm open to all arguments; yet religion seemingly rests on grounds which are publicly unarguable. The reigning solution to this problem, of course, is confining religion to the private realm, where choices need not be determined by convincing argumentation. It is gradually being recognized, however, that this is far from a satisfactory way of meeting the liberal dilemma. On the one hand, it falsifies religion. Implicitly, it treats religion as an avocation, a mere subjective interest; it asks the religious to regard their faiths as merely "true for them" rather than true universally. At the same time, it tends to trivialize not only religion but public life as well by separating it from ultimate issues. Public debate, it is assumed, must steer clear of the things people care about most. A conflict between the passion for liberty and the longing for transcendence, both arising from the depths of the human spirit, is potentially of tragic proportions. I want to show that the concept of dialogue can contribute to the resolution of this conflict.

To state my thesis in this way is by implication to define it more precisely. If the proper role of religion in public life can be worked out only through public dialogue, it follows that religious believers, *with the full panoply of their beliefs*, must be admitted into the public realm. The italicized proviso is crucial. No one, even now, would deny believers entry into the public realm—so long as they leave their religious beliefs behind. This, however, places them in the unsatisfactory situation already mentioned. The only kind of dialogue which can remove them from that situation is one which is all-inclusive, allowing believers *as believers* to engage in open debate with doubters and unbelievers. Someone may say, "Well, they can do that now; but they'd better back up their arguments with something other than the Bible if they expect to be heard." But that is tantamount to saying that, *as believers*, they will be ignored. In short, the public realm is closed to them.

But how *can* they be heard, in the sense of being thoughtfully listened to, by those who do not share their faith? In other words, how can a public realm that is open to expressions of faith, and in that way departs from the rule of public reason, be acceptable to those who try to base their political choices (and perhaps their private choices as well) exclusively on public reason—that is, on ground accessible to all alike? I shall discuss this question in the first main section of this essay. But there are similar questions concerning those on the other side of the great divide. Can believers, with all of their beliefs, fully and honestly enter into public debate? Is it in the nature of authentic faith to mix so indiscriminately with multifarious humanity? I shall discuss these questions in the following two sections of the essay. Throughout, I hope readers will remember that we are dealing not with a mere theoretical difficulty but with a profound dilemma of the spirit—the seeming antithesis between unfettered communication and uncompromising devotion to the ultimate good.

Two methodological postulates must be briefly specified. First, by public dialogue I mean conversation concerning public issues that is fundamentally democratic, in the sense of allowing participation by all adult citizens; that recognizes reason as essential to, although not necessarily the exclusive rule governing, the conduct of the conversation; and that has settled procedures by which the transition from talk to action can be made without either making action unduly difficult or curtailing conversation contrary to the minimal demands of reason. My other postulate concerns the nature of religion. I shall use generic words like "believers" and "unbelievers" whenever I can. But I shall be thinking mainly of Christianity and often I shall have to speak of Christianity. This is not because I assume Christianity to be the only legitimate religion, but because the term religion must be given flesh and blood. To speak in terms of mere religion would sometimes be too vague to have any theoretical value. I therefore ask—somewhat apologetically—that adherents of Judaism and other religions apart from Christianity be prepared to adapt and refashion my arguments as their own particular concerns may occasionally require.

UNBELIEVERS IN THE PUBLIC REALM

The question before us concerns the possibility of fully open public dialogue. In this section we are considering the question from the standpoint of unbelievers. How can they be expected to listen respectfully and honestly to expressions of faith, which by their very nature cannot be grounded in reason? In other words, how can those who try to guide their lives by reason, and not by faith, enter into unreserved discourse with those who give faith priority over reason? These questions have two basic answers.

The first is that unbelievers should accord believers the respect due every person. Such respect entails listening (we feed and shelter animals, and may even protect their lives and see to their comfort, but we do not listen to them). The respect owed to human beings is based on their intrinsic humanity, not on their opinions or even on their intelligence. By listening, you accord recognition. Hence we should listen to people we disagree with and we should do this even when our disagreement is based on divergent premises, such as those dividing believers and unbelievers. How, it may be asked, can you seriously listen when someone asserts principles that are at once unarguable and, in your view, in error? How, for example, can an atheist attend sincerely to a Catholic who affirms the truth of a doctrine as guaranteed by the infallibility of the Pope? There are two answers to this question. One of them derives from the principle that a person is not reducible to opinions and propositions. In facing someone with whom you disagree, even if your disagreement pertains to every conceivable principle of public life, you still face the mystery of a human personality, and listening is an indispensable way of acknowledging the mystery. Maintaining through sheer attentiveness a relationship attenuated by fundamental, principled differences is a perplexing and trying task. It is a necessary element, however, in the ethos that constitutes a realm of public dialogue. Reason alone does not suffice.

But neither does respect for personality, apart from reason, suffice. Hence the need for a second answer. This is one made familiar by classical liberalism: to reject an opinion unheard is contrary to reason, for only by hearing an opinion can you know whether it ought to be rejected. You should listen in order to discover the truth. Still, how is this possible when basic premises, that is, principles grounding reason and thus not themselves grounded in reason, are in conflict? It is possible partly because one's premises do not determine all of one's views; some views depend mainly on empirical or merely personal considerations. An economically illiterate unbeliever might learn from a believer who happens to be well-versed in economics. Moreover, an unbeliever might find even views rigorously deduced from a believer's faith to be acceptable, not on grounds of faith, but on grounds discerned by intuition or by reason. Archbishop Tutu's contention that crimes committed during the era of apartheid ought to be forgiven arises from his faith that human sins have been expiated by the death of Christ; an unbeliever might agree with Tutu—from a conviction that only through mutual forgiveness can peace in South Africa ever be attained. Religious and irreligious premises need not govern debate unconditionally.

There is a more radical reason, however, why unbelievers should attend to the voice of believers: their very unbelief may be in error. Dogma is commonly deplored by unbelievers; they should be wary, therefore, of dogmatic unbelief. If it is bad to be a dogmatic theist, presumably it is bad also to be a dogmatic atheist—a seemingly appropriate designation for an atheist unwilling to confront the fact that neither the existence nor the nonexistence of God is rationally demonstrable. The trouble with dogmatic unbelief, arguably, is not that it is dogmatic, and not even that it is atheistic, but that it is shallow. It refuses to acknowledge the rational abyss that underlies belief and unbelief alike.

It would be unrealistic to advance this argument, however, without recognizing that the radical openness of mind I am calling for will rarely, if ever, be encountered. People are not often sufficiently at ease in their ultimate commitments. Thus the only people truly open toward transcendence—open, that is, to revelation, to disclosures not certified by reason—may be those who are tacit, if not avowed, believers. The principle of openness is nevertheless important, for the question before us is not, in the final analysis, whether unbelievers are *likely* to listen to believers, but whether they *ought* to. The issue is moral rather than practical. How can believers address unbelievers *in good faith*, that is, on the presupposition that they have a right to be heard? That question seems to find an adequate answer in the principle of openness. A realm that is truly public presupposes unqualified care for the truth, hence unreserved attentiveness.

It may seem unfair that I have placed hard demands on unbelievers without placing commensurate demands on believers. Shouldn't believers be asked at the very least to frame their arguments in a way that will enhance to the greatest possible degree their acceptability to unbelievers? In other words, shouldn't they conform, to the utmost possible degree, to the requirements of public reason? Thus Walker Percy, arguing for legal restrictions on abortion, does not, as a Catholic, assert that abortion is murder because the Magisterium has so defined it; rather, as a physician, he states as a matter of plain biological fact that human life begins with conception. According to practically all Christian theologians (even Karl Barth), the knowledge to be drawn from revelation can also, in some degree, be drawn from secular sources. This means that Christians in the public realm can in many cases avoid arguing on grounds that divide them from non-Christians. Shouldn't they do so whenever they can?

The answer is not quite as obvious as one might suppose. It goes without saying that believers should not be any more objectionable in their public pronouncements than they have to be. Hence they should very often avail themselves of any common ground they share with unbelievers. Moreover, in referring to transcendence they should not always fall back on standard theological phrases of the kind that are apt to offend unbelievers. This is partly a matter of political prudence and of charity—of being as persuasive and as sincerely communicative as possible. But it is more than that. It dishonors God to reduce his Word to a handful of overused human words. If God is rich in wisdom and creative powers, then the translation of his Word into human words surely calls for translators who are rhetorically imaginative and resourceful. To say no more than this, however, would come close to saying that believers in the public realm should, whenever they can, disguise themselves as unbelievers. Once that is said, the public realm is again subjected to a secular closure. Public dialogue cannot unite believers and unbelievers unless the former can bring forth their faith, naked and unadorned, and count on respectful attention.

This, however, throws into doubt a restriction placed on believers by some of the most thoughtful defenders of their rights in the public realm. The restriction is this, that while believers may introduce matters of faith into public debate, they should not seek legislative enactments except on grounds that can be publicly argued. The logic of such a restriction is easily seen. Arguments are one thing, coercion another. When people are compelled to act contrary to their desires, they should be provided with reasons, even though the reasons will presumably seem inadequate to those coerced. To start with, however, one might ask, Why? Coercion is always an immediate evil, however beneficial its consequences, and it is not manifestly less evil if grounded on a process of reasoning you reject rather than on a faith you reject. To claim that you can argue against inadequate reasons but not against faith is not quite valid, for you *can* argue against faith, in the sense of arguing that it should not be embodied in a particular law. And you can do this not only before but after the law in question has been enacted. Statutes are not exempt from criticism or repeal. Procedures that turn discourse into action can, in turn, subject action to renewed discourse. The debate can continue. But this is not the major objection to the proposed restriction.

To say that statutory enactments must rest on publicly arguable grounds is to say that, while believers may base their arguments on faith if they like, they should not be permitted to win such arguments. To do that, they must be silent about the religious considerations which for them are finally persuasive. In other words, they must disguise themselves as unbelievers. This is the case, at least, if we assume that a political debate is usually not a mere theoretical inquiry but is a preface to legislative action. So again, however unintentionally, the public realm has been closed to believers.

Unbelievers (at least in the Western democracies) are typically outspoken, and sometimes courageous, defenders both of the dignity of persons and the value of truth. My argument, summarily, is that both standards dictate a fully open public realm, where believers are not under pressure to conceal their ultimate premises and are as sure of being heard as are unbelievers. I have tried to show that the latter have every reason to hear them. Can it be said, however, that believers have every reason to be thus heard? Is participation in public dialogue in their interest? More fundamentally, is it in character? In the following section, I shall address the second question.

BELIEVERS IN THE PUBLIC REALM

There is no skirting the embarrassing fact that Christianity, which we have taken as our model of religion, has not always been very dialogical in its relations with its adversaries. Not that it has been tyrannical. As uncompromising a figure as Augustine was strongly disposed to reason with his opponents and was reluctant to resist them with force. But he finally did resist them with force, as in the well-known case of the Donatists. And Augustine reflected the assumptions of the Christian empire he inhabited. As soon as Christianity became the established faith, efforts to stamp out paganism and suppress heresy began. The link between faith and official force was not severed until, under the impact of the religious diversity arising from the Reformation, it had to be. Given such a record, how can it be argued that religious faith belongs, *by virtue of its basic character*, in the public realm? Broadly I wish to argue that we learn more about the true nature of Christianity from Augustine's hesitations than we do from their eventual abandonment. Force is antithetical to fundamental Christian principles.

First of all is the principle (a principle important to Augustine) that faith is worthless unless it is freely chosen. More precisely, faith is not faith unless it is freely chosen; freedom belongs to its essence. Faith is an engagement of the whole person, and the concept of coerced faith is a contradiction in terms. Someone might say that this oversimplifies the usual situation. Coercion is not ordinarily used in order to drive a potential believer into actual belief but rather to silence a third party which might draw the potential believer away from belief. Coercion serves to suppress the alternatives to faith and thus to create an atmosphere in which faith is natural and easy. Such an objection has much validity and no doubt expresses the views that often animated the use of force by Christians. But is faith altogether freely chosen where, because there is nothing else at hand to choose, it is natural and easy? That is doubtful. It is arguable that faith embodies the freedom that belongs to its essence, and is thus complete, only in those believers who are fully cognizant (as was Augustine, for example, at the time of his conversion) of the claims of unbelievers. To the degree that this is so, faith is more than compatible with dialogue; it requires it.

Often, however, what unbelievers fear is less that believers will try through force to spread their faith than that they will try to exact conformity with their own versions of the moral law. They will attempt forcibly to make people good. I cannot claim that such a fear is groundless; there is too much historical evidence to the contrary. Nonetheless, the principle that faith is essentially voluntary applies also to morality. Moral actions have little worth unless they are free. Thus the burning moral consciousness that often and quite properly accompanies faith—the will to universal righteousness—is not necessarily repressive. It encounters the fact of freedom. The issue of abortion is a ready example. There is a strong argument, obscured by the polarities the controversy has created, that abortion is always, or almost always, wrong, yet that it ought, subject to procedures and delays designed to assure full deliberation on the part of the prospective mother, ordinarily to be allowed. Only thus can the bearing of children be undertaken altogether freely, thus realizing the moral quality intrinsic to it.

It may seem that a dialogic attitude of this sort is so far from traditional Christianity as to be implausible. But is it so far from the true character of Christianity? The wrath and severity of the God depicted in the Old Testament are so commonly commented on that it is often unnoticed that the Old Testament God is also dialogical; he is a God who speaks and listens. He is not out of character when he says to the Israelites, through the prophet Isaiah, "Come now, and let us reason together." (Isaiah 1:18.) Christianity has never entirely ignored the prophet's injunction. Christian evangelists have not ordinarily said to their hearers, "Simply believe, and don't ask why!" Paul was one of the most forceful reasoners in Western history. And from the time of the Church fathers to that of the great twentieth-century theologians, Christianity has provided the world with so many reasons for believing that few have had the time or patience adequately to weigh them. Indeed, in scholasticism Christianity produced a school of thought that has come to symbolize—however unfairly—reason run riot. These dialogical proclivities, stemming partly from the nature of the God encountered in Jewish Scripture, have been reinforced, as everyone knows, by Greek philosophy. More often than anyone could count, Christianity has been Socratic, or Platonic, or Aristotelian, or Stoic. Such rationalistic and dialogical proclivities are more securely anchored in the ocean-floor of Christian faith, however, than these remarks adequately indicate.

Jesus is conceived to be the Word—the Word which *in the beginning* was *with* God and which *was* God. God is God (one might almost say that God constitutes himself as God) through an act of communication, or dialogue. Jesus' appearance was God addressing the human race. Redemption came through a divine act of speech. That such speech ruled out violence seems plain from Jesus' submission to the Crucifixion; he told Peter to put away his sword. It is easy to think that the frequency with which Christians have resorted to force in support of their faith has obscured the very nature of their faith and of their relations with those not sharing it. We can gain some sense of all that was obscured by noting that if God defined himself in speaking the Word—if the Word *was* God—it is insufficient to say that God engaged in dialogue as though he might, while remaining the same God, have refused to engage in dialogue. God is dialogic in his innermost nature. It could be argued, indeed, that the doctrine of the Trinity is a dialogic symbol: the procession of the Holy Spirit consummates the act of communication which begins with the generation of the Word.

It would be well, in order to understand my argument, not to strip it of every qualification that common sense might suggest. Christians striving to do justice to the God of the Word are not obliged to plunge heedlessly into the torrents of public dialogue, nor need they entrust their faith to every current and caprice of public discussion. The proposition that God in his innermost nature is dialogic cannot be translated directly into political doctrine. Christians can hardly ignore the fact that Paul did not evince much enthusiasm for dialogue. Typical are the words in which he deplored "disputes about opinions" and (assuming the letter to the Ephesians to be reflective of his views, even if not written by him) the way in which Christians allow themselves to be "tossed to and fro and carried about with every wind of doctrine."[1] It may be that dialogue among creatures who are as distant from the truth in their finitude and fallenness as are human beings is workable only when balanced by stable doctrine and authority. Perhaps, for example, public dialogue will be most fruitful among those belonging to relatively authoritarian ecclesiastical structures. A certain tension between doubt and dogma may be dialogically healthy. Such matters, no doubt varying with time and place, cannot be examined here in detail. The point I am making is simply that a commitment to dialogue does not imply a repudiation of every restraint. Dialogue is a civilized practice and presupposes not only deliberative abilities but also the kind of civilized instincts that express themselves in qualities like prudence. Seeking the absolute, dialogue is also a religious practice; it belongs consequently in the company of the kind of reverential attitudes that can sanctify a tradition.

My argument so far might be summarily restated by saying that believers, at least in the case of Christians, are constrained by their own beliefs to rely heavily on words. For a wise and experienced Christian, the intellectual posture required by public dialogue is not strange or contorted. Unbelievers may be forgiven their suspicions in this matter, given the intolerance Christians have often displayed. May we not think, however, that the intolerance of believers tells us more about their human weaknesses than about their deepest principles? The latter suggest that Christians, and perhaps religious believers of various kinds, can be as fully at home in the realm of public dialogue as are disciples of the Enlightenment.

Indicative of the deep congruence between Christianity and public dialogue is the question of whether a dialogical society could long endure without Christian support and involvement. Dialogue depends on respect both for truth and for persons. Such values are so commonly spoken of that we tend to assume that they are obvious. But they are not. It is not obvious that truth is worthwhile regardless of whether it is useful or pleasant; nor is it obvious that every person, even one who is ignorant, unintelligent, or selfish, is a possessor of dignity and a rightful participant in public dialogue. In a thoroughly secularized society, truth tends to lose its inherent splendor and to be prized on pragmatic grounds alone. Persons in like fashion are apt to be looked on as mere consumers and voters, no more than targets of advertising and political manipulation. Under a secularist impulse, therefore, public life may degenerate into the cultivation of popularity and the play of propaganda; culture may become entertainment, and intellectual life may fall under the dominion of fashions like deconstruction; democracy will tend to decline from universal discourse into the mechanics of majority rule, or, more often, majority acquiescence in varieties of minority rule; and liberty will be apt to enfranchise self-indulgence rather than an inquiring life. It is doubtful that any recovery from these diseases of the mind and spirit is possible except on the basis of foundations which religion alone can provide.

If there is truth in my argument, it goes a long way toward meeting the most common objection to the uninhibited presence of believers in the public realm, namely, that it exposes unbelieving minorities to unreasonable risks. Public debate, it is said, may prove to be only an antechamber to political power. This is why believers, as believers, should be confined to the private realm. Thus in the abortion controversy, those favoring restrictions are often denounced on the grounds, not that their arguments are invalid, but that they are implicitly religious. As such, they are out of order in a free society. My response can easily be inferred from all I have said. Christian support for public dialogue is not casual or accidental; it mirrors the core of their creed. When Christians resort to force, they compromise their faith. Consequently, even when they "win," when they are persuasive enough to have their convictions expressed in laws, *they must allow the argument to continue.* Otherwise, they betray their very character as Christians. They might of course do this. Nonetheless, it cannot be maintained that faith in its very nature imperils public freedom.

Even if participation in public dialogue is in character for believers, however, it may seem to many of them not to be in their interest. There are several far-from-contemptible reasons why Christians might, in spite of all that has been said, hesitate to engage themselves fully in public dialogue.

CHRISTIAN HESITATIONS

The burden of proof, we should note at the outset, is on the side of the hesitations. Christians are under strong obligations to take part in public life, and these are outweighed by only the most compelling counter-considerations. Those who believe that the Savior of the human race came among us as one comprehensively true and sufficient *Word*—speech addressed to the human race by God—cannot casually turn their backs on the human world of discourse and talk. That would be to flout the dialogical ethic implicit in the act of divine redemption. Moreover, there are commonsense considerations dictating Christian participation in public dialogue. Christians are members of the human race and to be human and Christian must think and live accordingly. That means they must think and live politically, for politics can be summarily defined as the affairs of human beings collectively. Those who spurn politics abstract themselves from the human race. Christians who do so defy the precept of love. Finally, there is the matter of representing Christianity accurately before the world. A Christianity carrying no political meaning and no political responsibilities would look—and be—unreal. It would justify the notion that Christianity is in the nature of an idiosyncratic interest rather than an orientation of life pertinent to universal humanity. In that way it would lend substance to the prejudices of unbelievers.

These obligations have nearly absolute authority. They overrule all Christian hesitations about entering into public dialogue except those sustained by some uniquely strong justification, such as a strict and often-repeated scriptural injunction. It is doubtful that any are thus sustained. Consider, for example, the fear some Christians may feel that confessing their faith in the public realm would be casting their pearls before swine.

Jesus' warning against doing this indicates that such hesitation may at times be appropriate. Faith may properly be reticent. On occasion, then, believers can in good conscience wear disguises and translate their theological convictions into secular terms. Shielding their faith from the scorn of unbelievers may express an awareness of what is owing to the honor of God. At other times, however, it may involve a sin that Christians should especially dread: that of being embarrassed by their faith. Jesus warned his followers explicitly on this score. He would be "ashamed" at the end of the ages, he said, of those ashamed of confessing his name before men. One scriptural injunction, then, is counterbalanced by another. Faith cannot always be reticent; Christians must sometimes render their certainties vulnerable to the most corrosive criticisms unbelievers can bring against them. We need not try to decide when reticence, and when candor, should be the rule. The significant point is that the rule of reticence is not absolute. There is room—left by Jesus' own words—for Christians to observe the obligations of public dialogue.

Another far-from-negligible, yet inconclusive, reason some Christians draw back from the public realm is apprehension that the pressures and allurements of public debate will induce Christian participants to identify Christianity with some particular political program or ideology. This has happened often in our time. Christians have spoken as though the cause of Christianity were roughly the same as that of free enterprise or racial integration or some other, often commendable, political aim. Admittedly, there are circumstances in which Christianity seems to demand a particular political stand. Opposition to Nazism is an example; Dietrich Bonhoeffer did not falsify his faith. But many Christians, involved with political issues less primal than Nazism, seem to have forgotten that Christianity is not a political program. Jesus made this clear not only by the overall character of his ministry, but also by particular words and acts, as when he demanded of a man who requested help in getting his brother to share their inheritance fairly, "Man, who made me a judge or divider over you?"[2] Anyone taking into account the extent to which the work of government consists in judging and dividing will appreciate the full antipolitical force of Jesus' words.

Simply abstaining from politics, however, would violate the obligations discussed above. The danger therefore must be met not by withdrawal but by discretion. Christians in the public realm must be as wise as serpents. They must be not only politically astute, but spiritually tactful, placing above every political concern their concern for the integrity of the Gospel. They must be unfailingly cognizant of certain crucial distinctions: between the responsibilities of clergy and laity; between the dangers attending clerical speech (which may be construed by the public as the official voice of the Church) and lay speech; between demands arising in times of crisis (as in Germany in the 30s) and those arising in more ordinary times; between stating moral principles which may help voters ponder public issues and binding them to particular actions (for example, by distributing voters' guides in church); and so forth. We see again that for Christians to behave well in the public realm they need not only faith but prudence as well.

Yet another source of hesitation about participation in public dialogue may be fear of weakness. The Christian drive toward power goes back at least to the Age of Constantine; that it survives in the twentieth century, despite the fragmentation and disempowerment of the Church, will be manifest to any observer of the political activities of religious groups in the United States. By no means is this drive always reprehensible; in many cases it manifests an appropriate concern for Christian survival and influence. And if, as I have suggested, dialogue is compatible, and even needs to be counterbalanced, with authority, the same may be true of power too. Still, the aspiration to office and influence sits uneasily with what we might call dialogic integrity. It places one in quite a different relationship with people than does the pure desire to inquire with them into the truth. If a single word can signalize the difference, it might be said that the latter relationship is intersubjective. Power, in contrast, objectifies those over whom it is exercised. If this be true, then dialogue implies powerlessness. To invite others into an intersubjective realm is to relinquish power over them. A premonition of this weakness probably causes many believers to recoil from the dialogic ideal. And not without reason: it is realistic to think that if believers committed themselves more fully to public dialogue, and moderated their drive toward office and influence, they would often be the losers in political contests. Stripped of everything but words and faith, they would be weak. But would that be intolerable? Wasn't Jesus weak? Can't it be claimed, indeed, that the "power" of the Cross is inseparable from the weakness it symbolizes? Doesn't the Cross tell us that *truth is crucified* in the world at large and only in that way is vindicated and made known?

More troubling, perhaps, than questions deriving from fear of political weakness are those deriving from fear of spiritual weakness. Believers may be apprehensive that faith itself will be shaken in confrontations with unbelievers in the public realm. It is not confrontations confined to the political level, obviously, which are dangerous. An atheist may have keener insight into the likely consequences of a bill bearing on public finances, or of a proposed change in foreign policy, than a believer. The latter, in such circumstances, can learn from the former without risking a crisis of faith. We are concerned rather with confrontations of the kind that may occur when believers appeal in public debate to the religious commitments underlying their political commitments. Can it be asked of believers that they place their most cherished beliefs in harm's way?

Not always need they do this. There is a difference between the substance of one's faith and the words in which the substance is cast. Although these are not entirely separable, neither are they the same. The assurances on which a life is based are often not adequately reflected in the words which represent them in public. Thus the phrase "justification by faith," and even extended explanations of that doctrine, are not apt to convey the inner confidence of devout Christians that they have been transfigured by the Crucifixion and Resurrection. This distinction can have a significant bearing on public dialogue. It is often merely the verbal clothing of one's faith, and not the faith itself, which is placed in jeopardy in the public realm. The idea that faith seeks understanding, and does this through rational inquiry, is ancient and well-established in the Christian tradition. In many dialogic situations, Christians can feel that the substance of their faith is well shielded from attack and that there are prospects, through debate, of coming to understand it better. In confessing their ultimate premises, they are not challenging others to blow up the ground they stand on. Along these lines it can be explained how it is logically possible for "true believers" to be tolerant of and talk freely with unbelievers.

Not always, however, can faith and understanding be neatly separated. A clash of political opinions will sometimes become a clash of religious convictions, as in the abortion controversy. When this happens there seems no way for believers to avoid a hard imperative. They must strive to practice the same unqualified openness of mind which they ask of unbelievers. I have argued that unbelievers must have the courage to imperil their fundamental convictions by facing fairly the counterconvictions of believers. Can one ask less of believers? There are serious Christians who will deride such open-mindedness; they will see it as exemplifying the dilution of religion by liberal pieties. And Jesus' denunciation of those who, having begun the journey of faith, look back, would add weight to their protest. It is difficult, however, to see how believers in our pluralistic times can close their minds to the intellectual possibility of unbelief without cutting themselves off from that great host of conscientious and intelligent people who happen, in our time, to be unbelievers. And how can believers close their minds to unbelief without falsifying the spiritual situation of human beings in a fallen world, a situation consisting in the necessity of apprehending God by faith rather than by objective knowledge? Finally, there is the question of whether believers can refuse to expose their certainties to doubt without compromising the certainties themselves. Christian believers, after all, regard their faith as derived not merely from their own discernment and intelligence but from God. Faith is given them by the Holy Spirit. Anxious concern that it may grow dim and disappear in the heat of some public controversy seems singularly inappropriate. Christians believe that through the unifying power of the Holy Spirit the inner dialogue that constitutes the mind of God unfolds. Shouldn't they be willing to take the risk of allowing human dialogue to unfold through that same power?

Experience shows that it often does. Faith does not always, or even ordinarily, crumble when confronted with doubt. Sometimes it becomes broader and deeper; the clashes of believers and unbelievers can be spiritually fruitful. The role in recent intellectual history of Friedrich Nietzsche—as profound and impassioned an enemy as Christianity has ever had—exemplifies these phenomena. Twentieth-century Christianity would have suffered incalculable impoverishment had Nietzsche been dismissed without a hearing. And in the dialogue between Martin Heidegger and Rudolf Bultmann—a Nietzschean philosopher and a Christian theologian—one sees a mutually-enriching interchange between unbelief and belief. Comparable comments could be made about Freud, Marx, and other writers. As everyone knows, innumerable Christian theologians have learned from Freud, and "Marxist-Christian dialogue" has been a common occurrence in recent decades. Of course Christians often deplore the power and prominence of atheistic and anti-Christian writers in modern times, and in a sense they are right to do so. From the standpoint of faith, the flourishing of unbelief, particularly when brilliantly articulated, cannot be a pleasing spectacle. It is not at all manifest, however, that the flourishing of unbelief has weakened belief. In spite of a flood of anti-Christian writers, our time has witnessed also a flood of profound and original theologies—all produced by theologians well-versed in the anti-Christian writers.

Many voices today, however, raise more radical questions about the possibility of dialogue than any we have so far considered. They ask with Pilate, "What is truth?" The principles underlying public discourse are challenged more boldly today, perhaps, than ever before in history. The philosophical issues thus presented are far too large and intricate to be adequately considered here. They cannot, however, be passed by without notice.

POSTMODERNISM AND PUBLIC DIALOGUE

The ideal of public dialogue rests on the assumption that there exist what often are called "foundations," that is, fundamental, enduring realities which human beings can know and which enable them to speak of the true and the good as matters transcending our prejudices and preferences. Foundations provide standards against which varying human opinions and emotions can be judged. Given foundations, we can inquire together and anticipate conclusions to which everyone, regardless of social background or personal idiosyncracies, can be expected to assent. In short, we can aspire to community and not merely to domination.

Contemporary concern with foundations is due largely to a movement often called "postmodernism." The currents of contemporary thought making up postmodernism are various. Some take the form of philosophical inquiry, others of literary inquiry; some are subtly ironic, others overtly nihilistic. Politically, not only are they divided between left and right; some are hard to place on the political spectrum. The names of the most prominent postmodernist writers are familiar to everyone: Nietzsche, Derrida, Foucault,

Lyotard, Rorty. The tone of most postmodernist writing is pagan or atheistic. There are, however, postmodernist currents even in Christian theology. Here the key names are Kierkegaard and Barth. It is striking that such diverse ways of looking at the world are seen on all hands as making up a single intellectual force. What is the nature of this force? What binds together the various "postmodernist" writers? All, in some degree, and in some fashion, call into question the "foundations" on which Western culture has been based. And in doing this they conspire together to undermine public dialogue.

The impact of postmodernism on public dialogue is easily seen. On postmodernist premises, we cannot enter into common discourse in the assurance that eventual agreement, concerning either the actual or the ideal, is possible. In this sense we are strangers, not merely socially—and thus accidentally—but rather, so to speak, ontologically. Unbelievers have no reason whatever to listen to believers for they do not differ from them merely in their interpretation of realities we might all come to understand in the same fashion, that is, objectively. They differ from them in personal and social orientation and such orientation is not determined by, but rather determines, their version of reality. Believers, in like fashion, have no reason to listen to unbelievers. Everything they know (speaking of postmodernist Christians) is derived from revelation. The old idea that secular disciplines such as philosophy and history provide truths that pagans, atheists, and Christians all can share is an illusion destructive of Christian faith. Dialogue, then, must consist mainly in the elucidation of revelation and can be fruitful only among Christians. With sentiments such as these, believers and unbelievers join together, not to talk, but, in the words of one well-known postmodernist literary critic, to "shut down the marketplace of ideas."

To undertake here anything like a refutation of postmodernism would be quixotic. It would be to underestimate drastically the profundity and the heterogeneity of postmodernist writers. All we can do is note briefly some considerations which might amount to a refutation were they adequately developed.

Postmodernism is weaker in its secular, than in its Christian, versions. This is because as soon as it speaks it necessarily presupposes the objective truth which in theory it wishes to deny. Perhaps this embarrassment could be in some measure lessened were postmodernists willing to speak only in novels, plays, and poetry. But ordinarily they express themselves in philosophical discourse and literary criticism and in doing this they cannot avoid implicitly claiming knowledge of universal truths. This means that they presuppose, in some form, the foundational realities which in theory they deny. And when they not only argue that the case against foundations is universally true but also affirm that certain political principles also are universally true (as many of them do) their theoretical operations become acrobatic if not absurd.

Religious postmodernists, while denying as emphatically as their irreligious counterparts that philosophical reason can attain to universal truth, affirm revelation, and this puts them in a stronger position. They affirm foundations of a sort. These are not foundations on which anyone but a believer can stand, and they cannot, therefore, undergird a public realm. They do, however, make it possible to assert without contradiction that there are objective truths (thus Barth argues eloquently the *objectivity* of *revelation*). There are two considerations which might be developed into a refutation of Christian postmodernism.

The first is what seems a plain fact: that there are great natural theologies, or religious philosophies. According to Christian postmodernism this should not be the case. Theology without revelatory grounds is at best parasitic, a secularized version of Christian theology. There is of course no way of proving that the great religious but non-Christian philosophies that have been developed since the time of Christ (that of Plotinus, for example, or, in our own day, that of Karl Jaspers) are not parasitic. But the greatest of these philosophies predate Christ. Plato, Aristotle, and Stoicism—all in one way or another religious, all originating independently of Christianity—are mammoth obstacles in the way of anyone trying to make a case for Christian postmodernism.

The second consideration militating against Christian postmodernism is that it puts Christians in a nearly unlivable situation. They are completely cut off from the world. If all genuine truth is derived from a revelation which most people do not recognize, then Christians are almost unbearably set apart from the rest of the human race. They cannot learn from anyone but Christians (a strictly "Christocentric" Christian could not learn from Plato or Kant, from Thucydides or Gibbon, from Sophocles or Proust). Nor can they teach anyone but Christians; indeed, it is not clear that a consistently postmodernist Christian could engage in evangelization. The postmodernist Church would be an impermeable and self-enclosed society. Such a condition is humanly almost insupportable. The result is that the premised principle—that truth derives solely from revelation—is either compromised at the outset or is gradually broken down. It is my guess that a careful study of the intellectual development of the greatest of contemporary Christian postmodernists, Karl Barth, would show both of these things occurring.

Where does all of this leave us? More precisely, where does it leave the argument that through dialogue believers and unbelievers can be participants in a common life? We can say at least this much, that postmodernism is not beyond doubt. Strong arguments can be brought against it. In this unsettled state we simply do not know how much truth we can reach through common reason; we do not know whether there are foundational realities on which common discourse can be based. It does not follow, however, that dialogic efforts must be abandoned until we have demonstrated the possibility of their succeeding. Rather, we must proceed experimentally. Whenever we speak or listen, without regard to religious boundary lines, we are testing the limits of common understanding. And so far as we actually reach common understanding we are effecting a practical refutation of postmodernism.

Never, of course, will the refutation be final. Nihilism—of which postmodernism can fairly be considered a manifestation—is as old as civilization and arises from metaphysical uncertainties and psychological forces that will pass away only with the end of history itself. Owing to these uncertainties and forces, which arise from our finitude and our moral failures, a finished and unimpaired dialogic community is not within our grasp. Hence, to be realistic, we should aim not so much to build a dialogic utopia as to cultivate and maintain dialogic attitudes, that is, to be resolutely inquiring and steadily respectful of truth and persons. We may in this way discover that after all there are "foundations"—an encircling and sustaining order of things—and that we are therefore able, in spite of elemental disagreements, to accomplish occasional acts of genuine communication and to carry on a common life and history. To say this, however, calls for a final comment on the core significance of the standard of public dialogue.

THE PROPHETIC STANCE

Plato, taking cognizance of the improbability that a perfectly just city will ever be constructed, somewhere remarks that the individual must become the ruler of his own inner city. Plato's remark indicates what is being done by an individual who maintains dialogic attitudes. By being steadily attentive and inquiring one constructs and inhabits an inner public realm. A single person, related through attentiveness and readiness to speak, to humanity at large and to particular human beings, is the founder and ruler of an inward dialogic community. Such a community, of course, like every outward community, will be imperfect. Yet the imperfection of the inward community is not quite on a footing with that of the outward community. We readily assent to the proposition that an individual *ought* to be perfect ("You must be perfect," Jesus said, "as your heavenly father is perfect"[3]), whereas the proposition that a society ought to be perfect is apt to strike a sober person as dubious and even dangerous. There have been many saintly persons, but never a saintly society. There is much sense, then, in Plato's suggestion that a wise person, contending with the normal turbulence of history, is called on to undertake a kind of inward statecraft. The standard of public dialogue implies that such statecraft must consist in a determined, and more or less solitary, communality.

We are speaking, clearly, of a personal stance—of a way in which individuals may stand amid and against adverse currents of history. Such a stance is illustrated dramatically by figures such as Dietrich Bonhoeffer and

Aleksandr Solzhenitsyn, who, virtually alone, and in spite of profoundly inimical historical forces, have sustained responsible relationships with particular human beings and implicitly with the whole human race. The stance of someone like Bonhoeffer or Solzhenitsyn may be maintained through various activities—by helping members of a persecuted race to evade their enemies, taking part in a conspiracy to bring down a tyrant, investigating and publicizing the crimes of a government. Preceding reflections suggest, however, that an essential element in such activities must always be attentiveness to the situation and suffering of other human beings; and attentiveness, we may assume, is accompanied normally by a readiness to speak where speech is possible. The communicative demeanor of such people as Bonhoeffer and Solzhenitsyn confirms this suggestion. On this basis we may characterize the posture of one who rules a properly ordered inner city as a dialogic stance.

It may occur to the reader, however, that such a stance is not an end in itself but, rather, is anticipatory. From a Christian standpoint, the idea of a finished and perfect community, although not a realistic historical goal, forms an image of a future beyond history. It is an eschatological goal, like Augustine's City of God. In short, the dialogic stance is informed with an ultimate hope. It is prophetic. Standing dialogically is a way of waiting for, and so far as possible furthering by means of attentiveness and speech, the coming of a community so complete that the alienation and ignorance which are the primal conditions of history would be dissolved. For Christians, the prophetic stance is not willful or subjective or fainthearted. It is an attitude of settled receptivity to the Word which will not return to God void but will accomplish the thing for which it was sent.[4]

Americans have an historical emblem of the prophetic stance in their most revered president, Abraham Lincoln. Amid the chaotic and lethal tides of the Civil War, Lincoln much of the time had to stand alone. He seemed to be the only person in the nation's capitol who saw plainly, and all of the time, the end to be pursued—preservation of the Union, with the ultimate extinction of slavery. But solitary and sorely tried as he was, Lincoln was spontaneously and enduringly sociable, and his sociability was characterized always by serious, if playful, talk. His posture was habitually dialogical. That his posture was also prophetic will be plain to anyone familiar with his tragic sense of his own times, and his own fate, along with his consciousness of the national destiny which rendered the saving of the Union a compelling goal. Lincoln often made himself available, during his time in the White House, to anyone willing to wait in the line leading up to his office. Thus we may think of Lincoln, conversing—with deep, if unostentatious, seriousness—with a variety of ordinary people just off the streets of Washington, as symbolizing a life devoted to the statecraft required, not only for restoring order to a nation but for building an inner city. Dare we think that this was a city in which, ruled by one who was at once gregarious and beleaguered, shrewdly humorous and tragically profound, unpretentious and unafraid, Socrates and Isaiah alike might have felt at home?

NOTES

1. Romans 14:1 and Ephesians 4:14 (Revised Standard Version), respectively.
2. Luke 12:14 (RSV).
3. Matthew 5:48.
4. See Isaiah 55:11.

Index

About the Contributors

Elliot N. Dorff was ordained a Conservative rabbi by the Jewish Theological Seminary of America in 1970 and earned his Ph.D. in philosophy from Columbia University in 1971. Since then he has directed the rabbinical and masters degree programs at the University of Judaism in Los Angeles, where he currently is rector and professor of philosophy. Since 1974 he has also team-taught a course on Jewish Law at UCLA School of Law. He has chaired two scholarly organizations: the Academy of Jewish Philosophy and the Jewish Law Association. In the spring of 1993 he served on the Ethics Committee of the Clinton Health Care Task Force, and in March 1997 and May 1999 he testified on behalf of the Jewish tradition on the subjects of human cloning and stem cell research before the president's National Bioethics Advisory Commission. He has written eight books and over one hundred articles on Jewish thought, law, and ethics. He is married, has four children, and is looking forward to grandchildren.

R. Bruce Douglass is associate professor in the Department of Government of Georgetown University in Washington, D.C. He served as Dean of the Faculty of Georgetown College from 1995 to 1999. He has also been a director of the Social and Political Thought Program of Georgetown College and the School of Foreign Service. He is currently one of the editors of *The Responsive Community*. He has edited a number of books, including *The Deeper Meaning of Economic Life* (1986), *Liberalism and the Good* (1990), and *Catholicism and Liberalism* (1994). His writing has appeared in *Political Theory*, the *Journal of Politics*, the *Review of Politics*, *Commonweal*, *The Christian Century*, and the *New Oxford Review*, among other journals.

Eldon Eisenach's research interests center on the relationship between religion and liberal political thought in America and England. His first book was *Two Worlds of Liberalism: Religion and Politics in Hobbes, Locke and Mill*

(1981). His latest book, *The Next Religious Establishment: National Identity and Political Theology in Post-Protestant America* (2000), extends some of the ideas developed in *The Lost Promise of Progressivism* (1994) and "Progressive Internationalism" in *Progressivism and the New Democracy* (1999). "Mill and Liberal Christianity" appeared in a book collection he edited, *Mill and the Moral Character of Liberalism* (1998). Next year he plans to have published earlier articles and essays under the title *Sacred Narrative Power and Liberal Political Truth: Essays on Hobbes, Locke, Bentham and Mill.* His next book length project "The Inner Light of Liberalism" will examine the writings of a group of close followers of John Stuart Mill. Except for a year as a visiting professor at Cornell University in 1991-92, he has served as chair of the Department of Political Science at the University of Tulsa since 1985.

Daniel J. Elazar, until his untimely death in December, 1999, was professor of political science at Temple University in Philadelphia, where he directed the Center for the Study of Federalism, the world's leading federalism research institute. He was the founder and president of the Jerusalem Center for Public Affairs, the major independent Israeli policy studies center concerned with analyzing and solving the key problems facing Israel and world Jewry. Professor Elazar wrote or edited over sixty-five books and many other publications ranging from an analysis of local governments in the Midwestern United States to a handbook surveying and classifying federal systems and autonomy arrangements throughout the world. Among his books are: *The American Partnership*; *American Federalism: A View from the States* (now in its third edition); *The American Mosaic*; *Cities of the Prairie*; *Cities of the Prairie Revisited*; *Exploring Federalism*; and *Israel: Building a New Society.* He was the co-editor of *Publius: The Journal of Federalism* and editor of the *Jewish Political Studies Review.* He was also the author of several books exploring practical solutions to the Israeli-Palestinian conflict based on federal principles.

Jean Bethke Elshtain, a political philosopher whose task has been to show the connections between our political and our ethical convictions, is the Laura Spelman Rockefeller Professor of Social and Political Ethics at the University of Chicago. She has been a visiting professor at Oberlin College, Yale University, and Harvard University, and is a recipient of four honorary degrees. She is the author of fifteen books, over 400 essays in scholarly journals and journals of civic opinion, and some 175 book reviews. She also writes a regular column for *The New Republic.* Of her several hundred guest lectures at universities in the United States and abroad, over two dozen have been endowed lectureships. Professor Elshtain has been a Fellow at the Institute for Advanced Study in Princeton, New Jersey; a Scholar in Residence at the Rockefeller Foundation Bellagio Conference and Study Center in

Como, Italy; a Guggenheim Fellow (1991-92); and a writer in residence at the MacDowell Colony in Peterborough, New Hampshire. She currently serves as a member of the Board of Trustees of the Institute for Advanced Study, Princeton, and is on the Board of Trustees of the National Humanities Center in Research Triangle Park, North Carolina. Professor Elshtain also currently serves as the chair of the Council on Families in America; she also is a member of the National Commission for Civic Renewal, the Penn Commission on American Culture and Society, and is chair of the Council on Civil Society. She served as vice-president of the American Political Science Association during the 1998-99 academic year. Among other projects, she is currently writing an intellectual biography of Jane Addams.

Joshua Mitchell is associate professor in the Department of Government at Georgetown University, in Washington, D.C. He is the author of *Not by Reason Alone: Religion, History, and Identity in Early Liberal Political Thought* (1993); and *The Fragility of Freedom: Tocqueville on Religion, Democracy, and the American Future* (1995). His articles on the relationship between religion and democracy in the West have appeared in *Political Theory*, the *Review of Politics*, the *Journal of Politics*, and the *Journal of Religion*. He is currently working on a book-length manuscript entitled "Reinhold Niebuhr and the Politics of Hope" as well as a study of the significance of divine gifts in Plato's thought.

Michael J. Perry holds the University Distinguished Chair in Law at Wake Forest University. From 1982 to 1997, he taught at Northwestern University, where, from 1990 to 1997, he held the Howard J. Trienens Chair in Law. Perry has lectured widely in the United States and around the world. He is the author of seven books and more than fifty articles and essays. Perry's books include *Morality, Politics, and Law* (1988); *Love and Power: The Role of Religion and Morality in American Politics* (1991); *Religion in Politics: Constitutional and Moral Perspectives* (1997); *The Idea of Human Rights: Four Inquiries* (1998); and *We the People: The Fourteenth Amendment and the Supreme Court* (1999).

Mary C. Segers is professor in the Department of Political Science at Rutgers University in Newark, New Jersey, where she teaches courses in political theory, gender politics, and religion and politics. Her most recent book is *A Wall of Separation? Debating the Role of Religion in American Public Life*, coauthored with Ted Jelen (1998). She has also published books on equality and affirmative action, abortion politics, and on the American Catholic church's role in American politics. In 1985-86, Professor Segers served as visiting lecturer in the Women's Studies Program at Harvard Divinity School, where she taught a course on the American Catholic Bishops and Public Policy. She held a Henry Luce Fellowship in Theology at Harvard from 1987 to 1989. In 1998 she received the Charles Pine Award for Excellence in Teaching at Rutgers University. She held the Fulbright Distinguished Chair in American Studies at the University of Warsaw in the Spring 1999 semester.

Glenn Tinder is professor emeritus in the Department of Political Science at the University of Massachusetts at Boston. His recent books include *The Political Meaning of Christianity* (1989); *Tolerance and Community* (1995); and *The Fabric of Hope* (1999). He has published articles in *The Atlantic Monthly*, *The Christian Century*, *First Things*, *The Responsive Community*, the *Review of Politics*, *The Bulletin of the Harvard Divinity School*, *Christianity Today*, and *Commonweal*. He is currently writing a book-length manuscript on liberty.

David Walsh is professor in the Department of Politics at the Catholic University of America, where he offers courses in the problems and the history of political theory, with a special emphasis on Christian political thought. He is the author of *The Third Millennium: Reflections on Faith and Reason* (1999); *Guarded by Mystery: Meaning in a Postmodern Age* (1999); *The Growth of the Liberal Soul* (1997); *After Ideology: Recovering the Spiritual Foundations of Freedom* (1990); and *The Mysticism of Innerworldly Fulfillment: A Study of Jacob Boehme* (1983). In addition, he is a frequent contributor to periodicals both academic and popular, as well as one of the editors of *The Collected Works of Eric Voegelin*. His current project is a book on the modern openness toward transcendent reality, tentatively titled "The Transparence of the Modern World." He has served a number of terms as department chair, as director of off-campus programs, and co-chair of the university's Middle States Reaccreditation Self-Study. He received his Ph.D. from the University of Virginia, and previously taught at the University of South Carolina and the University of Florida.

John Witte, Jr. (J.D. Harvard) is Jonas Robitscher Professor of Law and Ethics, and director of the Law and Religion Program at Emory University in Atlanta. A specialist in legal history and religious liberty, he has published ninety articles and ten books, including *From Sacrament to Contract: Marriage, Religion, and Law in the West*; *Religion and the American Constitutional Experiment*; *Religious Human Rights in Global Perspective* (2 vols.); *Proselytism and Orthodoxy in Russia*; and *Sharing the Book: Religious Perspectives on the Rights and Wrongs of Mission*.